The Innovation Systems Cycle

T0384109

The Little Big Book Series

Edited by

H. James Harrington and Frank Voehl

OTHER BOOKS IN THE LITTLE BIG BOOK SERIES

The Innovation Systems Cycle

Simplifying and Incorporating the Guidelines of the ISO 56002 Standard and Best Practices

H. James Harrington
and
Frank Voehl

CRC Press
Taylor & Francis Group
Boca Raton London New York

CRC Press is an imprint of the
Taylor & Francis Group, an **informa** business

A PRODUCTIVITY PRESS BOOK

CRC Press
Taylor & Francis Group
6000 Broken Sound Parkway NW, Suite 300
Boca Raton, FL 33487-2742

CRC Press is an imprint of Taylor & Francis Group, an Informa business

No claim to original U.S. Government works

Printed on acid-free paper

International Standard Book Number-13: 978-0-367-34220-3 (Paperback)
International Standard Book Number-13: 978-0-367-34264-7 (Hardback)

Library of Congress Control Number: 2019948058

Visit the Taylor & Francis Web site at
http://www.taylorandfrancis.com

and the CRC Press Web site at
http://www.crcpress.com

I dedicate this book to all the TUCKERS. These are the magic elves who come to you nightly when you go to bed and pull covers around you. I sleep on my side, and there is always a little cold airway between my back and the covers. Every night, I remember that my wife Marguerite would make it her job to tuck the covers around my back. Oh, there are so many reasons I miss her so much.

H. James Harrington

Contents

Preface

It is always surprising to me how American business can go through massive swings based upon fads, regurgitation of old approaches, and name changes. The following outlines some of the many "silver bullets" that American business has shot itself in the foot with over the last forty years:

- Total quality management
- Business process improvement
- Organizational change management
- Six Sigma
- Lean
- Innovation—The current buzz word that most organizations are embracing.

I believe for the last thirty years we have been overly fascinated by Toyota's manufacturing process, believing it is America's answer to its loss of production capabilities. We need to ask ourselves the question, "Why do people buy Toyotas?" It is not for the initial quality. We buy Toyotas because their long-term reliability is far better than any American- or European-made autos. Toyota's manufacturing process had little or nothing to do with reliability. Its reliability was designed in, rather than built-in. The trademark of the last thirty years' performance improvement initiatives has been focusing on doing it with less, eliminating unnecessary activities, and now, at long last, with innovation, our focus is on changing from *doing it with less to doing it best.*

Today's best hope for the American business plan is not in the manufacturing process design or delivery processes. Our future is going to be based greatly upon improved innovation leadership, design engineering capability, and sales and marketing innovation. These three areas have been sadly lacking significant performance improvement over the last 20 years. Technology has moved forward with great leaps and bounds, but our support engineering processes have not kept pace with these advances. Our engineering capabilities continue to degrade as we graduate more lawyers and fewer engineers. Our innovation in sales and marketing has not kept up with its competition from Japan and Europe. We primarily forgot about the customer in favor of reducing manufacturing costs. The two organizations that have the primary interface with the customer are sales and marketing and development engineering. A number of companies' customer satisfaction index dropped significantly as they installed programs like Six Sigma. After-sales support and service systems are at an all-time low. In many companies, it is almost impossible to talk to a real person. I was recently pleasantly surprised when I called an organization and their phone *was answered* by a real person saying, "Would you like your concerns handled by me or would you rather work with the computer?" I was far less surprised when I called another service organization and the computer explained to me that there was an estimated two-hour wait to talk to someone. In fact, it took two hours and eighteen minutes before someone came on the call to address my concerns.

Another example is an organization that I am currently doing volunteer work for. They have a special program that you need to use to interface with them. It took me five to ten minutes to make the connection to leave a ten second message. My cell phone has so many features, it seems I can do everything with it except make a phone call. When I get a telephone call, by the time I push all the right buttons, I've missed the phone call. I believe that the magic word for American business is "SIMPLIFICATION."

We need a radical change in the way our businesses function/operate because of the shift to a global market and the birth of a global competitor base. Looking back at history prior to 1990s, the consumer buying pattern fits a standard bell-shaped curve, with the right-hand side of the curve being specialty products and the left-hand side of the curve being mass production products. The high point of the curve with the point in between the two extremes was impacted by both specialty and mass production products (see Figure F.1).

In the 21st century, there has been a major change in the global market. In these cases, the high points are mass production and specialized outputs. This transformed the normal bell curve into what IBM calls the "well shape curve" (see Figure F.2).

The last area really needing major focus is the board of directors and executive management decision-making system. One of the most costly failures are projects that are started, but turn out to of no-value-added. Project failure rates higher than 75% have been reported in many organizations. Upper management needs to insist on having data sources available to them that provides sufficient information so that they can make an intelligent decision. This means a major upgrading of most

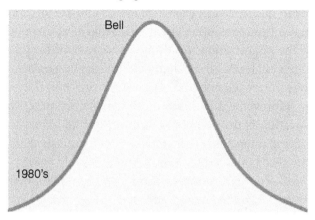

Changing Global Markets

Mass Production	Specialized
Low Cost	High Personnel Value
Good Enough Quality	High Cost and Quality
Low Emotional	High Emotional

FIGURE F.1
Global markets prior to 1990.

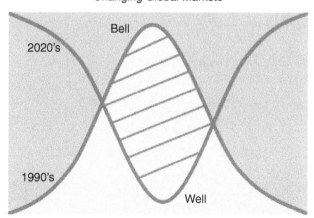

Changing Global Markets

Mass Production	Specialized
Low Cost	High Personnel Value
Good Enough Quality	High Cost and Quality
Low Emotional	High Emotional

FIGURE F.2
Customer buying patterns: well-shaped curve.

organization's business plan analysis. It also includes establishing an effective way to measure each executive team's and executive's error rates. In many cases, these executive errors are behavioral errors that vibrate throughout the organization, resulting in many poor decisions made at lower management levels rather than decision-making errors.

Continuous improvement and innovation are not the same thing. Continuous improvement is the result of many small practical improvements. Innovation is the combination of unique and creative ideas that have a significant impact on positive value added to all stakeholders. Every organization needs innovation. Many companies rely heavily on innovation to drive their organization forward and keep it competitive on the market. Other companies, like trendsetters, invest heavily in innovation so as to be the first to market with the latest technology. When the trendsetters' new products start up the steep part of the S-curve, the cautiously reserved organizations make slight improvements to the trendsetters' outputs and, in many cases, walk away with major portions of the market.

I repeat—the three areas that need to put a major focus on performance improvement are as follows:

1. Product Engineering
2. Marketing and Sales
3. Board of Directors and Executive Management Decision-Making Excellence

It is time to act before we have to react.

H. James Harrington

Acknowledgments

I recognize Candy Rogers for taking my rough draft manuscript and transforming it into a completed manuscript, reformatting it, and correcting technical and grammatical errors. I would like to recognize the many individuals who have coauthored books with me and exchanged ideas over the past year. Some of them are:

- Leslie C. Anderson
- Marcos E.J. Bertin
- Richard Charron
- Daryl R. Conner
- Praveen Gupta
- James S. Harrington
- Nicholas L. Horney
- Glen D. Hoffherr
- Alan Knight
- Robert Lewis
- Kenneth C. Lomax
- Thomas McNellis
- Chuck Mignosa
- Carolyn Pexton
- Robert P. Reid, Jr.
- William Ruggles
- Dr. Brett E. Trusko
- Christopher F. Voehl
- Frank Voehl
- Hal Wiggins
- John Wolf
- Rick Fernandez

Authors

Dr. H. James Harrington
Chief Executive Officer

HARRINGTON MANAGEMENT SYSTEMS

In the book *Tech Trending*, Dr. Harrington was referred to as "the quint-essential tech trender." The *New York Times* referred to him as having a "…knack for synthesis and an open mind about packaging his knowledge and experience in new ways—characteristics that may matter more as prerequisites for new-economy success than technical wizardry…." The author, Tom Peters, stated, "I fervently hope that Harrington's readers will not only benefit from the thoroughness of his effort but will also 'smell' the fundamental nature of the challenge for change that he mounts." Bill Clinton, former president of the United States, appointed Dr. Harrington to serve as an Ambassador of Good Will. It has been said: "He writes the books that other consultants use."

Harrington Management Systems (formerly Harrington Institute) was featured on a half-hour TV program, Heartbeat of America, which focuses on outstanding small businesses that make America strong. The host,

William Shatner, stated: "You (Dr. Harrington) manage an entrepreneurial company that moves America forward. You are obviously successful."

PRESENT RESPONSIBILITIES

Dr. H. James Harrington now serves as the chief executive officer for the Harrington Management Systems. He also serves as the chairman of the board for a number of businesses. Dr. Harrington also serves as the chairman of the Walter L. Hurd Foundation. He is recognized as a world leader in applying performance improvement methodologies to business processes. He has an excellent record of coming into an organization, working as its CEO or COO, resulting in a major improvement in its financial and quality performance.

PREVIOUS EXPERIENCE

In February 2002, Dr. Harrington retired as the COO of Systemcorp A.L.G., the leading supplier of knowledge management and project management software solutions when Systemcorp was purchased by IBM. Prior to this, he served as a principal and one of the leaders in the Process Innovation Group at Ernst & Young; he retired from Ernst & Young when it was purchased by Cap Gemini. Dr. Harrington joined Ernst & Young when it purchased Harrington, Hurd & Rieker, a consulting firm that Dr. Harrington started. Before that, Dr. Harrington was with IBM for over 40 years as a senior engineer and project manager.

Dr. Harrington is past chairman and past president of the prestigious International Academy for Quality and of the American Society for Quality Control. He is also an active member of the Global Knowledge Economics Council.

CREDENTIALS

Dr. H. James Harrington was given a lifetime achievement award for his work in process improvement and in innovation by the International Association of Innovation Professionals.

Dr. Harrington was elected to the honorary level of the International Academy for Quality, which is the highest level of recognition in the quality profession.

He is a government registered quality engineer, a certified quality and reliability engineer by the American Society for Quality Control, and a permanent certified professional manager by the Institute of Certified Professional Managers. He is also a certified Master Six Sigma Black Belt and received the title of Six Sigma Grand Master. Dr. Harrington has an MBA and PhD in engineering management and a BS in electrical engineering. Additionally, in 2013, Harrington received an honorary degree of doctor of philosophy (PhD) from the Sudan Academy of Sciences.

H. James Harrington's contributions to performance improvement around the world have brought him many honors. He was appointed the honorary advisor to the China Quality Control Association and was elected to the Singapore Productivity Hall of Fame in 1990. He has been named lifetime honorary president of the Asia-Pacific Quality Control Organization and honorary director of the Association Chilean de Control de Calidad. In 2006, Dr. Harrington accepted the honorary chairman position of Quality Technology Park of Iran.

H. James Harrington has been elected as a fellow of the British Quality Control Organization and the American Society for Quality Control. In 2008, he was elected to be an honorary fellow of the Iran Quality Association and Azerbaijan Quality Association. He was also elected an honorary member of the quality societies in Taiwan, Argentina, Brazil, Colombia, and Singapore. He has presented hundreds of papers on performance improvement and organizational management structure at the local, state, national, and international levels.

RECOGNITION

- The Harrington/Ishikawa Medal, presented yearly by the Asian Pacific Quality Organization, was named after H. James Harrington to recognize his many contributions to the region.
- The Harrington/Neron Medal was named after H. James Harrington in 1997 for his many contributions to the quality movement in Canada.

- Harrington Best TQM Thesis Award was established in 2004 and named after H. James Harrington by the European Universities Network and e-TQM College.
- Harrington Chair in Performance Excellence was established in 2005 at the Sudan University.
- Harrington Excellence Medal was established in 2007 to recognize an individual who uses quality tools in a superior manner.
- H. James Harrington Scholarship was established in 2011 by the American Society for Quality (ASQ) Inspection Division.

H. James Harrington has received many awards, including the Benjamin L. Lubelsky Award, the John Delbert Award, the Administrative Applications Division Silver Anniversary Award, and the Inspection Division Gold Medal Award. In 1996, he received the ASQC (American Society for Quality Control)'s Lancaster Award in recognition for his international activities. In 2001, he received the Magnolia Award in recognition for the many contributions he has made in improving quality in China. In 2002, Dr. Harrington was selected by the European Literati Club to receive a lifetime achievement award at the Literati Award for Excellence ceremony in London. The award was given to honor his excellent literature contributions to the advancement of quality and organizational performance. Also in 2002, Dr. Harrington was awarded the International Academy of Quality President's Award in recognition for outstanding global leadership in quality and competitiveness, and contributions to International Academy for Quality (IAQ) as nominations committee chair, vice president, and chairman. In 2003, he received the Edwards Medal from the ASQ. The Edwards Medal is presented to an individual who has demonstrated the most outstanding leadership in the application of modern quality control methods, especially through the organization and administration of such work. In 2004, he received the Distinguished Service Award which is ASQ's highest award for service granted by the society. In 2008, Dr. Harrington was awarded the Sheikh Khalifa Excellence Award (UAE) in recognition of his superior performance as an original Quality and Excellence Guru who helped shape modern quality thinking. In 2009, Harrington was selected as the Professional of the Year (2009). Also in 2009, he received the Hamdan Bin Mohammed e-University Medal. In 2010, the Asian Pacific Quality Association (APQO) awarded Harrington the APQO President's Award for his "exemplary leadership." The Australian Organization of Quality NSW (New South Wales)'s Board recognized Harrington as "the Global Leader in Performance Improvement Initiatives" in 2010. In 2011, he was honored to receive the Shanghai Magnolia Special Contributions Award from the Shanghai Association for Quality in recognition for his 25 years of contribution to the advancement of quality in China. This was the first time that this award was given out. In 2012, Harrington received the ASQ Ishikawa Medal for his many contributions in promoting the understanding of process improvement and employee involvement on the human aspects of quality at the local, national, and international levels. Also in 2012, he was awarded the Jack Grayson Award. This award recognizes individuals who have demonstrated outstanding leadership in the application of quality philosophy, methods and tools in education, healthcare, public service, and not-for-profit organizations. Harrington also received the A.C. Rosander Award in 2012. This is ASQ Service Quality Division's highest honor. It is given in recognition of outstanding long-term service and leadership, resulting in substantial progress toward the fulfillment of the Division's programs and goals. Additionally, in 2012, Harrington was honored by the Asia Pacific Quality Organization by being awarded the Armand V. Feigenbaum Lifetime Achievement Medal. This award is given annually to an individual whose relentless pursuit of performance improvement over a minimum of 25 years has distinguished them for the candidate's work in promoting the use of quality methodologies and principles within and outside of the organization they're part of. In 2018, Harrington received the Lifetime Achievement Award from the Asia Pacific Quality Organization. This award recognizes worthy role models and committed APQO leaders who have made significant contributions to the betterment of APQO.

CONTACT INFORMATION

Dr. Harrington is a prolific author, publishing hundreds of technical reports and magazine articles. For eight years, he published a monthly column in *Quality Digest Magazine* and is syndicated in five other publications. He has authored 55 books and 10 software packages.

You may contact Dr. Harrington at the following:

Address: 15559 Union Avenue #187, Los Gatos, California 95032.

Phone: (408) 358-2476

Email: hjh@svinet.com

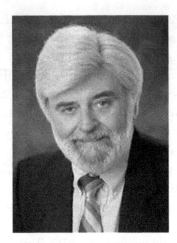

Frank Voehl
President, Strategy Associates

PRESENT RESPONSIBILITIES

Frank Voehl now serves as the Chairman and President of Strategy Associates, Inc. and as a Senior Consultant and Chancellor for the Harrington Management Systems. He also serves as the Chairman of the Board for a number of businesses and as a Grand Master Black Belt Instructor and Technology Advisor at the University of Central Florida in Orlando, Florida. He is recognized as one of the world leaders in applying quality measurement and Lean Six Sigma methodologies to business processes.

PREVIOUS EXPERIENCE

Frank Voehl has extensive knowledge of NRC, FDA, GMP, and NASA quality system requirements. He is an expert in ISO-9000, QS-9000/14000/18000, and integrated Lean Six Sigma Quality System Standards and processes. He has degrees from St. John's University and advanced studies at NYU, as well as an Honorary Doctor of Divinity degree. Since 1986, he has been responsible for overseeing the implementation of Quality Management

Systems with organizations in such diverse industries as telecommunications and utilities, federal, state and local government agencies, public administration and safety, pharmaceuticals, insurance/banking, manufacturing, and institutes of higher learning. In 2002, he joined The Harrington Group as the Chief Operating Officer and Executive Vice President. He has held executive management positions with Florida Power and Light and FPL Group, where he was the Founding General Manager and COO of QualTec Quality Services for seven years. He has written and published/co-published over 35 books and hundreds of technical papers on business management, quality improvement, change management, knowledge management, logistics, and teambuilding, and has received numerous awards for community leadership, service to the third world countries, and student mentoring.

CREDENTIALS

The Bahamas National Quality Award was developed in 1991 by Voehl to recognize the many contributions of companies in the Caribbean region, and he is an honorary member of its Board of Judges. In 1980, the City of Yonkers, NY, declared March 7th as "Frank Voehl Day," honoring him for his many contributions on behalf of thousands of youth in the city where he lived, performed volunteer work, and served as Athletic Director and Coach of the Yonkers–Pelton Basketball Association. In 1985, he was named "Father of the Year" in Broward County, FL. He also serves as President of the Miami Archdiocesan Council of the St. Vincent de Paul Society, whose mission is to serve the poor and needy throughout South Florida and the world.

Introduction

In 1995, James M. Higgins wrote a book titled *Innovate or Evaporate: Test Your Organization's IQ,* in which he points out three components for an individual to become more creative:

- Accepting one's own creative potential (20%)
- Learning the process that can produce new ideas (60%)
- Developing intuition (20%)

Twenty-three years later, his words still ring crystal clear like a church bell calling the peasants to come to the Sunday sermon. The developed countries in the world have no option but to become more innovative if their standard of living is going to survive. I have toured Asian and African countries where the government and people were very happy to build their capacity based upon cheap labor. This thought pattern is changing drastically as countries like China, India, and Japan become less and less willing to compete in the physical labor market and ever increase their emphasis to the high-tech middle class jobs that have been falling out of United States. Silicon Valley copycats are being developed in many countries around the world. These companies are focusing on penetrating the high-tech industries as they realize they are faced with an escalating cost of living that requires increased wages to keep up.

As customer's personal preferences changed to focus on customized unique products and services, it has opened the door for a smaller organization to focus on a very small niche market. Small unique focused brand names are becoming more and more desirable in comparison to the mass production quantity that manufacturing today treats as their bread-and-butter. With the growth capital value rapidly increasing for individuals throughout the world, there is a growing change in buying patterns.

Along with buying trends, a new type of executive is being formed. Fortunes are being made with just ten people as well as with two thousand people in the factory. Customized unique marketing approaches are opening new opportunities that have never been available to innovative organizations. More and more organizations are now interested in "what" the individual can do than in what they have memorized in classroom lessons.

To get started, let's address the most debatable subject in the innovative cycle. That is, "What is innovation?" Is it

- A new and unique idea?
- Any time an individual does something or learns something?
- Whenever an individual does something they have never done before?
- The real sense that they have never done something before?
- A new product that adds value to the consumer?
- A new product that adds value to the stakeholders?
- Any continuous improvement?
- A step-function improvement?
- Anything that is different from the individual's standpoint?
- Anything that adds value to anyone?
- All of these and more?

To some people, innovation is all of these and more. Depending upon whose definition you want to use, one or more of these would be covered in the definition. It could be as general as anytime a person does something different than has been done before. For example, when a child learns to read, that would be innovative. In this case, everyone is an innovator, and any change to any output is innovation. It could be as specific as a new unique, original, idea that results in a measurable value added to all stakeholders. In this case, it is extremely difficult to originate an idea that has a positive value-added impact upon all the stakeholders.

In 2013, *ISO TC 279*, a technical committee of the International Organization for Standardization (ISO), was formed. Its purpose was to develop, maintain, and promote standards in the fields of innovation management. As defined by ISO TC279 Working Group, the preliminary definition of innovation is defined as

A new or changed *entity* (3.36), realizing or redistributing *value* (2)

- Note 1 to entry: Novelty and value are relative to, and determined by the perception of the organization and interested parties.

- Note 2 to entry: An innovation can be a product, service, process, model, method, etc.
- Note 3 to entry: Innovation is an outcome. The word "innovation" sometimes refers to activities or processes resulting in, or aiming for, innovation. When innovation is used in this sense, it should always be used with some form of qualifier, for example, innovation activities.

Source: ISO 56001 Fundamentals and Vocabulary

As a general overview, the definitions of innovation tend to be a combination of anything that is an improvement and/or different from what was done in the past. I personally disagree with the broad general definition of innovation that includes small, medium, and large changes/improvements, but I'm in the minority. I have a tendency to want to think of an innovative output as being something special that sets the originators apart from the average. For a continuous improvement activity to be considered innovative, it would have to be driving the total organization at an improvement rate that is greater than the three sigma limits of the improvement rate of other organizations. That typically indicates they need to be doing something different than what other organizations are doing. Typically that would be a sustained continuous improvement of greater than 15% for a minimum of three years.

For the purpose of this book, I'm going to define innovation as follows:

- Definition of innovation: Innovation is people creating value through the implementation of new, creative, and unique ideas that generate combined measurable added value to the organization's stakeholders. Innovation is how an organization adds value for the stakeholders from implementing creative ideas. An individual change can have a negative or positive impact (value) to each of the individual stakeholders.

  Note: A typical example of this would be a modern music group that composes their own original music and delivers it to their audiences. Unfortunately, today there are few, if any, modern music groups whose compositions are original and creative.

Can an idea be innovative if the concept is not implemented or if it's just creative or inventive? If you can patent the idea, does that indicate that it is an innovative idea? No, it must be a creative idea, but it has not met the criteria to be classified as an innovative idea.

THE 12 PROCESS GROUPINGS OF THE INNOVATION SYSTEMS CYCLE

It is important to remember that the innovative system that functions in most innovative organizations is made up of a series of interrelated processes. The system could be divided into many different ways. We have chosen to divide it into three major phases with four process groupings in each of the three phases for a total of twelve process groupings (see Figure P.1). The three phases are as follows:

- Phase I—Creation
- Phase II—Preparation and Production
- Phase III—Delivery

What businesses are looking for today is an individual who can take an idea and turn it into a profitable output. These new *Masters of Results* go by many different names; some of them are entrepreneur, creator, inventor, artist, or innovator. It does not matter what you call those individuals who take an idea and turn it into a successful value-added output. They each play a slightly different role in the Innovation Systems Cycle (ISC) (see Table P.1).

The ISC makes up the skeleton that supports the total innovation activities. As a result, it is imperative that you have a good understanding of what it is, how it functions, and how to use it effectively. This entire book is directed at defining how you can strengthen and take advantage of this framework called the *Innovation Systems Cycle (ISC)*. It's very important to understand that innovation is a complex system starting with opportunity identification and is only completed once the degree of transformation has been measured. Too many people think of innovation as the creative phase of ISC; in reality, this accounts for only 8%–15% of the total effort.

TABLE P.1

Innovation Systems Cycle

Phase I. Creation
- Process Grouping 1. Opportunity Identification
- Process Grouping 2. Opportunity Development
- Process Grouping 3. Value Proposition
- Process Grouping 4. Concept Validation

Phase II. Preparation and Production
- Process Grouping 5. Business Case Analysis
- Process Grouping 6. Resource Management
- Process Grouping 7. Documentation
- Process Grouping 8. Production

Phase III. Delivery
- Process Grouping 9. Marketing, Sales, and Delivery
- Process Grouping 10. After-Sales Services
- Process Grouping 11. Performance Analysis
- Process Grouping 12. Transformation

THE FOUR BASIC TYPES OF PEOPLE WHO DRIVE INNOVATION

Basically, there are four types of people who interact to drive the ISC. These include the inventor, the entrepreneur, the innovator, and the project manager. Each of these four interacts in a slightly different part of the total cycle.

1. The inventor—The inventor is an individual who comes up with a unique creative solution to a potential opportunity. Their primary drive is to see their idea come to market. Once the concept is validated and the associated patents are issued, the inventor's enthusiasm fades, and they head back to the lab hoping they can invent something bigger and better than their present invention.
2. The entrepreneur—The entrepreneur is always looking for a new idea that has marketing potential. They're not concerned with who originated the idea. These are usually extroverts who get a great deal of satisfaction out of making things happen. Their major objective is to get the concept out to market where they can make some money for the organization.

3. The innovator—The innovator is a combination of the inventor and the entrepreneur. The innovator comes up with a new release that is unique and different and has the capabilities to process through ISC. The innovator is involved in driving the cycle starting with Process Grouping 1. Opportunity Identification to Process Grouping 11. Performance Analysis.
4. The project manager—The project manager is assigned to a project during the business process analysis. On occasion, they could be assigned as early as the value proposition is approved. Their primary responsibility is to ensure that the project is implemented on time, within budget, and it is performing as required. They're held accountable for overseeing the project up until the time the output starts to be delivered to the external customer.

Figure P.1 provides a view of how each of these types of innovative work assignments related to the twelve Process Groupings that make up the ISC. You will note that there is considerable overlap, particularly in Phases I and II. Basically, the activities in the overlapping work assignments are the same. As a result, only one of the four types of work assignments is scheduled for an individual project. The exception to this would be when an inventor develops the project concepts and the project is picked up by an entrepreneur to develop and market. We will be discussing this type of interface in more detail in Chapter 1 of this book.

The twelve process groupings that make up the ISC provide an excellent model for a specific project and even for a small group of people who are part of a much larger organization (for example, product engineering or

Phase I. Creation	A	B	C	D	
• Process Grouping 1. Opportunity Identification					PG 1
• Process Grouping 2. Opportunity Development					PG 2
• Process Grouping 3. Value Proposition					PG 3
• Process Grouping 4. Concept Validation					PG 4
Phase II. Preparation and Production					
• Process Grouping 5. Business Case Analysis					PG 5
• Process Grouping 6. Resource Management					PG 6
• Process Grouping 7. Documentation					PG 7
• Process Grouping 8. Production					PG 8
Phase III. Delivery					
• Process Grouping 9. Marketing, Sales and Delivery					PG 9
• Process Grouping 10. After-Sales Services					PG 10
• Process Grouping 11. Performance Analysis					PG 11
• Process Grouping 12. Transformation					PG 12

Index: A = Creator, B = Inventor, C = Innovator, D = Entrepreneur

FIGURE P.1
The four types of innovative work assignments.

sales and marketing). For many organizations, there is a need to improve the creativity and innovation levels for the total organization. In these cases, a cultural change is needed to obtain the desired impact.

For this book, I decided to primarily focus on the activities that go on in Phase I of the ISC, as it seems to be a part of the cycle that people are most interested in improving.

THE WORLD IN A WHIRL

Innovation is changing the world so fast today that it's hard to keep up with the latest technologies and products. By the time, I get all my apps and names added to my new telephone (telephone seems like an obsolete name; it would be better off calling it a technaphone), it's obsolete and a new telephone that does a great deal more and does it faster is on the market. It wasn't long ago that Dick Tracy's telephone watch was just a cartoon artist's fantasy. Today, many of us are wearing watches that allow us to make telephone calls and much more.

Since the turn-of-the-century, innovation has caused the earth to change so fast that you can't keep up with it even if you study twenty-four hours a day. As we look ahead, technology and innovation are going to drive change at a much faster rate than it ever had been driven before. It's almost like we will have to implement the old song lyrics, "I'm going to change my way of walking, my talk, and my name; nothing about me is going to be the same." Innovation is now going at supersonic speeds, making it more and more difficult for any individual to stay well informed and up-to-date.

It's scary to think of what can be done with artificial intelligence and cloning. Just think what will happen when we have direct brain stimulation? Anyone will be able to put on their thinking cap, and in a matter of a few minutes, they will have completed the four-year college curriculum. Basically, our whole education system will undergo a radical innovation change. Within the last ten years, the online university programs have given anyone in the world an opportunity to graduate from a recognized university at a much lower expense and do all of this without ever leaving home. It provides us with the advantage of studying at our own pace and go to class on our own schedule without being away from home or traveling long distances to get to the university. The University of Phoenix is a prime example of a very successful online training program.

Practically, the more minds you have thinking about improvement opportunities will result in a higher level of innovation. Today, China has more engineers available in the work force and far more engineers in the university than we have in the United States. In the 1980s and 1990s, China was a copycat country. They relied heavily on other countries during the design development work, and they specialized in producing the product faster and less expensive. But things are changing rapidly in China; they now have the world's fastest computers and have now focused on shifting away from putting another country's trademark on the product that they produce. Today, their goal is to develop their own brand reputation. Trademarks like Good Baby are readily recognized around the world. This company produces 90% of the children's car seats. After giving a speech at their headquarters, they sent me a children's motorized replica of the 300 SL Mercedes that I used to drive. See the following picture of the children's model of my car and a picture of me in my car (see Figures P.2 and P.3).

FIGURE P.2
Children's 300 SL Mercedes.

FIGURE P.3
Harrington's Model 300 SL Mercedes.

China is being driven into a new industrial revolution as they concentrate on bringing out their own innovative products. This focus is on product from the very low end all the way up to artificial intelligence. Watch out Silicon Valley—China has your product in its product bomb sites. Admittedly, United States is the leading developer of artificial intelligence, but unless you increase your innovation activities, you are going to go the same way that Ford and General Motors went. For many years, China has been the biggest, and now their goal is to be the biggest and best. Their goal is to do everything better than anyone else. Just look at the show they put on at the closing of the last Olympics. But China is not the only nation coming after our innovative reputation. India already has a surplus of engineering talent that has a huge potential of generating and producing innovative products. Both of these two great countries have a huge internal market that they can use to pilot their potentially innovative outputs before they start shipping to the rest of world.

The world's first virtual shopping center was opened in Korea. All the products are just liquid crystal display (LCD) screens that allow you to order the items by touching the screen. When you get to the counter, your items are already bagged and ready to go. As you walked through the store and select items, the screen on your telephone shows the items you have selected, its cost, and total cost of all the items you selected (Figure P.4).

FIGURE P.4
Shopping in a virtual store.

FIGURE P.5
Google's self-driving car.

Here is a recent personal example of how innovation is changing our world. A few months ago, I was stopped at a red light (I usually stop for red lights) in Santa Clara, California when a small blue car pulled up beside me. I casually glanced at the car, and my focus went back at the red light. My mind quickly came back to me saying, "Did you see what I thought I saw?? There was no one driving that blue car!" My head quickly swung 90° to the right. My first impression was right there was no one in the car. I then remembered there is work going on in Silicon Valley to develop a driverless car. This was one of these models. When the light turned green, my foot pushed the accelerator all the way to the floor, my wheels spun for a few seconds and off I took like a bat out of hell. I made sure I was well ahead of that blue car for the next five blocks when it turned off in a different direction. A driverless car is a technical reality using today's technology (see Figure P.5).

TOTAL INNOVATION MANAGEMENT EXCELLENCE

The Total Innovation Management Excellence (TIME) Pyramid shown in Figure P.6 is what we are using for developing an organization's innovative culture. So far we've been focusing our discussion on how to manage innovative projects, processes, and/or products. This approach is good for starting the transformation process. In the long run, you want the innovation

TIME PYRAMID

Total **I**nnovation **M**anagement **E**xcellence

Rewards & Recognition

Comprehensive Measurement System

Innovative Organizational Structure

Innovative Design

Innovative Robotics/ Artificial Intelligence

Knowledge Assets Management

Innovative Management Participation

Innovative Team Development

Individual Creativity, Innovation & Excellence

Innovative Supply Chain Management

Innovative Organizational Assessment

Innovative Executive Leadership

Performance & Cultural Change Management Plans

Commitment to Stakeholders

Innovative Project Management Systems

Value-Added to Stakeholders

FIGURE P.6
TIME Pyramid.

concepts spread throughout the organization and penetrating into every aspect of your culture. The best way to accomplish a cultural transformation is to instill innovation activity into everyone's behavioral patterns and by focusing on the sixteen Building Blocks (BBs) that make up the TIME Pyramid.

The TIME Pyramid will only be discussed briefly in this book, since the focus of the book is on increasing creativity in small groups and/or projects, rather than changing the culture of the organization. Changing the culture of the organization requires a much broader comprehensive action plan than focusing on specific natural work team programs or projects.

The TIME Pyramid—Sixteen Building Blocks

The following are the sixteen BBs that make up the TIME Pyramid:

- BB-01 Foundation—provides value to stakeholders
- BB-02 Innovative Organizational Assessment
- BB-03 Innovative Executive Leadership

- BB-04 Performance and Cultural Change Management Plans
- BB-05 Commitment to Stakeholders' Expectations
- BB-06 Innovative Project Management Systems
- BB-07 Innovative Management Participation
- BB-08 Innovative Team Development
- BB-09 Individual Creativity, Innovation, and Excellence
- BB-10 Innovative Supply Chain Management
- BB-11 Innovative Design
- BB-12 Innovative Robotics/Artificial Intelligence
- BB-13 Knowledge Assets Management
- BB-14 Comprehensive Measurements System
- BB-15 Innovative Organizational Structure
- BB-16 Rewards and Recognition System

It is these individual BBs and how they work together to strengthen the total organization that makes a real difference. It is now TIME to introduce TIME into one or more of your three key innovation driving parts of your organization. Normally, they are

- sales and marketing
- product engineering
- management

Once you have the approach embedded in one or more of these areas, it is time to roll out the innovation attitude to the total organization.

TIME is ready for you. Will you be on time?

H. James Harrington

ISO TAG 279—INNOVATION

Innovation is not just a phenomenon in the United States. People in small, medium, and large size countries are also focusing on capturing the international market by increasing the number of new and innovative products that they are able to produce. The International Standards Association (ISO) has recognized this trend and has established a special group called ISO TAG 279 to develop international standards relating to innovation. Four TAGs (Committees) have been formed to develop standards for the innovative process, innovative definitions, innovation tools and techniques, and innovation process audits. This international group of experts' output is designed to minimize, if not even eliminate, the main discussions that are going on related to the ISO in terms and definition.

In 2019 two major documents were released by ISO that give guidance in implementing and reviewing an efficient and effective Innovation Management System. These documents that will make up the 56000 series will be coming out soon. We recommend that you purchase ISO 56002 and 56004 from ISO or from your national standards organization when it is formally released to the general public. For the complete documents, you will need to purchase a license from ANSI and/or ISO.

Much of the information presented in this book was the result of knowledge captured as the authors worked with the ISO TC 279 Working Group. Although we were not allowed to include either of these two documents in this book, we have been authorized to present a summary that you can find in Appendix C of this book. The summary was prepared by Richard Fernandez and Frank Voehl.

Although this book is focused on the process to take advantage of an innovative opportunity, we have kept in mind the system that the process needs to operate in.

THE 4 INNOVATION PROFICIENCY MEDALS

Based upon this model, Harrington Management Systems has defined four levels of innovation proficiencies. Rather than using the martial arts approach of belts to indicate different levels of proficiency, we chose the Olympics' medal designations for competencies. They are as follows:

- Bronze Innovation Medal (Introduction to Innovation)—Employees who have received two days of training to improve their creativity/innovation and have passed the exam.
- Silver Innovation Medal (Innovation Process Specialist)—Employees who are capable of managing an improvement opportunity from identifying the opportunity to measuring transition.
- Gold Innovation Medal (Innovation Cultural Specialist)—Employees who are trained and capable of changing the organization's culture to make the organization more creative/innovative.

- Platinum Medal (Innovation Systems Expert)—Managers who set the example for other individuals related to their actual use of the innovative system.

This book is designed to support the training needs for individuals to become a Silver Innovation Medal level performer. The Silver, Gold, and Platinum Innovation Medal levels require the user to complete a project and pass a written exam and an oral interview.

You will note that this approach is directed at the total organization rather than random individuals throughout the organization although we offer classes to the general public.

OUTLINE FOR TWO-DAY BRONZE INNOVATION MEDAL CLASS

1. What is innovation and how does it differ from entrepreneurship, invention, and creativity?
2. How to recognize improvement opportunities
3. Exercise
4. How to evaluate an improvement opportunity
5. Exercise
6. Creativity workshop
7. Exercise
8. Preparing a value proposition
9. Exercise
10. Discussion and closing
11. Presenting bronze medals

OUTLINE FOR THE TWO-DAY SILVER INNOVATION MEDAL CLASS

1. Conduct the innovation walk.
2. Why is innovation important to you? Why is it important to the organization?
3. Understanding the differences between innovation and creativity, continuous improvement, entrepreneurship, and invention.

4. Just before the break in the morning have each member of the class fill out a small innovation survey.
5. Exercise: list of innovations you did in the last 12 months. Classify each one into the different types of innovation four boxes.
6. Explain how to recognize an improvement opportunity.
7. Exercise: make a list of the improvement opportunities within the classroom.
8. Exercise: make a list of self-improvement opportunities.
9. Exercise: make a list of improvement opportunities within your city government.
10. How to select the best improvement opportunity.
11. Exercise: the team combined improvement opportunities related to the classroom and a second list was created related to city government. Using the longest list of improvement opportunities, plot each opportunity on the different types of innovation for box matrix, based upon this analysis for further study.
12. While the exercise is going on, the instructor will make a list of the tools/methodologies that are part of the Green Belts toolkit. When the exercise is over, each of the students will be given three poster notes to put behind the three tools that they are most interested in learning about first. As a result of this exercise, select six tools/methodologies with the highest number of votes to be scheduled for training on the second or third day. The instructor will choose four additional tools/methodologies making up a book for a total of ten tools/methodologies that will be presented on the second or third day.
13. Introduction to the Innovation Systems Cycle.
    - Phase I—Creativity
    - Phase II—Production
    - Phase III—Delivery
14. Process Grouping 1—Opportunity Identification.
15. Process Grouping 2—Opportunity Development.
16. Exercise: Rain Coat Exercise. One person to be the model and the remainder of the group are the designers.
17. Process Grouping 3—Value Proposition.
18. Exercise: for the improvement opportunity you rated the highest, the following is a close will be and what will be the impact on each of the stakeholders.
19. Process Grouping 4—Concept Validation.
20. Process Grouping 5—Business Case Analysis.

21. Exercise: Each member of the team should quickly prepare a 1–2-min elevator speech to sell the improvement opportunity that the group selected. This will then be read out aloud to the entire group and combine them together into one that will be presented to the class.
22. Process Grouping 6—Resource Management.
23. Process Grouping 7—Documentation.
24. Process Grouping 8—Production.
25. Process Grouping 9—Marketing, Sales, and Delivery.
26. Exercise: the team should turn the treatment elevator speech into a sales commercial.
27. Process Grouping 10—After-Sales Service.
28. Process Grouping 11—Performance Analysis.
29. Process Grouping 12—Transformation.
30. Plus–Minus Analysis of the Class.
31. Two- to Four-Hour Exam.

Upon reaching the Silver Innovation Medal proficiency level, this individual becomes an Innovation Process Specialist who is capable of recognizing a problem or improvement opportunity and taking advantage of ones that do not involve large quantities of resources and/or are classified as apparent solutions or minor improvements. Typically Innovation Process Specialists do not set up major improvements, new paradigms, or discovery inventions. Although they may coordinate the ISC related to these opportunities, they are greatly dependent upon other individuals to take the lead in their part of the cycle. The Innovation Process Specialist frequently does not follow the solution all the way through the ISC. Usually these individuals are part of an already established organization that supplies the resources for the project. Often their projects are limited to value added within the organization.

We recommend that the training for Innovation Process Specialists be conducted over a two-week period with four hours of training for ten days in the morning and four hours of consulting in the afternoon, where the instructor works with the students on one of their improvement opportunities. This formula produces knowledge plus results.

After reaching the Gold Medal proficiency level, an individual becomes an Innovation Culture Specialist who has the knowledge and capabilities to lead the change in the organization's culture, planning, and products so that it is significantly more innovative. They work closely with the Board of Directors all away down to the hourly worker.

This individual addresses upgrades/changes to the organization's mission, vision, and operating plan. Their focus is directed at bringing about increased creativity and innovation in every department within the organization. This is often accomplished over a two-year part of the strategic plan. This new culture will be capable of creating added value for the organization and its customers by defining improvement opportunities and the creation of new and unique ideas or concepts all the way through the ISC from recognizing an opportunity to evaluating the actual value added.

INNOVATION MATURITY GRID

There is an extremely wide range of sophistication and effective utilization of the innovative management systems within organizations. Some organizations have not started the journey while other organizations are leading the pack. This evolution from no activity to best-of-breed has been defined as a stair-step made up of twelve innovation maturity levels. Each maturity level requires the organization to be performing at a higher sophistication than the previous level. Moving up the maturity grid staircase is an excellent way to set goals and develop action strategies for your innovation system. The following is a short definition of how the organization would be performing at each of the maturity levels.

- Level I—No innovation is required as we do the same old things the same old way for years, and there are no plans to change.
- Level II—Everyone does what the CEO tells us to do, the way he tells us to do it, and when he wants it done.
- Level III—We do just exactly what we are told to do. If we don't, we get in trouble. We learn from the mistakes we make. We learn that if you make a mistake, you're going to get fired.
- Level IV—If you come up with an idea that increases productivity, this results in someone being laid-off.
- Level V—We get paid to work, not to think.
- Level VI—It is the doer, not the thinker, who gets ahead here. Do exactly what the boss wants and never challenge his or her ideas; that's the way to get ahead.

- Level VII—We don't need R&D because we work only on already-proven products/concepts. Let the competitor waste their money on research.
- Level VIII—Our R&D groups are thinkers; we are the doers.
- Level IX—We all are encouraged to make suggestions, but you soon learn that it is a waste of time.
- Level X—Everyone is encouraged to make suggestions about their job, and the products and management implement the best ones.
- Level XI—Time has been set aside every day for every employee to spend time thinking about what they are doing, how things could be better, and to refresh themselves. Individuals are encouraged to implement their own ideas whenever possible.
- Level XII—Every employee is encouraged to generate ideas that can be implemented. The managers are required to sit down with an employee who has an idea and help him or her develop into a value-added solution. The quality and value-added content of an individual's history file plays a major factor in deciding if he or she will be promoted and when promotions will occur. Employees are encouraged to take rest breaks whenever they are tired, and taking an occasional nap is acceptable.

MIND EXPANDERS OR SUSPENDERS FOR OUR MINDS

Children are born creative, and yet we do our best as adults to stamp it out of their behavior patterns.

- 90% of our five-year-olds are creative
- 10% of our seven-year-olds are creative
- 2% of our fourteen-year-olds are creative

Our education system is based upon conformity, not on originality. Independent thinking is discouraged. There is only one way to spell anything. As a result, we have created a highly educated population of robots that only do what they're told, and anything they are told is the gospel.

The world is full of conventional thinkers, but it is not too late to change these conventional thinkers into innovative thinkers. There are many tools that are available to transcend the usual way of thinking. These tools can

FIGURE P.7
Missing mind expanders.

make a big difference in your life at home and at work. These tools are often called "mind expanders" or "suspenders for our mind" (see Figure P.7).

Today's world is full of people with small minds pointing at a specific point. We are a lot like a pack of wolves hungry to follow the pack and afraid to take a position that is not in keeping with the pack. We don't understand something, but we don't ask the question to get clarification. Why? Because we're afraid it will make us look different. However, often there are many other people just as lost as you and who are not afraid to stand out in the crowd.

Many tools are available that transcend the usual way of thinking. As a result, we don't question our thought patterns that reject any pattern that does not agree with our past experiences. Why risk being different, being unique, and being yourself?

Being creative and innovative can make a big difference in your success at home and at work. There was a time for a management style that was very dictatorial. People were poorly educated, so they told themselves that they should keep quiet and listen to the PhDs. Today, environment is moving more and more toward a participative environment. Executives no longer want yes men or women setting at the conference table with them. They realize that the yes man or woman has no value to the decisions. Today, creativity and innovation have replaced physical labor as a valuable way that an individual can contribute to the organization.

I've been watching some of the people training for the Olympics. They are out there every day stressing the body as far as they can in order to make half a second improvement that means the difference between a Gold medal or not being on the stand at all. We are all competing in our own private Olympics to make things better for ourselves and our families. You're in the innovative competition. You have other competitors in

Germany, Japan, China, Great Britain, Canada, and all other nations. It is a very competitive category with literally billions of people competing against you. Most Olympians focus on exercising the body first and the mind second. In your classification, the mind has to come first; to be competitive, you need to think creatively, better and faster than anyone else. You don't want to find yourself sitting in the stands clapping for somebody else receiving a Gold medal.

The Typical 14 Mind Expanders

Exercising the mind is equally, if not more, important than exercising the body. There are a number of tools called "mind expanders or suspenders for our minds" that are particularly designed to help you develop new and more progressive thought patterns. All of us should be exercising with them a minimum of two hours per week. Some of these exercising tools are as follows:

- The alphabet
- The numbers
- A nursery rhyme
- Common objects
- Personal creativity
- Analyzing outrageous ideas
- Pictures to drive creativity
- Words to drive creativity
- Differences and similarities
- Defining other applications
- Creative progress reports
- Dreaming in color
- Recording your evening's activities
- Discarding the boom box

Note: These exercises are included in the book titled "The Creativity Tools Kit."

To improve your innovative and creative ability, you need to think outside the box. These exercises are designed to challenge the way you think about a situation. Keep track of how many you answer correctly, and at the end of the book, we will provide you with your personal analysis of your creative abilities.

1

Innovation—What Is It?
How Do You Do It? Who Does It?

INTRODUCTION

What is an innovator? That's very simple. An innovator is an individual who takes an idea, sprinkles a little fairy dust on it and magically turns it into a product that people are lining up to buy. Oh, yes, we need to make one clarification. An innovator has to have knowledge about the total Innovation Systems Cycle (ISC) plus a whole lot of drive and pure luck.

> All organizations – not just businesses – need one core competency: INNOVATION.
>
> **Peter Drucker, author and management consultant**

Since the late 1970s, America's focus has been on the elimination of waste, elimination of problems, reducing cycle time, eliminating risks, and adding more value-added activities. This was a period where we focused on efficiency, effectiveness, adaptability, and reducing cost while eliminating defects. Although a great deal of talk was directed at improving customer satisfaction results from programs like Six Sigma, Supply Chain Management, Customer Relations Management Software, TQM, BPI, and Lean, these often had a negative effect on customer satisfaction level (see Table 1.1).

We need to ask ourselves the following question: "Is it Quality Assurance's job to solve problems, reduce costs, or to ensure that we ship products that will meet customer requirements?" I believe our role is to ensure that our products and services as delivered to the customer/consumer meets their requirements. Customer satisfaction ratings' improvement is the single major measurement of the quality initiative

TABLE 1.1

National ACSI Scores

	1st Quarter	2nd Quarter	3rd Quarter	4th Quarter
1994			74.8	74.2
1995	74.1	73.7	73.7	73.7
1996	73.0	72.4	72.2	72.0
1997	70.7	71.7	71.7	70.8
1998	71.9	72.2	72.3	72.6
1999	72.1	72.0	72.1	72.8
2000	72.5	72.8	72.9	72.6
2001	72.2	72.1	72.0	72.6
2002	73.0	73.0	73.1	72.9
2003	73.8	73.8	73.8	74.0
2004	74.4	74.4	74.3	73.6
2005	73.0	73.1	73.2	73.5
2006	74.1	74.4	74.4	74.9
2007	75.2	75.3	75.2	74.9
2008	75.2	75.1	75.0	75.7
2009	76.0	76.1	76.0	75.9
2010	75.9	75.9	75.7	75.3
2011	75.6	75.7	75.7	75.8
2012	75.9	75.9	75.9	76.3
2013	76.6	76.5	76.7	76.8
2014	76.2	76.1	75.6	75.2
2015	74.7	74.3	73.8	73.4
2016	73.7	74.3	75.4	76.8
2017	77.0	76.7	76.7	76.7

excellence. Consumer spending accounts for 70% of US gross domestic product (GDP), which means that changes in customer satisfaction, as measured by the American Customer Satisfaction Index (ACSI), correlate with the changes in GDP. Increases or decreases in the national ACSI score have been shown to predict changes in GDP growth (see Figure 1.1).

During the last twenty years, a high percentage of executive teams have questioned the effectiveness of the different performance improvement programs that were implemented. Although there were significant savings claimed for a number of implemented projects, the impact on the bottom line was nonexistent. Much of the labor savings was reassigned to other projects that weren't being done before, because it was not previously needed or cost justified. This has resulted in the executive team

FIGURE 1.1

Changes in the National ASCI since Q2 1995. Note: Since the low point in 1997, there has been a continuous positive change in the overall customer satisfaction index. Despite a major drop in the index during 2015 and 2016, there has been a major recovery, and at the present time, the customer satisfaction index is higher than the baseline. If you look at a 3-year rolling average, the average is approximately 75.2, an improvement of 0.4 compared with the original baseline. That's not much progress for a 22-year effort.

turning their attention to the development of new products that were value added to the customer and to the organization. This also results in improved customer satisfaction and positive impact upon the bottom line, which has led to increased priority being focused upon creativity and innovation. Unfortunately, the culture developed in support of the elimination of waste was not in line with the culture needed to encourage innovation. The Lean methodology considered the elimination of waste as the primary performance improvement strategy. In the innovation culture, a failure was looked upon as a learning experience. In the Lean methodology elimination of waste culture, whenever the individual wasn't working, they were wasting time. In the innovation culture, large periods of time are set aside for quiet peaceful thinking. Companies like Apple and Google have become role models for the innovation culture. As these two companies have developed a more relaxed homelike culture, they were able to attract the best minds giving them an additional advantage over the elimination of waste culture. Office buildings became campuses, keeping the young and brightest students in an environment that they felt very comfortable in.

In the early 1900s, Ford, General Motors, and Chrysler developed employees who became the new middle class of workers. Unfortunately, in today's environment, the middle class is collapsing as these positions are being transferred to the developing countries. More and more we now have two classes, rather than three, in the United States. We used to have the poor, middle class, and rich populations. Now we just have a poor and rich population, as the middle class jobs are slowly being transferred out of United States. In the mid-1900s, an engineer was a much respected individual; today, everyone is focusing on becoming a doctor or lawyer. This means that a higher and higher percentage of our workforce is staying longer in education/training and has less available years to do productive value-added activities. Organizations that want to keep the middle class in the United States have major problems in trying to find engineering support (manufacturing engineers, industrial engineers, test engineers, etc.).

I love to go to school. It's much more fun than working.

WHY BE INNOVATIVE?

> Imagination drives creativity.
> Creativity drives innovation.
> Innovation drives the organization's reputation.
>
> **H. James Harrington**

Work is going on in the University of Alabama to develop a way to use gravity to propel an object into space rather than holding it on the ground (see Figure 1.2).

In the 1960s, the Star Trek TV series and their subsequent movies were favorites for many of us. Captain James Kirk commanded the battle star "The Enterprise," which took us on many far-out adventures and galaxies. The creators of these shows imagined unbelievable space equipment like laser pistols, handheld radios, talking computers, and teletransportation; these were so far out that not even dreamers could imagine these futuristic devices. All the imaginary things the science-fiction writers were dreaming about it have now become an everyday reality, even teletransportation. In fact, the Australian National University has developed a means for transporting the beam of light from one location to another.

(Super- Conducting Disc)
Dr. Ning Li, Researcher
University of Alabama

© 2007, Harrington Institute, Inc

FIGURE 1.2
Altering gravity.

Just think what this could mean to a transportation industry. There would be no need for airplanes, buses, or even cars; you would simply step into your teletransport unit in San Francisco, set the destination for Paris, and all of a sudden, your physical being would be in the Louvre looking at some of the world's great paintings (see Figure 1.3).

Ping Koy Lam
Australian National University
transported a beam of light

© 2007, Harrington Institute, Inc.

FIGURE 1.3
Teleportation.

Work is underway to use the three-dimensional printing technology to build low-cost housing. Successful pilots have been set up, although the production has been on a very limited scale. Projections are that they can build low-cost small housing in one-third of the time at half the cost (see Figure 1.4).

Furthermore, there's work underway at the present time focusing on direct brain stimulation for learning. Your eyes, your ears, and your mouth are extremely ineffective at taking an outside-of-the-body situation and transferring it to the mind. When we can stimulate the mind directly, we will be able to collapse a four-year college degree into wearing your learning helmet for ten minutes. With this new development, our entire education system would be collapsed down into a learning helmet where initially chips would be used to cover individual subjects, but in the long run, the information would be made public and be available to everyone in the world at no cost. At that point in time, everyone will be equally as intelligent; the differential will be in how they use this information (see Figure 1.5).

Today if you can dream it, you can do it. We used to say "the sky is the limit." That's no longer the case; the limit is what you place upon yourself.

The world is changing everyday. Our competition used to be a next-door neighbor, but today our competition is worldwide. Your competition may be an individual in Zimbabwe whose biggest problem today is getting fresh drinking water. I can imagine the day when water will be more

3 Dimensional Printed Home
IC OMA startup company

FIGURE 1.4
Mass production of housing using the three-dimensional printer technology.

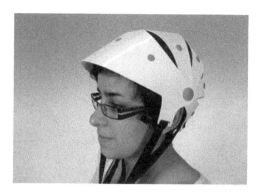

FIGURE 1.5
Leaning helmets.

expensive than gold. More and more developing countries are looking over your shoulder thinking, "Why can't we have everything that the developed countries have?" They feel that they work harder, work longer, and are more productive than the people born in the developed countries. As these developing countries advance, they are increasingly eating away USA's share of the world market. As the developing countries evolved, it was projected that the market would grow as their emerging needs are being defined. But the growth in market share is being offset as the developing countries produce more product than they can absorb. The percentage of World Equity Market Cap (USD) is over 35%, but our debt per citizen is $211,600 and getting bigger every day. We are not going to be able to hold our current position in the world market and hope to pay off some of our personal debts by working hard. The only way we are going to sustain our standard of living is through being more inventive, creative, and innovative. When I was young, anyone who was a graduate from high school had many opportunities to get and hold a good job. My son Jim, as he entered the workforce, needed a master's degree to be offered the same opportunities I was offered. When my granddaughter Grace enters the workforce, she will need a doctorate to have the same type of opportunities open to her or she will have to marry a very innovative husband.

> On a trip to Egypt, when I was talking to my guide he pointed out, 'We have been poor for generations; however, today although we are still poor, with television we now know we are poor.'
>
> **H. James Harrington**

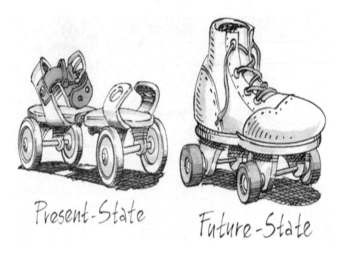

Present-State   *Future-State*

FIGURE 1.6
1920s: present and future state for roller skates.

THE EVOLUTION OF THE ROLLER SKATE

Today's world seems to be turning faster and faster. By the time you explain your innovative idea, someone else has already started to develop a comparable invention. The auto market now has more than ten models of self-parking cars; however, this automatic parallel parking system was not a feature in the car I bought just a few years ago.

Just think about the evolution of the roller skate. My father's roller skate was simply four wheels nailed to a piece of wood that he could stand upon. When I was a boy in the 1930s, roller skates were simply four wheels strapped on your shoes as is pictured in the present state of Figure 1.6. The roller-skate key that was used to adjust the width in the front was a key position for every boy and girl. This has given way for the roller board and today we have the electrical power roller boards.

Today, the present state of roller skates is pictured in Figure 1.7.

If the roller skate is reengineered again, the innovative roller skate could look something like the one pictured in Figures 1.8 and 1.9, which is how your grandson will look traveling to school one day.

> Why become more creative, inventive, innovative, and entrepreneurial? It's a question that is obvious and easy to answer for without it, the American way of life is in jeopardy.
>
> **H. James Harrington**

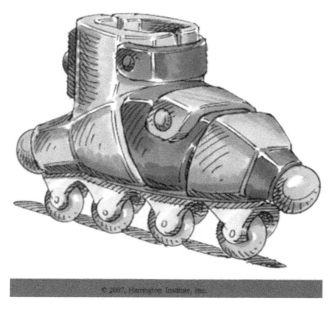

FIGURE 1.7
The present state of roller skate.

FIGURE 1.8
Tomorrow's innovative roller skate.

FIGURE 1.9
A boy traveling to school on an innovative roller skate.

THE TWO WAYS TO IMPROVE YOUR INNOVATION

There are two ways to improve an organization's innovative processes. They are as follows:

- Focused innovative improvement.
- Innovation cultural transformation.

Both of these are effective and provide significant value added to the organization. The one that you select and/or recommend is highly dependent upon your organization's financial, technical, and cultural combinations. Neither of these two approaches can be considered cookie-cutter approaches. Each of them has to be considered and modified based upon the conditions.

The two ways to improve your innovative activities are as follows:

1. Focused innovative improvement—This is an improvement directed at rapidly bringing about increases in the creativity and innovation within a specific part of the organization. It is not designed to bring about a cultural change within the organization and is often used as a pilot approach to validate the effectiveness and efficiency of a

change in the organization's innovative culture. Most often, this approach is used in research and development, product engineering, marketing, and sales.

2. Innovation cultural transformation—In all organizations, it is more difficult and requires more time to bring about a cultural change in the organization than to implement a focused innovative improvement change initiative that is much easier to implement, because the employees are simply told that this is what they must do. An innovation cultural change requires a great deal more time to implement, as it is directed at having management and employees truly believe that this is the best alternative.

THE 5 INNOVATOR DNA SKILLS

Organizations continue to fail because they believe that innovation is a passport that only the engineering departments have. Stephen R. Covey points out that, "Successful innovators exhibit common behavioral habits—habits that can boost one's creativity capacity." The truth of the matter is no organization can reach its full potential, unless innovation is part of its deoxyribonucleic acid (DNA).

In the book *The Innovator's DNA: Mastering the Five Skills of Disruptive Innovators,* the authors (Jeff Dyer, Hal Gregersen, and Clayton Christensen) have defined five discovery skills that are prevalent in innovators who create breakthrough innovation. They are as follows:

1. Questioning
2. Observing
3. Networking
4. Experimenting
5. Associating

Every individual from the CEO to the person mowing the lawns needs to be reexamining everything they do to determine whether their job can be done in a more creative way. The more creatively the individual is performing his or her assigned task, the more innovative the organization becomes. Take, for example, a mother's womb, which is the creative part of the birth cycle. The father injects stimuli that penetrates and fertilizes the eggs, which results in adding value to the world in the form of another human being. Just as the fertile egg is the creative part of the birth cycle, many creative ideas are required to feed the innovation's stimuli. No organization can survive for long without creativity being part of everyday requirements.

> An organization can have creativity without having innovation but cannot have innovation without creativity. Often the creative idea that has no customers is the stimulus that generates new and innovative projects.
>
> **H. James Harrington**

We recommend that a focused innovative improvement project be implemented as a pilot. Based upon the outcome of the pilot, an innovation cultural transformation project should then be implemented. Usually, a number of focused innovative improvement projects will be implemented in parallel with the innovation cultural transformation initiatives, because the organization wants to optimize their innovation activities/performance as soon as possible. The innovation cultural transformation takes additional time, as it is directed at changing the behavior patterns that impact long-term performance.

ORGANIZING FOR INNOVATION IMPROVEMENT

Yes, you are doing what you want to do better. You believe that your organization's performance would be greatly improved if your organization was one of the innovative leaders in your industry. The question is, "What type of organization will provide increased creativity and innovation?" I hear stories about companies like Google, one of the outstanding leaders in the innovation field, providing sleeping areas for their employees so that they can sleep during working hours. I will be damned if I will allow my employees to sleep during working hours. I put in twelve-hour days, and I expect my workers to give me a full eight hours work each day. I understand Minnesota Mining and Manufacturing Company (3M) celebrates noble failures. I don't need any noble people around. I expect the job to be done right the first time and every time. These innovation specialists say that failure is a learning experience that you must accept in innovative culture. I say failure is a very expensive way to provide education to employees.

It's a new world out there, and management needs to understand that the styles and approaches used yesterday are no longer effective in the very competitive international market that we all are part of. Both the executive team and the board of directors need to understand that the workforce has evolved significantly who are looking for different types of self-satisfaction and compensation (see Figure 1.10).

Before 1890, a vast majority of our people were making their living by farming and cattle raising. By 1910, the Model T had transformed the worker environment by putting most of our people to work as factory workers. This mobility brought large groups of people together surrounding large factories. By 1930, the support staff began to grow in stature and quantity of employees. The worker environment shifted days of the factory worker to an office worker. By 1950, it was obvious that the office worker required a great deal of knowledge in order to perform his or her job effectively. The individual's scope was reduced while their depth of knowledge in a specific field was lengthened. This opened the door to the training of employees and hiring office workers who had a significant formal education behind them. By 1970, the complexity of the support areas required highly trained individuals who maintained an excellent understanding of their chosen field. As a result, major organizations accepted the responsibility of providing information and training to their employees. The concept of lifelong employment that gave way to learning became a reality. The focus here was on becoming as effective and efficient as possible to eliminate waste of all kinds.

By 2010, the work environment had changed significantly. The United States became a service provider, rather than a manufacturer. Entry-level jobs that were performed by high school graduates were now being

Worker Evolution

Land Workers *Factory* **Office** *Knowledge* **Information** *Innovation*
(Farmers) *Workers* **Workers** *Workers* **Workers** *Workers*
Business Age (Wave)

FIGURE 1.10
Worker evolution over the last 150 years.

performed by MBAs and master's degree graduates. At one time, this work was interesting, challenging, and rewarding to the high school graduates, but it was boring and dissatisfying to these highly educated workers. A feeling took over employees in the United States of "I love my job, but I hate doing it." Problem-solving that was challenging to the high school graduate has given way to recognizing opportunities and understanding how to develop them. As a result, we now have the innovative worker. This individual is looking for ways to use his or her skills. They are bored with the old methods, and their attention span has collapsed to minutes. These are individuals who like to take risks. The loyalty is not to the company, but to their profession. It's obvious that these innovative workers need to have an environment that challenges them and provides them with a personal sense of accomplishment. This new environment provides management with a difficult, but rewarding, challenge. How do you save face when you have been preaching to them for the last thirty years and that they are expected to work without making errors and now you're saying, "I'm sorry you made an error. I hope you learned something from the experience. After all, it was a noble failure."

To fail is human, but to be paid for it is divine.

It's very true that you will be navigating through some very treacherous waters for the exposure from running aground is higher than it's ever been before. If you're going to successfully navigate these waters without running aground or ripping the bottom of your boat, you will need a very experienced helmsman getting you all the way to the consumer's pocketbook. This requires an assessment that tells you where you are and what your strengths and weaknesses are. Typical assessments that we use are the following:

- History Assessment—Determines the emotional impact of previous innovative projects on the employees.
- Is/Should Be Analysis—This is from focus groups of employees, first-line managers, middle managers, and key staff personnel. The same analysis is given to all of the executive team. Each question is analyzed related to where it is today, where it should be in 3 years, and how important is it that it reaches its objective.
- The McKinsey 7S Survey—This survey is directed at management, product, processes, services, and sales and marketing.

- Innovation Maturity Analysis for Your Organization—It is the usual initial online survey that provides the individual analyses feedback related to their personal use of the organization's innovation. You can get to the survey using the following link www.hjharringtonassociates.com. When you get to this web site, just click on breaking news. After you take the survey, the computer will analyze your inputs and provide a free customized report back to you within several minutes.
- Innovative Management System Review—This review compares the organization's innovative management system to best practices.

The Opportunity Center

To stimulate the creativity and innovation movement within their organizations, many of the more advanced US organizations are now establishing or replacing their suggestion departments with a new organization called "Opportunity Centers." These Opportunity Centers play a key role in stimulating creativity and innovation in all areas of the organization. However, in most cases, the Opportunity Center was the outcome of the evolutionary growth of the suggestion system. In some organizations, the Innovation Center and the Knowledge Management System responsibilities have also been delegated to the Opportunity Center. Having the Knowledge Management System part of the Opportunity Center provides an ideal organizational structure. The Opportunity Center then serves as the spearhead for the creative and innovative activities within the organization. In keeping with this responsibility, it maintains a database that collects best practices operations, both internal and external to the organization.

Often the Opportunity Center will be the champion for an idea that has been presented to them. Individuals who believe they have a good idea will often go to the Opportunity Centers where professionals help them clarify and document their ideas. For some ideas, the Opportunity Center will schedule meetings with key executives and assess the employee in presenting their concept, including the projected value added.

A typical mission statement for an Opportunity Center could read as follows.

The Opportunity Center is responsible for stimulating and activating the creative and innovative activities for all the organization's employees. This is accomplished by providing training on problem solving, creativity, and innovation. The Opportunity Center personnel provide one-on-one and group mentoring with the objective of helping employees clarify and develop their ideas. They then provide guidance and help the individuals and the organization to transform these concepts into tangible results.

Typical services that are provided by an Opportunity Center are as follows:

- Review suggestions to identify ones that have a high potential payback and putting them on a fast track to get them implemented.
- Review suggestions to identify ones that need additional clarification. Then sit down with the individual that made the suggestion to help the individual document his or her ideas.
- Serve as a resource that will work with an individual who is having difficulties in expressing and documenting their ideas.
- Help individuals prepare value propositions that are used to evaluate conceptual ideas.
- Provide training on various problem-solving tools, innovation approaches, and knowledge management methodologies.
- Serve as the ombudsman for individuals or teams that are presenting ideas and concepts to the management.
- Help individuals or groups to find executive sponsors for ideas that have significant merit.
- Help individuals develop their high potential ideas into documented value propositions that are presented to management.
- Provide mentors for teams or groups that are holding brainstorming or problem-solving meetings.
- Maintain a best practice database that makes up the Knowledge Management System.
- Establish and coordinate communities of practice to propagate knowledge exchange.

Typically, an individual, who is having problems in clarifying and documenting a concept that he or she has developed, will schedule a meeting with a member from the Opportunity Center. Often, these meetings are focused on getting a better understanding of the difficulties in implementing his or her concept and calculating potential benefits, costs, and risks related to the implementation of the concept. The Opportunity Center personnel are responsible for helping the individual clarify and refine their concept. The outcome of this activity can result in the concept being discarded or the preparation of a value proposition that will be presented to the management team. On occasion, the results from these meetings are a decision that the concept is not in line with the mission of the organization. When this is the case, in the more advanced organizations, the Opportunity Center personnel will help the individual to determine whether it is a marketable idea. Some organizations even encourage the employees, who have marketable ideas that do not relate to the organization's mission, to become entrepreneurs. In these cases, the personnel in the Opportunity Center will acquaint the employee with the risk, benefits, and activities required to form his or her own corporation or to market the idea to an organization outside of the one that presently employs them. These are organizations that are concerned about its employees and realize that small business is the heartbeat of the American economy. These are organizations that look beyond their own bottom line, thereby encouraging innovation and entrepreneurship throughout the organization.

Typical Objectives of the Opportunity Center

The following is a list of typical objectives that could be set when an Opportunity Center is established.

- Obtain 100% of all employees submitting ways to improve how they perform their assigned task each year. This includes everyone from the CEO down through the organization chain.
- Obtain an average of two implemented suggestions per month per employee related to how he or she performs his or her assigned tasks.
- Obtain from each major function in the organization at least one major improvement concept every year that will generate revenue or define operating savings equal to the operating cost of that function over the following three years.
- Obtain from each function creative concepts that will improve their productivity by a minimum of 5% per year. This will be measured by the function being able to increase its output by a minimum of 5% using the same resources or by producing the same quantity of output using 5% less resources.
- Help the organization generate 35% of its revenue each year from products and/or services that were not offered three years earlier.
- Provide training to 100% of the employees that will help improve their problem-solving ability and their creativity.
- Conduct the closing postmortem related to successful and unsuccessful projects. The results of these postmortems are entered into the knowledge database.

- Establish and maintain an online database of best practices and proven applied approaches that have been used by the organization and that may be used to create new solutions and products.
- Champion the implementation of good ideas developed in one part of the organization to throughout the organization (e.g., use of robotic cleaning devices throughout the laboratory).

You may wonder why an organization would include their Knowledge Management System as part of the Opportunity Center. Increasingly, today's improvements are based upon an evolution, rather than revolution, of concepts. A good Knowledge Management System collects information related to how problems have been solved in the past and groups them in a format that past experience can readily be applied to existing problems. Reapplying proven concepts, slightly modified to correct a current problem, is often the less risky path to take in your continuous improvement.

50+ INNOVATIVE APPROACHES/CONCEPTS

In our approach to transform organizations into innovation centers of competency, we use 50+ different approaches/concepts. The 50+ approaches/concepts are made up of 452+ elements. The following is a list of some of the 50+ innovative approaches/concepts:

1. The 4 Basic Types of People Who Drive Innovation
2. The 16 Building Blocks (BB)
3. The 5 Innovation Proficiency Medals
4. The 2 Ways to Improve Your Innovation
5. The 5 Innovator's DNA skills
6. The 24 Innovative Approaches/Concepts
7. The 12 Statements to Evaluate if Innovation Is a Core Value
8. The 4 Behaviors That Defined Corporate Culture
9. The 4 Innovation Targets
10. The 9 Ways to Finding Creative/Innovative Solutions
11. The 14 Innovator knowledge areas
12. The 2 Types of Innovative Improvement Initiatives
13. The 12 Innovation Systems' Groupings
14. The 5 Certification Levels

15. The 5 "I do it" Phases
16. The 6 "Must Being Willing to"
17. The 3 Reasons for Lack of Creativity Dilemma
18. The 12 Idea Evaluation Questions
19. The 5 Creativity Myths
20. The 13 Truths about Creativity
21. The 12 Creativity Killers
22. The 13 Rules for Individuals to Become More Creative
23. The 8 Foundations for Your Ideas
24. The 2 Creativity Levels
25. The 4 Styles of Creativity
26. The 5 Questions to Maximize Any Creative Effort
27. The 3 Thinking Styles
28. The 4 Resources to Consider
29. The 30 Impact Results
30. The 3 Thoughts about Developing AHA Solutions
31. The 6 Parts of the Value Chain
32. The 5-Phase Process Cycle
33. The 14 Typical Mind Expanders
34. The 3 Ways to Improve Innovation
35. The 4 Things to Remember
36. The 10 Typical Creativity Tools
37. The 14 Typical *What If* Questions
38. The 5 Problems with Most Databases
39. The 8 Questions to Evaluate a Solution
40. The 10 S's of Improvement Drivers
41. The 20 A's of Creative Behavior Patterns
42. The 5 Creative Fundamentals
43. The 6 Creative Time Rules
44. The 4 Drivers of Creativity and Innovation
45. The 5 Techniques for Managing Creative People
46. The 10 Fire Starters (Urgency Drivers)
47. The 5 Types of Invention
48. The 5 Levels of Improvement
49. The 76 Most Effective and/or Most Used Innovation Tools/ Methodologies
50. The 16 Questions to Evaluate Supplier's Processes
    Total = 468 + elements
    Total = 50 + approaches

An Overview of the 50 Innovative Approaches/Concepts

Throughout this book, we will be addressing the 50 innovative approaches/ concepts to define how each fits into the total transformation of the organization's activities and culture. The following is a partial list of some of these approaches with an explanation of what each is designed to accomplish.

- The 5 "I Do It" Statements: They explain how an individual feels as he or she moves a potential project from recognizing the problem to evaluating the value of the activity with real customer data.
- The 20 A's Creative Behavior Patterns: These are twenty things that an individual or organization needs to be able to perform in an innovative organization.
- The 10 S's Improvement Drivers: These are the ten drivers of the innovation culture within an organization. (Shared vision, strategy, systems, structure, skills, styles, staffing, specialized technologies, systematic change management, and systematic knowledge management.)
- The 5 Types of Invention: Inventions can range from the very simple to the very complex, from the obvious improvement to an idea that is totally unexpected. (Apparent solution, minor improvement, major improvement, new paradigm, and discovery.)
- The 4 Styles of Creativity: New creative ideas can be generated using different types of the management system. (Structured creativity, nonlinear creativity, provoking creativity, and Aha creativity.)
- The 12 Innovation Systems Groupings: The process of taking an opportunity and moving it through the ISC consists of three phases—Phase I. Creation, Phase II. Preparation and Production, and Phase III. Delivery. Each of the three phases has four process groupings that take place during the specific phase, making up a total of twelve process groupings in the ISC.
- The 76 Most Effective and/or Most Used Innovation Tools/ Methodologies: A list of over 250 innovation tools and/or methodologies was accumulated. This list was narrowed down to seventy six of the most effective and/or most used tools and/or methodologies for innovation. The list was divided into three different categories of approximately twenty five tools/methodologies for each category.

The three categories were organizational and operational, evolutionary and improvement, and creative tools and methodologies.

- The 24 Organizational and Operational: These are the twenty four tools/methodologies that are used to bring about major changes in organization and its culture.
- The 23 Evolutionary and Improvement Tools, Methods, and Techniques: These are tools and methodologies that are based upon changes/improvements to products or processes that provide value to the organization and to the customer. Many of these tools are total quality management tools, although there are some tools that are unique to the product development cycle.
- The 29 Creative Tools, Methods, and Techniques: These are tools/techniques that aid in the development of new and unique concepts. These are not used to bring about improvements to the already established product and/or processes.
- The 3 Ways to Improve Innovation: This lists three ways to improve the quantity of relevant ideas and/or the quality of ideas.
- The 14 Typical Mind Expanders: This is a list of fourteen exercises that have proven to be effective at improving an individual's capability to develop unique and creative ways of addressing an opportunity.

The 12 Statements to Evaluate Whether Innovation Is a Core Value

Almost every CEO I know tells me and even brags about how innovative their organization is. The critical important factor that needs to be foremost in the minds of board of directors and executive team and in the organization's strategic plan is making innovation a core value throughout the organization. Yes, an innovative research and development team is an excellent start, but it's only a start. There has to be a feeling of urgency sweeping through the entire organization, brushing out the old spider webs that keep us from dreaming big dreams and transferring those dreams into reality. Almost everyone has a war story that proves some point in time when someone in the organization was innovative, but that does not mean that innovation is a priority throughout the organization.

This only happens when innovation is a core value for every individual in the organization.

The following is a list of statements designed to help you determine if an innovation is or is not a core value in your organization. Think about each of the following statements honestly and without prejudice. Then ask yourself if your organization is truly innovative.

1. Products are becoming a commodity
2. Technology, products, or improvement processes are mature
3. Seems impossible to design around competition's patents
4. Busy dealing with recalls for failures or safety
5. System performance not meeting expectations or standards
6. Global competition is winning (shorter time-to-market)
7. "Innovation Director? I'll connect you to our Quality Dept."
8. "My idea was finally accepted despite the system"
9. Toughest problems seem unsolvable
10. "Innovation requires people with *genius genes*"
11. How many new and unique ideas have I had in the last 3 months?
12. Is your customer more satisfied with your organization than he was last year and if so, by how much?

KEY TERMS USED IN THIS BOOK

I debated long and hard if definitions should be given in Chapter 1 of the book or listed in its Appendix only. I finally decided to put them in both places because how you define an innovator or innovation greatly impacts the certification process. Someplace, between 50% and 70% of all patents issued never produce anything that is value added. If you are part of an established organization, probably no one in the organization is innovative as they are usually only involved in part of the ISC. If you're in a startup company, the innovator will need to know and understand each of the twelve Process Groupings or they will probably not be successful.

When we decided to certify people as Innovation Specialists, we chose to adhere to the most stringent requirements, rather than including ideas that create little or no value, adjusting it to their present specific assignments. Often, innovators are called upon to step away from the structured environment of an established organization to take on the excitement of building their personal brand. Based upon this, now is the time to establish a common understanding of the key terms we used throughout this book.

- **Breakthrough Innovation**: Innovation that changes the game or breakthrough ideas and their implementation that leads to substantial change in the organization business model and/or product/service offerings.
- **Create**: Make something: to bring something into existence.
- **Creative**: Using the ability of people to make or think of new things involving the process by which new ideas, stories, products, etc., are created.
- **Entrepreneur**: An entrepreneur is a person who organizes and manages any enterprise, especially a business, usually with considerable initiative and risk. They do not have to create the idea or concept.
- **Innovation Management**: The systematic development of innovation in an organization, including designing and implementing business processes, workflows, systems, and activities to generate insight, creative ideas, evaluate them, develop business cases, prioritize experiments, and execute projects based on the new concept developed to manage innovative investment.
- **Innovation Systems Cycle (ISC)**: The way a typical project for products would progress through the innovative activities from identifying opportunities to measuring the value added to stakeholders. There is a trend to use the term "interested parties" in place of "stakeholders." We personally like the word "stakeholders," as it indicates that these are the people who are impacted by the organization's operations. In my age, I am interested in almost everything, but that doesn't mean I'm going to cook shortlists tonight for supper. I'm interested in what's new at the movies, but I'm not going to the unhappy and/or take action because an Errol Flynn movie is not playing.
- **Innovative Idea**: An innovative idea is a new and unique one that adds greater value to the customer and the organization than it cost to produce it.

- **Innovator**: An individual who is capable of creating added value for the organization and its customers by being capable of taking new and unique ideas or concepts all the way through the ISC, from recognizing an opportunity to evaluating the actual value added.

  Note: The definition of innovator greatly varies from company to company and consultant to consultant. At one end of the spectrum, an innovator is defined as anyone who creates a value-added idea/concept. It does not have to be unique/original, nor does it need to be marketable. An extreme example is an employee who tells his manager that the filing cabinet needs to be bolted to the wall so that it won't fall over and hurt someone.

  At the other end of the spectrum, an innovator is defined as a person who generates a unique and original idea or concept for some portion of the product or service that adds value to both the organization and the external customer. For example, defining a new material that is less expensive and less breakable than the present material for the face of an iPad.

  A third definition of an innovator is an individual who defines a new and unique idea that has potential value to the organization and the consumer and is then responsible for managing it through the total ISC. Due to the smokestack organizational structure in most large companies, it is difficult, if not impossible, for any one individual to lead the innovative project throughout its entire cycle. In each of the major functions Research and Development (R&D), project management, production control, purchasing, manufacturing, quality, personnel, sales and marketing, etc.), there are individuals who are experts in specific parts of the ISC, and they must be creative in the way they conduct these activities. With this definition, there is no employee or manager who is innovative, although they may all be very creative. The organization itself may provide output that is very innovative.
- **Intrapreneur**: An employee of a large corporation who is given freedom and financial support to create new products, services, systems, etc., and does not have to follow the corporation's usual routines or protocols.
- **Natural Work Teams**: A natural work team is any group of individuals that report to the same individual. It could be employees that report to the first-line manager, first-line managers that report to a second-line manager, etc.

- **Organization**: A company, corporation, firm, enterprise, or association of any part thereof, whether it is incorporated or not, public or private, has its own function and administration (source: ISO 8402—1994). It can be as small as a first-line department and as large as the government in the United States.
- **Organizational structure**: It is a system used to define a hierarchy within an organization. It identifies each job, its function, and where it reports to within the organization. This structure is developed to establish how an organization operates and assists an organization in obtaining its goals to allow for future growth. The structure is illustrated using an organizational chart.
- **S curve**: A mathematical model, also known as the logistic curve, describes the growth of one variable in terms of another variable over time. S curves are found in fields from biology and physics to business and technology. In business, the S curve is used to describe, and sometimes predict, the performance of a company or a product over a period of time.
- **Structure**: The arrangement of and relations between the parts or elements of something complex.

Many company's weakness is the inflexibility of its management structure.

H. James Harrington

Notes:
- **Innovative versus Creative**: The output from an innovative process must create added value, while the output from the creative process does not have to be valued.
- **Innovator versus Entrepreneur**: The entrepreneur does not have to originate the idea/concept. An innovator needs to create new and unique concepts that are value added to the organization and the external customer. To be considered successful, they both have to produce an output that is value added to someone other than themselves.
- **Innovation versus Invention**: Innovation differs from invention in that innovation refers to the use of a better and, as a result, novel idea or method, whereas invention refers more directly to the creation of the idea or method itself.
- **Innovation versus Improvement**: Innovation differs from improvement in that innovation refers to doing something different rather than doing the same thing better.

THE 4 BEHAVIORS THAT DEFINE CORPORATE CULTURE

There are four values and behaviors that contribute to the unique social and psychological environment of an organization. Organizational culture includes an organization's expectations, experiences, philosophy, and values that hold it together, and is expressed in its self-image, inner workings, interactions with the outside world, and future expectations. It is based on shared attitudes, beliefs, customs, and written and unwritten rules that have been developed over time and are considered valid. Also called corporate culture, it's shown in

1. The ways the organization conducts its business, treats its employees, customers, and the wider community.
2. The extent to which freedom is allowed in decision-making, developing new ideas, and personal expression.
3. How power and information flow through its hierarchy down to the rest of the organization.
4. How committed employees are toward collective objectives (business dictionary).

THE 4 INNOVATION TARGETS

There are four innovation targets:

- Target 1. Structures—Reflects the way the organization is organized, its job descriptions, organizational chart, and reporting relationships, and also includes rewards and recognition.
- Target 2. Processes—The way work is accomplished (financial processes, information processes, communication processes, human resource policies and procedures).
- Target 3. People—This includes the skill level of all personnel, their ability to work together, their commitment to the organization, their ability to accomplish difficult tasks, the level of management support required, and the ability to see and appreciate the differences in other people.
- Target 4. Products—This includes keeping up with the technologies that are related to your product even if it is a service or a tangible

hard product. It includes being able to develop and deliver products that are innovative in nature to the point that they are distinguished from your competition. It includes product reliability, quality, environment, availability, function, and maintainability. It is the point where the value to the customer/consumer is evaluated. You cannot have an innovative product if for any reason the customer would prefer to buy the product from another source.

Is It a Good Idea?

A truly creative individual will be identifying improvement opportunities every place they go. It could be while parking the car, going to a meeting, giving instructions to another employee, getting a cup of coffee, talking with a neighbor in the next cubicle, swimming with their family, sweeping the floors, watching over the building in the night, etc. There are literally hundreds of improvement opportunities out there just waiting for you to identify. Some of these are worthwhile and should be on anyone's hit list. Others may look like improvement opportunities but turn out to be negative value added when analyzed. The question is, "How do you know what should be on your list of good improvement opportunities?" The following are nine of the things that should be considered related to each potential improvement opportunity.

1. Is it creative or merely original?
2. Does it result in significant value added?
3. Will it be implemented?
4. Will it create true value to the stakeholders?
5. Will it work and get the results you want?
6. Is it better than the current situation and why?
7. Will it be accepted and is it in line with the organization's culture?
8. Is this the right time?
9. Is it worth the effort?

For potentially worthwhile improvement opportunities, we suggest that you record the following five impressions, because many of the improvement opportunities may be value added but are not a priority on your schedule.

1. What is the improvement opportunity?
2. How will the improvement add value and how much value will it add to the stakeholders?

3. How will this impact the external customer?
4. Is it difficult or simple to correct?
5. Who will define how the improvement opportunity will be taken advantage of?

You don't have to be extremely accurate in your estimates. Your opinion will be good enough, but you should be able to explain why and how you made the estimates to the management team. Realizing what you are doing is asking the organization to commit sufficient resources to develop a plan to take advantage of the improvement opportunity. These resources may be just your personal time or could be the financial as well as personal time from other employees.

THE 9 WAYS TO FINDING CREATIVE/ INNOVATIVE SOLUTIONS

When it comes to being creative or being innovative in designing an existing product or process, there are nine general ways to develop an innovative solution. This approach will provide you with a satisfactory answer 98% of the time. For each of the nine general ways to improve, ask yourself this question "WHAT IF?" (for example, What if I combine the three activities together?)

1. Divide
2. Add
3. Subtract
4. Magnify
5. Combine
6. Simplify
7. Substitute
8. Minimize
9. Redesign

Once you answer the "WHAT IF" question, you are now ready to ask the "IF I" question. If I divided it into three parts, how would that add value? If I added another function to it, how would it add value to the item? Do this for each of the nine individual ways to innovation and select the two or three best approaches to develop further. Sometimes, it's necessary to combine two to four improvement ways in order to get a satisfactory result. Of course, there are a number of other ways to stimulate your creative juices, but we think this is one of the very best approaches. We will be discussing some of these other alternatives later on in this book.

THE 14 INNOVATOR KNOWLEDGE AREAS

Individual creativity is directed at finding solutions to personal problems, improving financial and/or living standards, organizational, and providing a level of personal satisfaction. Organizations need to be innovative to provide increased value-added content to all of their stakeholders (stakeholders include management, investors, customers, suppliers, employees, the employees' families, and the community).

I'm often asked the question, "Would you rather have creative employees or innovative employees?" The answer to this question is obvious when you realize you cannot have innovation without creativity, but you can have creativity without innovation. The key is to interest your employees enough so that a higher percentage of their creativity is directed at taking advantage of organizational opportunities. Usually, as you increase the number of creative ideas, you increase the number of ideas that provide added value to the organization. Increased creativity drives increased opportunities, because creativity drives innovation (see Figure 1.11).

- Priority 1—opportunity recognition.
- Priority 2—creativity
- Priority 3—innovation

  - *Creativity* is idea generation

  - *Innovation* is implementing ideas in ways that create economic value in your business world

FIGURE 1.11
Creativity versus innovation.

To be an innovator, we need to be knowledgeable about the following knowledge areas:

1. Opportunity identification
2. Creation/problem-solving
3. Business planning
4. Finance/accounting
5. Human relations
6. Computer/software support
7. Supply chain management
8. Patent processing
9. Data analysis/value propositions/business case analysis
10. Documentation and document control
11. Resource and equipment acquisition
12. Production/manufacturing engineering
13. Sales and marketing
14. Measuring value added to stakeholders

TWO TYPES OF INNOVATIVE IMPROVEMENT INITIATIVES

We believe that there are two distinct types of innovative improvement initiatives. Each type can stand alone if designed to accomplish a specific task or the two can be implemented in parallel to maximize their impact and to minimize the time required to make innovation a part of the organization's culture. The following are the two types of innovative improvement initiatives.

1. Managing a single innovative opportunity. This involves taking an individual improvement opportunity and managing it through the complete ISC. The results are easily measured as a single process/product is used and a single set of output is measured related to its value added.
2. Transforming the organization's culture into one that is more innovative. Typically, this requires a major initiative that penetrates every function within the organization. It typically requires changes to the job descriptions, organization values, strategic plan, performance

measurement systems, etc. As a result, it typically takes two years to complete the initiative.

INNOVATION PROCESS GROUPINGS

Not only does the innovator need to know and how to use the 14 innovator knowledge areas, they have to know when and how to put them together to create an active innovation process. A typical hardware-type process will be made up of three phases that are subdivided into twelve process groupings. When studying the twelve process groupings, each event may look relatively simple to master, but when you try to tie them together into an effective process, they become interrelated activities that require a great deal of skill and experience to optimize their efficiency and effectiveness. Figure 1.12 lists the three phases of the ISC with the supportive process groupings.

The ISC is uniquely developed for hardware and new products, as it usually is the most complicated. Usually, software and organizational improvements follow a general cycle. However, they don't have to penetrate into the details related to each activity that a hardware improvement or

Phase I. Creation

- Process Grouping 1. Opportunity Identification
- Process Grouping 2. Opportunity Development
- Process Grouping 3. Value Proposition
- Process Grouping 4. Concept Validation

Phase II. Preparation and Production

- Process Grouping 5. Business Case Analysis
- Process Grouping 6. Resource Management
- Process Grouping 7. Documentation
- Process Grouping 8. Production

Phase III. Delivery

- Process Grouping 9. Marketing, Sales, and Delivery
- Process Grouping 10. After-Sales Services
- Process Grouping 11. Performance Analysis
- Process Grouping 12. Transformation

FIGURE 1.12
Innovation Systems Cycle.

release goes through, although their impact on the organization can be greater than a new product release. We will be discussing the ISC in much greater detail later on in the book.

> Everyone can be creative, but not everyone can be an innovator. It takes a very special person with a good understanding of how the business operates to be an innovator. Many established organizations are very innovative and they often have creative people working for them.

H. James Harrington

BOOK OBJECTIVES

The objective of this book is to prepare an individual to perform the duties and activities of an innovator, as defined later. Unfortunately, because the innovator needs to be the person who is familiar with the entire product cycle, it will require an individual to complete the Silver Innovation Medal and Gold Innovation Medal training activities and successfully pass the test for each level. The Silver Innovation Medal training is heavily focused on improving creativity and potentially innovative ideas and solutions. In order for the Innovation Process Specialist to function, they will need to have knowledge of the remaining parts of the ISC.

Typically anyone who has obtained a Gold Innovation Medal focuses on solutions for more complex opportunities and on much greater capabilities related to the total ISC. They also will need to have the understanding and abilities to guide the board of directors and the executive team as they implement an innovative culture across the organization. The Innovation Culture Specialist usually serves as the innovation champion for the organization. Upon completing the training and test for the Innovation Process Specialist and Innovation Cultural Specialist, a demonstration of capabilities needs to be performed. Individuals who have successfully completed the course and to read passed the required tests, but who have not demonstrated capabilities, will be given a certificate of attendance. After completing the capabilities' demonstration satisfactorily, they will receive the Silver Innovation or Gold Innovation medal.

A well-known saying by Angels in Silicon Valley is, "You're not an entrepreneur until you've had a minimum of four failures." By reaching Innovation Cultural Specialist status, you should be able to greatly reduce this number.

SUMMARY

The elimination of waste approach to increasing customer satisfaction and reducing costs has been in practice for many years. It may work for some of the developing countries as they are frequently competing based on inexpensive labor, but in industry and governments of the developed countries, they need to increase their focus on developing more advanced innovative products and services. That's easier said than done, for most established industries have been focusing on increasing the product performance while decreasing the product costs for many years. The National Standards Association has been extremely active in collecting good practices and procedures like ISO 9000 and ISO 14000.

There are many ways to improve your organization's performance. Everywhere you look and every book and magazine you read list new ways to run your business better. Everyone has been claiming that they have the road map to put the organization ahead of its competitors. However, there is no silver bullet, but there is a combination that can lead you to win the gold medal. The mistakes many organizations make are each time their managers read a new book or go to a new conference, they come back with new concepts to implement. Most of these concepts are just different names given to the same tools and methodologies in order to set the organization apart from its competition. With so many things out there to try, it's difficult to stay with one concept long enough to make it successful. It's a lot like a boy going into a candy shop when the clerk is not there. He helps himself to as much candy as he can carry out and heads directly for the back of the barn where he eats all of it. An hour later, he's in terrible pain and wonders why his stomach aches. Too much of a good thing can be worse than doing nothing (see Figure 1.13).

MIND EXPANDER'S EXERCISE

To improve your innovative and creative ability, you need to think outside the box. These exercises are designed to challenge the way you think about a situation. Keep track of how many you answer correctly, and at the end of this book, we will provide you with your personal analysis of your creative abilities.

Defining How to Change

FIGURE 1.13
Too much of a good thing.

Chapter 1. Mind Expander's Exercise

There is a clerk at the butcher shop. He is 5 feet 10 inches tall and he wears size 13 sneakers. What does he weigh?

RECOGNITION AND COMMENTS

The following books and/or PowerPoint presentations of H. James Harrington were used as references, and information from them was included in many of the chapters.

Presentations on innovation

- *Innovation*—The International Association of Innovation Professionals (IAOIP) annual conference by H. James Harrington (Boston 2016)
- *Hmmm—Creativity* presentation by H. James Harrington conference (Jamaica 2008)
- *The Innovation Process* presentation by H. James Harrington at American Society for Quality (ASQ) Section Meeting (Sacramento 2017)

- *Creating a Creative Culture* presentation by H. James Harrington (UAE 2012)
- *Status of Innovation* presentation by H. James Harrington (Mexico 2017)
- *Using TRIZ* presentation by H. James Harrington (Dubai 2016)
- *Innovate or Evaporate* presentation given by H. James Harrington (Abu Dhabi UAE 2010)
- *Organizational Excellence* given by H. James Harrington (Shanghai China 2003)
- *The Innovation Works* given by H. James Harrington (UAE 2014)

Books authored or coauthored by H. James Harrington that were used in this chapter

H. James Harrington is a prolific author, publishing hundreds of technical reports and magazine articles. He has authored or coauthored over fifty-five books. The following books were written or coauthored by H. James Harrington and were used as reference with parts of them.

- *Innovative Change Management (ICM): Preparing Your Organization for the New Innovative Culture* (2018)
- *The Framework for Innovation: A Guide to the Body of Innovation Knowledge* (2018)
- *Project Management for Performance Improvement Teams* (2018)
- *Creativity, Innovation and Entrepreneurship* (2018)
- *Total Innovation Management Excellence (TIME)*—technical report published by Quality Progress magazine (2019)
- *Innovative Medal Handbook*—classes being taught/manuscript being prepared and released 1st quarter 2019. Technical paper published 1st quarter 2019
- *Total Improvement Management—The Generation in Performance Improvement*—(1995)
- *Creativity Toolkit—Provoking Creativity in Individuals and Organizations*—(1998)

2

The Creative and Innovative Story

INTRODUCTION

In the movie "How to Succeed in Business without Really Trying," a young college graduate gets a job in a major company owned by his father's friend. He was told he was going to have to start at the bottom and work his way up. As a result, he started in the mailroom and delivered mail to the various offices. During his first interview with the mailroom supervisor, he was told, "When I joined the firm, I told myself, 'Don't get any ideas' and I haven't had one in years. I play it safe—that's the company way." It looks a little funny seeing this comment in writing, but it actually is the underlining culture within many major organizations. That is—keep quiet, agree with the boss, and never voice your opinion. This is believed to be the secret to getting ahead in these organizations. Just try to remember the last time one of your staff who reports directly to you has said, "No, you're wrong; it's better to do it this way." If it has been more than ten days, you're probably working in one of these types of obsolete cultures.

The only people who never fail are the ones who never try. If you don't do anything, it's hard to do it wrong. Do everything just as your boss tells you to do it, so you can blame him if something goes wrong. When things go right, the boss gets all the credit, no matter how hard you worked for it.

KEEPING UP WITH THE COMPETITION

The office next door, the office on the other side of town, an office in a different state, an office in Beijing—yes, an office any place in the world represents a potential competition for you and your products.

FIGURE 2.1
Business area in Dubai at the start of innovation.

Innovation is not a US secret. Private and public organizations around the world have realized that the key to prosperity is being innovative. Governments in various parts of the world are investing large sums of capital to make their country's products more innovative. The United Arab Emirates (UAE) is an excellent example of the way countries are encouraging and supporting the development of the innovative culture. Figure 2.1 shows a picture of the business area in Dubai in 1990.

Figure 2.2 shows a picture of the same business area in Dubai twenty years later.

FIGURE 2.2
Current picture of business area in Dubai.

His Highness Sheikh Mohammed Bin Rashid's Vision: UAE's National Innovation Strategy

His Highness Sheikh Mohammed bin Rashid has a vision for UAE's National Innovation strategy. He is not only dreaming or just talking about it; the UAE government is pouring billions of dollars into the project to make the dreams become a reality. The following outlines the UAE's National Innovation Strategy:

> The UAE will become one of the most innovative countries in the world through a focus on seven sectors: renewable energy, transport, education, health, technology, water, and space.
> - Innovative leadership using different methods and tools.
> - Growth of distinctive skills and capabilities across the nation.
> - Creativity in every field.
> - Shape specialized entities such as innovation incubators.
> - Institutionalizing innovative practices with the support of an integrated system of modern tools.
> - National training and education programs on innovation will also be launched.
> - Encourage private sector innovation by stimulating companies to establish innovation and scientific research centers, to adopt new technologies, and to develop innovative products and services.
> - Qualify individuals with highly innovative skills.
> - Global indicators include an overall measure comparing countries' innovation capabilities, as well as indicators for the protection of intellectual property, the creation of patents and the availability of scientists and engineers.
> - Establish innovation labs in schools and universities as part of a drive to equip students with targeted skills such as critical thinking, problem-solving, creativity, perseverance, and adaptability.

Do you know what the US government's innovation strategy is? Is it building a wall so you keep other cultures out? Or is it developing technologies that make other countries output obsolete? How much money has the federal government set aside to encourage the innovative organizations to develop more new and unique test technologies that will give us a favorable balance of trade with countries like Canada, China, and Japan? What are the states and cities doing to foster innovation in the government operations? Are we as serious about innovation as the UAE is? How can we hope to do anything but go downhill and lose our competitive advantage if we're not serious about developing new and unique products that can be produced at a profit?

It's nice for US to give aid to struggling countries like Egypt, Israel, etc. However, it is our first obligation to give aid to our struggling business communities' fighting high healthcare costs, high labor costs, lack of proper skills, and high taxes? Maybe a good objective for federal government is to be acquiring 30% of its tax money three years from now from products and/or services that are not in existence today. Wouldn't an objective like that change the way the Congress and our President used the federal budget to set their priorities. Impossible you say! Jim, be realistic; there is no earthly way that this could happen. Again you're right—as long as we say we can't do it, we won't do it. If we think it's impossible, we make it impossible. But, what if we had a can-do spirit? We believe that nothing is outside of your reach if you really want to accomplish it. Anything we can dream about could be possible, and if we didn't quite reach our stretch goals, we have moved a long way forward in the positive direction.

I ask again, "Do you know what the United States' innovation strategy is?" Well, don't feel bad; I don't know what it is either probably because we don't have one. It's up to you and me to insist that Congress and our President establish a logical strategy that will ensure we remain the most innovative country in the world.

The 5 "I Do It" Phases

Way back when I was a young man, the resident number of really great comedians relied on their wit, rather than sex, to entertain. Two of the greatest were Bob Hope and Red Skelton. Red Skelton had a number of different personalities; he transformed himself into Clem Kadiddlehopper, Freddie the Freeloader and Junior, "the mean widdle kid." Junior's favorite saying was, "If I dood that, I get a whippen!... I dood it!" (see Figure 2.3).

In the early 1930s, Red Skelton was famous for his "I dood it" statements which we have converted to 5 "I do it" phases. For those of you who are in your mid-40s or younger, you probably do not remember the "I dood it" statements made by Red Skelton too many years ago. We have used the "I do it" Red Skeleton statement to jokingly define the innovation activities. They are as follows:

1. The opportunity identification (dream) phase—**Should I do it.**
   During this phase, you question if it is as good as it could be. You question why the opportunity hadn't been improved by someone

FIGURE 2.3
Red skeleton.

else, and if no one has done it, it probably can't be done. Why should I stick my neck out?

2. The vision phase—**Will I do it.**

    During the vision phase, you begin to think about how things would be different if it was done. You paint the picture in your mind of how things could be. You eventually convince yourself that you can do it.

3. The creative plan phase—**How will I do it**

    During the creative phase, you developed a number of potential ways to take advantage of the opportunity. You then selected the best combination of potential changes that maximize the value added for the stakeholders.

4. The installation phase—**I am doing it**

    During the installation phase, concepts are turned into realities, and the realities are turned into output that can be secured by a customer/consumer.

5. The evaluation phase—**Should I have done it?**

    During the evaluation phase, you estimate the impact the change might have on the organization and the customer. Outputs are turned into hard cash and increased or decreased customer satisfaction. It is at this point in time a creative idea is determined to be or not to be innovative. It must be original and unique. Output that generates significant real value to the customer/consumer and the organization can be classified as innovative. If the change does not produce added value to the organization and its customer, it is considered a poor creative solution. For a change to be classified as innovative, it must produce value added for the stakeholders.

I realize that there are many knowledgeable people who will disagree with me that an innovative idea has to be unique, different, and provide added value to the organization and its consumers. I understand how these requirements may not be applicable to the US government and not-for-profit organizations. Both categories may have a number of creative solutions that do not provide added value to the organization and many a times did not provide added value to the customer or humanity.

All organizations—not just businesses—need one core competency.

Peter Drucker, management consultant and author

WHERE, OR WHERE, DID OUR CREATIVITY GO?

Our culture and education systems are designed to kill our creativity. When my son was three years old, he wrote with his blocks the word "regt." As a good father showing interest in my son, I asked him, "What does that mean?" He quickly replied, "Dad—it means I love you." Being a good, well-educated Dad I quickly replied, "Let me show you how to spell *Dad.*" With this act, I put a quick stop to his creativity. He had created his own language and was able to express in four letters that took me eighteen letters to express after more than thirty years of education. Our education system and our culture frown upon creativity. We become similar to the robots—systematically doing the things that we were programmed to do. Those of us who do something different are treated as outcasts. For example, in the TV program "Boston Legal," one of their lawyers starts to "purr" when he gets nervous and thus gets treated as an outcast.

- 90% of our five-year-olds are creative
- only 15% of our 7-year-olds are creative
- only 2% of our fourteen-year-olds are creative

You have to be creative before you can be innovative

H. James Harrington

"The 6 *Must Be Willing to*"—The Black Knight of Innovation Conditions

I doubt if anyone from the quality assurance organization could ever be an innovator. It seems like the key traits that drive an innovator are the same key traits that a quality professional should not tolerate. The following are the principles and makeup of an innovator. They are called "The 6 *Must Be Willing To*" Conditions:

1. **Must be willing to** tolerate ambiguities.
2. **Must be willing to** be uncomfortable.
3. **Must be willing to** be lonely at times.
4. **Must be willing to** risk it all.
5. **Must be willing to** bend the rules.
6. **Must be willing to** take negative criticism.

If your ISO 9000 quality system was designed to reflect these six traits, you have so many deviations that your organization could never be certified. Certainly, one of the big problems that organizations face today is how to integrate the quality system with their innovation system.

The Shark Tank

As an innovator, I really enjoy the TV program called "Shark Tank," where entrepreneurs present their product to a group of mediators/billionaires in order to get them to invest in their product (see Figure 2.4).

Figure 2.5 shows an example of two innovative products they invested in along with how these two organizations succeeded.

The 3 Reasons for Lack of Creativity Dilemma

People are born with a natural ability to creatively solve problems. Given this, why has the lack of creativity around the world become such a problem? Well, the answer has several major causes. The following outlines several of the reasons this is occurring.

- Education through memorization of facts.
- Lack of creative exercise.
- Avoiding risk.

FIGURE 2.4
Primary investors that make up Shark Tank TV program.

SHARK TANK INVESTMENTS

- Cheong Choon Ng- The Rainbow Loom
  - ✓ Rubber band bracelet making kit.
  - ✓ Over 5 million sold the first year
- Mary Beth Luogo - The Kazam Bicycle
  - ✓ No balance wheels or pedals
  - ✓ One of the hottest selling items last Christmas

FIGURE 2.5
Typical companies that the Shark Tank invested in.

Education through Memorization of Facts

There is so much data in the world today that we can't afford the luxury of letting everyone recreate their own database. If everyone was allowed to create their own basic concepts without a degree of standardization, we would not be able to effectively interact with each other. For example, imagine how hard it would be to communicate if each person spoke a unique language, or how hard it would be to pay a bill if every individual used a different numbering system.

Often, our education keeps us from conceiving truly creative solutions. It is important to realize that education does not make an individual creative. In fact, it often has just the opposite effect on the individual, because there is less need to use our creative powers on a continuous basis. Someone else is always giving us the answers. Of course, being educated does not mean that an individual won't be creative. Highly creative educated individuals do not rely on their education to solve their problems. They use it to develop new improved solutions.

Due to the complexity of today's environment, we start reducing a child's natural creative urges very early in a child's life by saying, "Don't try to be creative. We already have an answer that is better than anything you can create."

That's what education (not learning) is all about. Maximizing and memorizing what we already know, not focusing much on creating anything new. We are not suggesting that education is bad. In fact, we just feel the opposite. The more knowledge an individual has, the better they can perform. The problem is that while we are collecting knowledge, we are not creating. Figure 2.6 shows what we mean.

Most of the time, the learning process is going on as we accumulate more information. The learning process includes education, observation, and experience. These three provide us with information. We filter the information into two different categories.

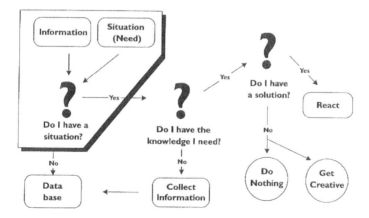

FIGURE 2.6
Creating versus using collected information.

- Knowledge, which is information that is always correct within its context. Knowledge includes physical laws, mathematics, and similar concepts.
- Wisdom, which is the insight to make sound decisions and to take actions that are based on our knowledge. Our sound decisions also keep us open to new information and to keep learning, improving, and contributing to the welfare of our world (see Figure 2.7).

The next activity is the reaction process. This process consists of evaluating or finding out if you have the knowledge that you need. You must now determine whether you have acquired the knowledge to react to a situation. If you believe you have the knowledge required, you take the appropriate action. If you believe you don't have that knowledge, you need to collect more information and pass it on to your knowledge base.

Definition: A **situation** is defined as anything that requires a response. It can be an opportunity to take advantage of, a choice between options, or as simple as a need to make a verbal response.

When you have sufficient knowledge, you react to the situation. Whether you already have or need to collect new information, you may find that you are stuck using it in the same way because your assumptions are conventional and have never been challenged. You may need an outside catalyst to help you break out of your conventional perspectives (see Figure 2.8).

The 4 Reasons for Being Stimulated

In the days of kings, the individual who challenged conventional thinking was known as the court jester. In a number of organizations today, there is an individual who serves this function. The court jester's job is to

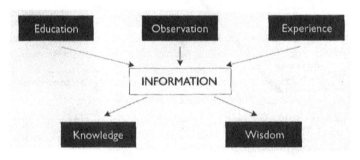

FIGURE 2.7
The learning process.

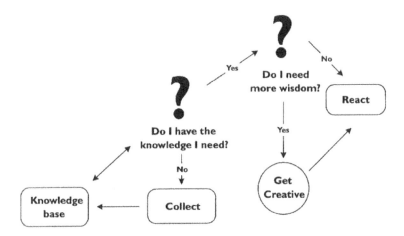

FIGURE 2.8
Reaction process.

ask questions and present possibilities in such a way that it opens people's minds to possibilities that had not been considered.

If you don't have enough information, it is usually because of one or more of the following:

- It takes too long to get the information.
- The information is not available.
- You believe a better solution exists.
- You get more satisfaction from creating a new solution.

In this case, you use all of the knowledge you have available to you and create a new solution. It is easy to see that as you analyze more information, there is a lesser need to be creative, because you have the required knowledge to react to situations you are encountering.

Inspiration is the impact of a fact on a prepared mind.

Louis Pasteur

Lack of Creativity Exercise

An individual's creative capabilities are a lot like their physical capabilities. The more you use them, the better you can perform. And if you don't exercise then, your capabilities diminish—sometimes fast. Just as you have an exercise program to sharpen your body muscles that are not used in your normal activities, you need a creativity exercise program that stimulates the creativity "muscles," that you may not use too frequently.

Avoiding Risk

Creative people are willing to take a risk to challenge the rules, expected behaviors, and status quo.

Definition: **Status quo** is a condition where the environment and the individual's expectations about the environment are in harmony. It does not mean the individual's expectations are being met.

There is an old Japanese saying: "The nail that sticks up the highest is the first to be driven down." We'd like to reword this statement to: "The nail that sticks up the highest is the one that rips your paints." The individual or group that tries to be creative is like the nail sticking up. It will cause you problems if you don't take care. Of course, when you think you might challenge the status quo, there's always the danger of failing—So why try new things. A conservative individual who tries to be creative is at as great a disadvantage as a five-foot tall individual who is competing for a position on a professional basketball team. As Woody Allen puts it, "If you're not failing every now and again, it's a sign that you are not doing anything very innovative." Too many individuals spend their lives worrying about failing, and because of that, live in a mire of mediocrity. They are afraid to change. Confucius once said, "Our greatest glory is not in never failing, but in rising every time we fall."

Definition: **Change** is a condition where an individual's expectations are no longer aligned with the environment. Change occurs when expectations are not met.

To be creative, you must be willing to take risks. We are not talking about skydiving or Indy-car racing or anything like that. We are talking about the risks we need to consider when we don't do the same things in the same old ways. Trying new ways of acting or getting something done involves risk, risk in the sense that we might be embarrassed, ridiculed, left out, talked about, or all those things that potentially can happen when one stands out from the norm. As shown in Figure 2.9, the more radical the creative idea, the higher the risk.

The nature of our current society is strongly biased toward conformity and conservatism, where everyone is expected to stay within certain boundaries. Those who go beyond these boundaries are considered different and are in some way "punished." But thinking differently is required

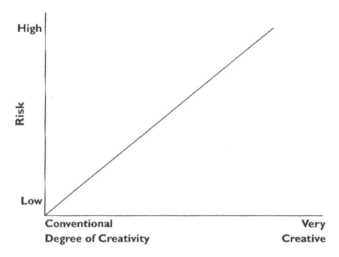

FIGURE 2.9
Risk versus level of creativity.

to think beyond these boundaries. We need to find ways to do this without endangering our mental selves. Being able and willing to take these risks is an essential step to becoming creative (see Figure 2.9).

Consider what almost everyone does when they ride in an elevator. You walk into the elevator, turn around, push the button for the floor you want, then either stare at the floor or at the changing floor numbers. Because of the "rules of elevator riding," you don't say anything. Have you ever noticed that few people talk, even if riding with somebody they know? Take a risk, and say something. Perhaps say, "I'm sure glad we are all going the same way" or "We are all sure quiet today" or if it's crowded, ask someone to push the floor button for you. It is not that you need to be a stand-up comic. But you are trying to use your risk muscles by doing something different that will help you think about the world in new ways. If you really want to take a risk, don't turn to the front of the elevator. Stand looking at the other people in the elevator and wait for them to say something.

Let's examine another situation. You are in a meeting (a class or a staff meeting, for example), and someone says something that you don't understand. What do most people do? They don't say anything, hoping that someone else will or maybe it will be explained later (usually, this never happens). Think of Tom Hanks in the movie *Big*. He took risks that most of us would not, because the barriers that we normally avoid were not in place because of the switch that had taken place. The age/creativity relationship had been changed. Learn to take a risk and ask the question. In almost every case, there are others who have the same question as you. This is especially difficult if the person talking is a senior (older, higher-level) person.

There is always some intimidation, even if unintentional, and it can be seen as a risk in that you might feel you might be subjected to ridicule (i.e., all eyes turn to you as if to say, "How come you don't understand?" or any number of things that you can imagine). So, with that fear, you just sit there silently. You follow the rule that you were trained to as a child: "Don't speak unless spoken to." The elevator, the meeting, and other similar situations give us an opportunity to use our risk muscles to think differently and to act differently. Thinking and acting go hand-in-hand, because the acting will strengthen our thinking.

HOW DO YOU KNOW YOU ARE CREATIVE?

A question we are frequently asked is, "What is the difference between creative and normal thoughts?" A simple answer is that you are not being creative when you are doing something the same way it was done before and getting the same results. Typically, you will know you are creative by the way you feel about the results of the activity.

One resulting experience from being creative is sometimes called "the WOW experience," because it is accompanied by an expression or feeling of "wow, that's great" or "wow, look at what I've done." The "WOW experience" is a true high. It will build spirit, enthusiasm, confidence, and contentment. It's the kind of experience that we can say, when you have it, you'll know it. It's often a kind of breakthrough or insight by which things just come together in a way that solves the problem or allows you to do or make something new and better that you haven't been able to do before.

Key Issues Calling for Creativity

Each of us addresses three different types of issues in our daily lives. They are setting our direction, planning for how we are going to move in that direction, and the tasks that we do to move us in that direction.

When you deal with direction issues, you are trying to answer questions like "Where am I going?" and "Why am I going there?"

Planning is essential in our daily lives. We often do it without even thinking about it. We must learn to set aside enough time to plan if we want to succeed. At a personal level when you are engaged in planning, you are trying to answer questions like "How am I going to get to where I am going?" "What are all of the steps I need to take to reach my goal?"

Not only do we set direction and make plans, we also complete tasks. For most, completing a task takes at least 80% of our time. With regard to task issues, you are trying to answer questions like "What do I have to do to follow my plan?" "What can I do differently to make my life easier?" In our experience, we have found that each of us spends about 3% of our time in setting directions, 17% of our time in making plans, and 80% of our time on completing tasks. Creativity can and should be applied to all three of these areas. However, the greatest rewards of creativity are usually found when we focus on the tasks that we do. Check out the following quotes:

Everything that can be invented has been invented.

Charles H. Duell, Director, US Patent Office, 1899

Sensible and responsible women do not want to vote.

Grover Cleveland, 1905

Who the hell wants to hear actors talk?

Harry M. Warner, Warner Bros. Pictures c. 1927

There is no likelihood man can ever tap the power of the atom.

Robert Millikan, Nobel Prize in Physics, 1923

Heavier than air flying machines are impossible.

Lord Kelvin, President, Royal Society, 1895

Ruth made a big mistake when he gave up pitching.

Tris Speaker, 1921

The 12 Idea Evaluation Questions—Is It Good or Is It Bad?

So you've just had what you believe to be a really creative idea. What do you do with it? Do you just share it right now so that everyone will know you are creative or should you wait and check it out? The answer is yes. Both actions are right depending on the idea and the environment you find yourself in. If it is a very important idea that will impact other people, you may want to sit on it for a day or so. Maybe even check it out with some friends to see if they can find a weakness that you had not thought of.

Often, you may only get a chance at selling the concept, so it must be presented right the first time. At other times, a spontaneous reaction is the best approach. You should develop a systematic way to evaluate your ideas before you decide how you are going to react. The following typical questions are helpful in evaluating an idea.

1. Do you really understand the situation? So many creative ideas fail because they are not addressing the actual situation.
2. Will your idea address the situation in a way that solves a problem or makes an improvement?
3. Is this the best action that can be taken?
4. Is your idea better than the present situation?
5. What are the advantages your idea has over the present situation?
6. What are the advantages the present situation has over your idea?
7. What will it take to implement your idea?
8. Who will need to approve your idea before it can be implemented?
9. Who will need to implement your idea?
10. Is your idea in line with the current culture?
11. Is this the right time to discuss the idea?
12. How long would it take to implement the idea?

> The Lord gave us two ends—one to sit on and the other to think with. Success depends on which one we use the most.
>
> **Ann Landers**

Rising above the Immediate

Too often, we define a path of action, and then spend all our time justifying that path rather than breaking down the perceived barriers we have built around ourselves. It is a lot like being in a canoe, paddling down a winding river to get to the sea as soon as possible. You can be so intent on

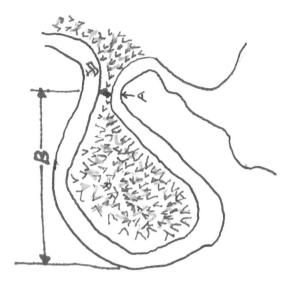

FIGURE 2.10
Paddling the canoe down the river of no return.

paddling that you go right past point A without realizing that by carrying the canoe twenty feet, the journey could have been shortened significantly (see Figure 2.10).

Truly creative people take a global view of the river to define an optimum path in contrast to the hardworking conventionalists who reason, "The harder we paddle, the faster we'll get to the sea." In addition, they welcome the input of outsiders that can help them perceive the problem in different terms. They are willing to take both a global view (this view is often called synthesis) as well as an analytic view. The ability to look at the same idea from more than one viewpoint is very difficult to master, but well worth the time. We will provide you with a number of tools and techniques in the later chapters to help you learn how to approach any situation from either viewpoint.

The 5 Creativity Myths

As children, we heard stories about ghosts and goblins, witches and vampires, and dragons and heroes. Soon, we lost sight of fact and reality. In school, we are taught that if it is printed in a book, it is a fact. We have a tendency to accept, without question, anything that we are told by a person who has Dr in front of his or her name. We draw conclusions based upon statistically unsound databases. We have a friend from India who is a superb mathematician. We begin to believe that Indians are systematic thinkers. My wife sees a movie about a psychotic killer, and for a week, she's worried every night when I am away. We have a tendency to develop beliefs that are often not based on facts. But we believe in them so strongly that our ability to see what's really going on becomes severely limited. The following are some myths related to creativity that have developed over the years, along with comments on the reality of these points.

1. **Creativity is a natural gift**. This is a half-truth. Nature provides us with the capabilities of thinking. How we use our thought patterns is based upon the environment an individual lives in and the individual's interests.

2. **Only some people are creative**. Everyone has the ability to be creative, unless they have a severe mental handicap. We all can be creative if we just want to work at it. It is usually easier to follow than to lead, but never as satisfying.

3. **There's no need for me to be creative. What we are doing right now is good enough**. The fact is that if we continue to do the same thing in the same way, the best we are going to get is the same result. If no one was creative, we would still be living in caves and protecting ourselves with clubs. Our ability to use our skills in creative ways is really an important key to succeeding in today's competitive marketplace. If you are not applying your creativity to how to become more efficient and how to deliver more value to customers, you are opening the door for competitors who are looking to take your business away from you.

4. **Creativity is always good**. Creativity can be both bad and good. It depends on your purposes. If you use your creative power to manipulate and take advantage of others, this is clearly not good in the eyes of most people. Hitler was creative but in a very negative way, as most people would see it. Conversely, creativity that leads to helping people perform better or develop something new and useful is clearly a good purpose to which to apply our creativity.

5. **Creative people are successful people**. This is not necessarily so. Often, creative people do not have the ability to sell the fruits of creativity and/ or do not care if anyone makes use of their ideas (Figure 2.11).

The 13 Truths about Creativity

It is important that we all understand what creativity is and what it is not. The following is a list of basic concepts that will help you understand creativity.

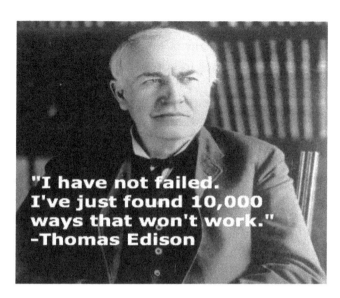

FIGURE 2.11
Thomas Edison.

1. **Creativity is not a single process**. Creativity is a number of different processes that make up the creativity system. A creative idea may come to you in a blinding flash or through a systematic approach that refine your thought patterns.
2. **Your creativity powers can be improved**. Methods are available today to exercise your creative powers and to change the way you think, allowing you to become a much more creative person.
3. **Creativity is often an explosion rather than a logical sequence of information**. Some of our very best ideas may occur at a golf course or in the shower. All of a sudden, you get a flash of inspiration. Be prepared for those flashes. Don't tuck them over in one corner of your mind saying, "I'll get back to that later."
4. **Creativity is random**. Although you can't predict when you'll have a creative breakthrough, you can increase the frequency of having such breakthroughs. You can do this by having an inquisitive mind and by understanding the process by which you increase the possibility of coming up with a creative idea.
5. **Frustration is often the father of creativity**. Most people take the easy way out and search for a rule that will allow them to complete a specific assignment or solve a specific problem. When our rules fail and we have no place to go, our creativity kicks in.

6. **Creativity is seeing the same old thing in a different light and/or in new combinations**. Many techniques you will read about in this book, in fact, are designed to help you change the context in which you view a problem or opportunity or to recombine elements in such a way that it leads to a creative breakthrough.

7. **Creativity is risky, but rewarding**. Doing a job the same way your predecessor did the job or your boss told you to do, the job provides you with a way out. You can always blame any problems that occur on somebody else. It requires no thought, very little risk, and results in little progress. It is only when we use our creativity to improve that we truly make progress and become recognized as superior performers by the people we come in contact with. In addition, we gain a degree of self-satisfaction that is never present when we are blindly following someone else's lead.

8. **Creativity is the ultimate source of self-indulgence and self-satisfaction**. When you exercise your creative powers, you develop a sense of self-confidence and self-worth. It is a way of proving to yourself that you are adding value to the rest of the world.

9. **The way you performed in the past does not always reflect your potential**. Just because you have not been creative in the past does not mean that you cannot be creative in the future. Likewise, individuals who have been creative often look backward and stop being creative as they mature. The will to create has to be renewed every day.

10. **Trust your own observations**. Don't be limited by others. Too often, someone in a higher position or someone we respect influences our thinking in a way that prevents us from applying our personal creative powers. Encouraging diversity, rather than conformity, is the key to creativity. It brings out many ways of understanding the same phenomenon and to build on one another's ideas.

11. **Creativity often comes when you reject your first acceptable solution**. People have a tendency to first look at a problem and define how it can be solved, and then devote their time to collecting information to prove their initial approach. Every opportunity should have at least three alternate solutions developed for it, before the best-value solution is defined.

12. **The more you use your creative powers, the better they work**. The brain is a muscle, and like any other muscle, it must be exercised to

stay in shape. Many people claim that creativity is a lot like riding a bicycle, you never forget how to do it. That may be true, but if you're racing against a person who rides ten miles every day, you are probably going to lose the race.

13. **Creativity turns work into fun**. Too often, we wear our conformity masks and are afraid to relax. We envy the child who has fun in everything they do. We complain about our daily chores. We complain it's too hot in the office when it becomes over 80°. But then, we stop on our way home to play tennis out in the sun when it's 90° and enjoy the experience. Free up our creative powers. Turn the monotony of our daily chores into a series of enjoyable experiences.

The 12 Creativity Killers

Are you a creativity killer? Do you encourage or repress creative thoughts? A newly hatched idea is fragile. We need to encourage it, cultivate it, and help it to develop and grow, not casually discard it. The following are twelve commonly used phrases that discourage creative thinking.

1. It won't work.
2. It makes me afraid.
3. We tried it already.
4. That can't be done.
5. It will never work here.
6. Let's be serious.
7. That's ridiculous.
8. What's original about that?
9. How dumb can you be?
10. You obviously don't understand the situation.
11. That's a silly idea.
12. That's impossible.

Look at each one of these statements and create a sentence or two that would encourage the person you are talking to rather than discourage him/her. As managers, we are taught to throw cold water on new or different approaches when what we should have been doing was throwing gasoline on the smoldering embers.

We can't build a better tomorrow by using yesterday's methods. Businesses that expect to make it in today's global marketplace must begin by tapping the creativity of all employees, not just a few maverick inventors or dynamic CEOs. Competitive advantage today comes from continuous, incremental innovation.

Harold R. McAlindon

The 13 Rules for Individuals to Become More Creative

Here are some quick techniques you can use to turn on your creative powers:

1. Create mental pictures in your mind and turn these pictures into reality.
2. Keep your mind open to new ideas by presenting new experiences to your senses. Be a keen observer of the environment that you come in contact with. Provide the mind with the raw materials that it needs to be creative.
3. Do something creative each day. Set aside a specific time each day to review the creative things that you accomplished.
4. Define alternative approaches to situations and problems. Don't use a one-track approach and gather data to prove you were right. Focus your creativity on simplifying the old and new approaches.
5. Maintain a questioning attitude. Remember, there is always a better way and, if you don't find it, someone else will and use it as their stepping stone to get ahead of you.
6. Don't be afraid to take a risk. You will never fulfill your true potential if you play it safe.
7. Record your ideas as soon as you get them. Keep a notepad with you at all times.
8. Take time to relax and unwind. Take a long walk or a long hot bath. Play golf or restful music. Try meditation or yoga.
9. Don't accept limiting factors as being unchangeable or correct.
10. Gain confidence and enthusiasm by first focusing your creative effort and ideas on things that are within your control to implement.
11. Help others to be creative by pointing out the good points related to their ideas, not the bad points. We already have too many devil's advocates. Be an angel's advocate.

12. Find your creative time of the day. Some people are morning people. Others are evening people. We all function differently. Sample your emotions and creative powers to determine when you are the most creative. Then, set that sacred time aside to work on developing new concepts.

13. Start today to improve your creative processes. It has been said, "Yesterday is history, tomorrow is a mystery. Today is a gift. That's why it's called the present."

I am a great believer in luck, and I find the harder I work, the more of it I have.

Stephen Leacock

The 5 Discovery Skills for Breakthrough

There are five common skills that truly innovative people have developed. These five skills help the individual to look at the world in a different way than others do. Truly innovative people are the individuals who come up with new and unique ideas. Often, people have good ideas, but do nothing with them. The highly skilled innovator thinks of better ideas and tries to get them implemented. The five common skills are as follows:

1. Opportunity identification
2. Creativity
3. Business analysis
4. Organizing
5. Selling

The 8 Foundations for Your Ideas

As we begin to review many techniques we can use to turn on our creative powers, here are some affirmations about you and others like you to serve as a foundation for our ideas:

1. We are confident that you are or can be creative.
2. We are confident that you can improve your creativity. It has been estimated that Leonardo da Vinci and Thomas Edison used less than 50% of their potential creativity capabilities.

3. We are confident that the regular use of the mind expanders defined in this book will improve your creativity.
4. We are confident that risks, creativity, and rewards go hand-in-hand.
5. We are confident that creativity will become even more critical to real success in the 21st century than ever before.
6. We are confident that creative people get more joy from life.
7. We are confident that if you do not use your creative powers, you will become less capable to using them.
8. We are confident that real success goes to creative people who can implement their ideas and concepts.

HARNESSING INFINITY: DEVELOPING CREATIVE FOCUS

Creativity is the ability to come up with something that did not exist before. There are many adjectives used to describe creativity, such as imagination, risk taking, independence of judgment, flexibility, curiosity, spontaneity, and perceptiveness.

We have described three different types of issues each of us face in our daily lives, setting our direction, planning for how we are going to move in that direction, and the tasks that we do to move us in that direction.

Our focus for creativity is either personal or enterprise. Personal creativity focuses on your values, helps you determine and examine your beliefs, sets your direction, provides a method to develop appropriate plans, and defines the tasks you should be doing. At a personal level, these functions are often intermixed and difficult to separate. It may be helpful for you to take some time and focus on one aspect at a time.

Enterprises may be as simple as your family or as complex as a multinational corporation. It may be a business, organization, nonprofit group, or government. Enterprises have the need for creativity just as individuals do. Their ability to be creative allows them to grow. Growth is the key to long-term success of the enterprise. Without growth, enterprises eventually wither and go out of business. Because of their structures, most enterprises have a difficult time maintaining a creative focus. Enterprises exhibit the same characteristics as aging and relation to creative focus.

The 2 Creativity Levels

The scale of use of creativity can be applied at either the personal or enterprise level. The scale with which you apply creativity is important because it will enable you to provide an appropriate focus for your creative efforts.

- Individual Level.

   As an individual, you can be creative in everything you do. Being creative can help you find easier and more effective ways of interacting with others and becoming more successful. There are a number of methodologies, tools, and techniques that lend themselves to being creative by yourself. Being creative can be an individual experience.
- Group Level.

   Groups of people working together often focus on being creative. Enterprises normally stress group creativity. Group creativity can be at least as powerful as individuals who are creative. It requires a somewhat different mindset. Not everyone is good at both types of creativity; however, with effort and patience, we can all get better at both of them. There are many types of groups, such as natural work groups, families, ad hoc groups, and those on special projects or assignments. The methodology, tool, or techniques you may use depend on the kind of group that is using it. Other factors include the expected outcome and the group's understanding of what creativity is and how to maximize it.

   When we describe the tools and methodologies of creativity in Chapters 5–7, we will provide you with the scale of individual or group usage that is the most frequent. The expected results and methods will vary depending on the scale of use. Individuals can be creative at personal and enterprise levels, while groups can normally work at an enterprise level.

The 4 Styles of Creativity

One famous statement about creativity says that it is 99% perspiration and 1% inspiration. This definition is a precursor to the four styles of creativity that we have identified. Tools play an important role in creativity. The four styles of creativity are as follows:

- Structured creativity
- Nonlinear creativity

- Provoked creativity
- Aha creativity

There are many tools that can help you to focus on each type of issue. There are tools that will help you to explore and set your direction, develop plans to follow that direction, and to identify and improve the tasks that you do. All these types of issues are what it takes to get you where you want to be. No one type is more important than any of the other.

> The ultimate creative capacity of the brain may be, for practical purposes, infinite.
>
> **Dr W. Ross Adley**

Structured Creativity

The first style is the structured approach to creativity. This approach to creativity occurs most frequently in organizations. One such approach is the linear model of problem identification, root cause analysis, breakthrough, and solution implementation.

Structured creativity can be described as follows:

1. Step by step
2. Detailed
3. Complex
4. Tool intensive
5. Tight control
6. Requires little facilitation
7. Works with individuals or groups

Structured creativity is good for improving tasks that already exist, and for developing a set of tasks to follow a plan. It is usually focused at the day-to-day task of an individual or the operating level of an organization.

For example, if you find water on the kitchen floor, there must be a cause for that water. Following the linear model may lead you to understand that the sink is leaking only when the dishwasher runs. This could lead you to find a clog in the dishwasher drain pipe. You replace the pipe and the problem goes away.

Nonlinear Creativity

The second style of creativity is a methodology that takes up much space in current literature. It builds on open-ended thinking. Nonlinear creativity provides a freeing up of human energy. Despite popular misconceptions, creativity does not require putting on goofy hats and blowing horns. An example of nonlinear creativity is brainstorming or ideas without concern about what they are connected to. Nonlinear creativity transcends rightness or wrongness.

Nonlinear creativity can be described as follows:

1. Exciting
2. Unpredictable
3. Fast paced
4. Focuses on quantity, not quality
5. Promotes involvement of people
6. Usually used in groups

Nonlinear creativity is good for getting people involved. It promotes high energy and promotes group ownership. It is best used to work on tasks that are understood and for developing plans for new tasks.

An example of nonlinear creativity is a brainstorming session to develop a new product for your company. Structured and nonlinear creativity are the most commonly used methods of creativity in organizations.

Provoked Creativity

The third style of creativity that is rapidly gaining popularity is provoked creativity. Provoked creativity uses a catalyst of some sort to provoke or evoke ideas and develop new insights and understanding. The mental movement generated by a catalyst comes from the use of analogies, metaphors, words in the dictionary, colors, or some other tangential approach to get the human intellect to evoke or create a new insight. Some people feel that this is the optimum method of being creative in a group. Techniques that are common include Six Hat Thinking developed by Edward DeBono and TRIZ (it is also called TIPS or Systematic Innovation) developed by G. S. Altshuller.

Provoked creativity can be described as

1. Catalyst focused
2. Provides a springboard for forward movement

3. Easy to build on
4. Easy to start
5. Requires active facilitation
6. Easily used by individuals or groups

Provoked creativity is good for getting creativity started. It helps you to address issues such as the context that you are in. It uses a mechanism, such as a random word or scenario. Provoked creativity is very effective when you are working on developing plans and setting direction, although it can also help with improving tasks.

Aha Creativity

The fourth style of creativity is the *Aha or Eureka* that occurs when a new unconnected idea suddenly bursts forth. Aha creativity has contributed the most to the major breakthroughs in the history of the planet, and yet is the least understood, the least studied, and the least practiced. Aha creativity is the new idea that comes from your ability to create that which did not exist before. Eureka creativity is that which Archimedes did when he measured the king's crown to find out it was lead, not gold. His description was Eureka. Aha or Eureka creativity is the truly creative breakthrough that occurs when something that did not exist before springs into someone's mind. For example, someone came up with the idea of the paper clip as a general conceptual breakthrough. Our experience has shown that Aha creativity produces less than 1% of the total creative ideas.

Aha creativity can be described as

1. Having no steps
2. Does not contain patterns
3. Focuses on big issues
4. Frequently has one defining moment
5. Uses simple methods
6. Is individually intense

Any style of creativity can be used to help you work each of the three types of issues of direction, planning, and tasks, although certain creativity styles are usually more effective on specific types of issues.

DESIGN THINKING

Design thinking is an approach to analysis and problem-solving tools that encourage the team to look at in developing many options before selecting the best value solution. It is particularly helpful in developing action plans to take advantage of complex improvement opportunities and difficult problems.

Here again, the basic team involved principles that are used to merge together thought patterns from different parts of the organization and different backgrounds. The has been a proven effective process to uniting different thought patterns, to come up a consensus solution that is frequently much better than any one of the concepts. We have talked for a long time about teams that make $1 + 1$ equals 3, but that is not always the case. Sometimes, the compromised decision is less effective $(1 + 1 = 0.8)$. Great care must be taken to ensure that compromised decisions are not immediately selected, as these may not be the best answer.

I personally like to take two or three of the best individual ideas and perform a value analysis on each of them. Another approach I like to use is to define different situations related to the improvement opportunity. Each opportunity has a different set of conditions that stimulate different thought patterns within the team. Each of the three different situations creates conditions that are used to stimulate new thought patterns. (The following are the typical different situations that the team will address.)

- The team can take the required time to develop an action plan and implement it. There is no cost limitation related to implementing the solution, but the solution must provide a significant five-year value-added output that would give the organization a significant competitive advantage.
- The team has three weeks to come up with a way to take advantage of the improvement opportunity that must be implemented in no more than four additional weeks.
- The competition has just came out with a new product that is performing at 25% better than our product and is selling for less than the cost for us to make our product.

It's easy to see that each of these three conditions will generate a different approach to fulfilling the conditions placed upon the improvement opportunity.

Design thinking can be described in six "What's." They are

- What #1—What improvement opportunities should the team work on?
- What #2—What is the definition of the improvement opportunity?
- What #3—What is the root cause of the improvement opportunity?
- What #4—What are the ways that the improvement opportunity can be taken advantage of?
- What #5—What is the best solution? What solution will produce the most value added based upon prototyping and situation analysis?
- What #6—What should the phase-in strategy be? (for example, small group of selected customers, model process for internal use only, full production to meet additional demands).

Using the synergistic efforts of the design team to answer these questions is a key benefit of the model. Early on, the team agrees to the problem definition and a set of design criteria by which the team will experiment and learn about the solution. This collaborative team approach allows the formation of a foundation from which further idea generation and feedback analysis is accomplished effectively and efficiently. Team members have contributed and "bought into" the process by which the solution will be designed, evaluated, and prepared for the user.

Design thinking was originally developed as a tool to be used in development engineering during the product development phase. It performs the function of providing a synergistic approach to bring together the development and marketing group to solve early problems and/or to get a common agreement on product specifications. It was an iterative approach of selecting potential solutions and/or conditions, evaluating them, and looking at alternatives. And it provides the team members with the opportunity to establish customer-centric objectives, proposals, and products. Although the objective was to define the ultimate approach, it frequently missed the mark by establishing an agreed-to compromise that was satisfactory to both sides.

We often question the similarity of the many different problem-solving and improvement approaches that are used. The question is, "Why can't we just use the following Plan–Do–Check–Act (PDCA) approach with the ten supporting activities that was generated back in the 1930s by Shewhart?"

Plan
1. Identification of targets (objectives and goals)
2. Identification of methods/procedures to achieve these targets
3. Identify control items and methods

Do
4. Communicate and train associates
5. Implement the plan (2 and 3)

Check
6. Check progress to plan (1, 2, and 3)
   - Against targets and goals
   - Within the strategy
7. Identify any problems

Act
8. Resolve/eliminate problems
9. Correct/modify plan (2 and 3)
10. Standardizing implementation

The answer is that most, if not all, of the problem-solving approaches are based upon the PDCA approach which have been slightly modified to reflect the personality of the individual presenting the subject, the organization's culture, the purpose of the analysis, and the inherent need to have something different from the one used in the past. Many consultants and engineers have a personal strong need to leave their mark on their subject-matter knowledge base. For example, I believe that the Six Sigma problem-solving approach is basically the PDCA approach that was repackaged and sold as a new concept in order to get funding from management. From my standpoint, what you call it is not important. What is important is that you do it.

Design thinking can be described in four phrases, or key questions, that form the process:

- Phase I. "What is?"—A deep dive into understanding the problem
- Phase II. "What if?"—Creating a list of potential solutions

- Phase III. "What wows?"—Finding potential solutions that most likely create value through prototyping and early analyses
- Phase IV. "What works?"—Begin to move the solution to the marketplace in small, limited environments

THE 5 QUESTIONS TO MAXIMIZE ANY CREATIVE EFFORT

There are hundreds of creativity tools that are available to individuals working alone or in groups. Creativity is a central ingredient to the success of any individual or organization. Success is the ability to be effective in generating desired results, being efficient in getting that result, being creative in finding new and better methods to produce those results, and being adaptive in what results need to be produced. Over the years, we have defined a lot of tools that we have shared with you in this book. You too can feel free to create your own tools to fit the situation you are facing. Let us know how your efforts turn out.

Organizing for creativity should maximize the impact of the four different styles of creativity. There are five questions that you can ask to maximize any creative effort. They are as follows:

1. How are we going to continue? In other words, which style are we going to use?
2. Who is going to do the creativity? Are we going to practice creativity as an individual, in a team, or in some formal or informal structure?
3. What topic are we going to work on? What is it that we are going to apply creative energies against?
4. When will this creativity occur? Will we do it on demand? Will creativity become structured and formalized? Will there be scheduled meetings and agendas to follow?
5. Where will the creativity occur? Will it occur in our home, our natural work area, or must we set aside some special place to make the creativity happen?

Creativity is not a spectator sport. You can only be creative by doing something.

THE 3 THINKING STYLES

Every individual's primary frame of reference for creativity is their own individual makeup. Each individual has their own unique way of processing and looking at things. This is your preferred thinking style. Here are the three thinking styles:

1. The top style of any organization is to understand the expected outcome.
2. The middle style of any organization is in planning, allocating resources, and in making sure that the plan is implemented.
3. The third style is the organization that performs majority of tasks primarily using short-term thinking.

Your thinking style has nothing to do with intelligence; rather, it has to do with the amount of time you are most comfortable thinking about. For instance, some people are able to conceptualize over a broad time event horizon and look at things, perhaps in decades and centuries in nature. Then there are those who prefer to think in years, months, and quarters. The types of events at this level are those that require us to have standards. The third style thinks in very short time frames. Their tasks occur in a localized area over days, hours, and minutes. Many individuals feel comfortable thinking about this type of time period. To be successful, creativity must focus on the appropriate time event horizon.

Traditional organizational structure reflects these thinking styles. The top style of thinking for any organization by its very definition is to understand the expected outcome. They should be most concerned with long-term thinking. This type of thinking can be related to President Kennedy's objective of putting a man on the moon.

The middle style of thinking for any organization is planning, allocating resources, and making sure what happens is consistent with the thinking of the top strata thinking style of the organization. They develop the tactics that keep the organization on track. To continue our analogy using this type of thinking, the colonels, majors, and captains had to develop plans to have the right troops and equipment in the correct positions to enable them to move quickly through the desert.

The third style of thinking is found in organizations that perform a majority of tasks primarily using short-term thinking. To use a military example, those performing at this level drive the tanks, load the fuel onto the trucks, and win the war.

Not one of these thinking styles is either good or bad. None is better or worse than the other. Every organization requires a very large percentage of short-term task thinking and creativity to make it operational. Usually, it is the executive team or the board of directors within an organization who perform longtime frame thinking.

We believe these thinking styles are a continuum. It is not so much that one is distinctively different from another. Instead, there is a blending like the rainbow from one to the next. It is not true that hourly people do all tasks, and owners and senior executives do all direction settings. There are many seemingly minor tasks that the highest chief executive in the highest office must do to accomplish his or her job. Conversely, seemingly minor tasks can require some long-term thinking. In addition, there are some long-term thoughts required in seemingly minor tasks.

Some work requires teams working together for $1+1$ equals 3 instead of 2. In other cases, the $1+1$ type organization's output equals 0.5, and the individuals are trying to develop a consensus. Highly developed organizations strive to empower individuals to work on their own in preference to team decision-making.

In other cases, the $1+1$ organized into a team equals 0.5 as the individuals strive to develop a consensus. There is the basic tendency in highly developed organizations to empower individuals to act on their own in preference to team decision-making. Your challenge is to understand how you can plan and organize for maximum meaningful creativity that provides added value to the organization and its consumers (innovation).

Our definition of success includes being effective in meeting customer requirements and expectations, efficient in doing the assigned task with a minimum amount of resources, being creative in establishing new and unique methods, and being adaptive in changing what you do in response to a changing environment. Being efficient, effective, creative, and adaptive in developing and applying new insights to your world determines your success in a changing environment.

There are many tools available to help you improve your creativity. Each of the succeeding chapters will highlight some of our favorite tools. Many of these tools have several applications; however, we have broken them into four styles. Each style is described in more detail as it relates to individual thinking styles and organizational structure.

First comes imagination, then organization of that thought into ideas and plans; the transformation of those plans into reality. The beginning, as you will observe, is in your imagination.

Napoleon Hill

USING CREATIVITY IN AN ORGANIZATION

The approach to creativity within an organization varies with the thinking style, the organizational stratum, and team issues being addressed.

The 4 Resources to Consider

When we address innovation and creativity, we are not limiting ourselves to improving the way people think. There are four other categories that must also be considered (see Figure 2.12). They are

1. Knowledge management
2. Technology application
3. People development
4. Process optimization

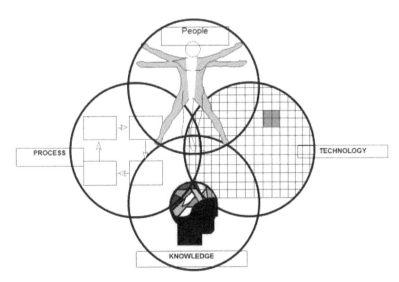

FIGURE 2.12
The four key innovation management factors.

Knowledge Management Overview

We need to pause right now and give a thought to knowledge management. In thinking about innovation, we immediately think about people, process, and technology. Seldom do we really set out to manage the knowledge that we have within the organization. We promise ourselves that we will save the lessons learned on each project and share them with the rest of the organization so that the problem will not be repeated. In my many years with IBM, I know I have solved the same problem with the same solution at least ten different times.

The people who have the vast amount of knowledge often never share it with rest of the organization. Sometimes, information is hoarded because the individual sees it as power, a way to get promoted, because other people do not have the information. At times, information is not shared because of the lack of time to record and communicate it. Often, information is not shared because the individual has already been transferred to a different assignment. A good postmortem, where the results are organized and fed into the database, is a crucial part of the innovation system today.

Without many new computers and many different ways of automatically collecting data, most of us are overwhelmed with data that should be supplied to a data warehouse, waiting to be analyzed and condensed (see Figure 2.13).

Once the data is analyzed and condensed into a usable format, it is fed into the information warehouse. But inputs into the information warehouse should be from many areas other than the organization's information. Information from the following typical sources should be collected and stored in the information warehouse.

- Colleges and universities
- Books

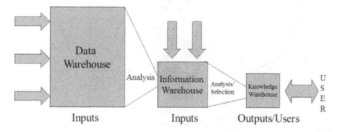

FIGURE 2.13
Knowledge management system.

- Internet
- Magazines
- Technical journals
- Conferences
- Tradeshows

Unfortunately, much of the data from outside sources and even from our own organization is questionable at best. Typical things that would make the data in the information warehouse questionable are as follows:

- Too small a sample size to get accurate projections.
- Data collected from one source may not be relevant to another source.
- Improbably analyzed data.
- An inaccurate measurement system.
- Bias presentation of the information.
- Errors in collecting data.

The following is a personal example of inaccurate information. We were using control charts, and I noticed that variation in the process was much lower on second shift than it was on first or third shifts. As a result, I sat down with the individual and asked her to pull a sample and make the measurement so that I could see what she was doing. I asked her to show me how she went about updating the control chart. She quickly grabbed the box of parts and went over to the tester. She tested one and put it aside, and then she tested another and put it aside. I noted that both were outside the normal range, but still within specification. "She then tested a third part and put it in a different box. When I pointed out that what she is testing had a greater variation than the one she had previously recorded on her control chart, her answer to me was, Sometimes I have to test twenty to thirty to find five parts that are good enough to plot. My manager told me that he wanted the average to be as close to the centerline as possible."

Time after time, I have seen management make important decisions based upon sample sizes that were so small that it had a 50% chance of being right and 50% chance of being wrong. It's absolutely imperative that the information in the information warehouse be analyzed to select the data that has a high probability of being correct before it goes into the knowledge warehouse. This is information where decisions and future directions can be legitimately based upon. If for some reason you want to put unproven data in the knowledge warehouse, it should contain a warning of potential problem to the individual who may be using it. In the knowledge warehouse, information should be segregated according to the communities of practice within the organization, thereby minimizing the amount of time and effort required for an individual to find the type of information they're interested in.

The other part of knowledge management is how do you protect your intellectual capital? Many companies have intellectual capital that is of greater value than all the hard resources owned by the organization. Certainly, one of the most important and complex ways of protecting intellectual capital are the patent and copyright laws that many countries outside the United States respect. We have covered the subject in detail in one of our previous books, and as a result, to keep the length of this book to a reasonable size, we will not repeat it here. We will just point out two factors.

1. If you think it is patentable and worthwhile, get the aid of a legal expert in the patent process to ensure it is done correctly as it is complex.
2. If you think you may be infringing on someone else's patent, get the aid of a legal expert in the patent process to ensure it is done correctly as it is complex.

Yes, you got the idea—the patent and copyright process is best handled by those who have a good understanding of the patent laws to ensure that your interests are well covered. It's the regular person that can handle processing a patent or copyright that can be treated as a do-it-yourself project.

SETTING DIRECTION

We start with the driving part of any organization from the top. At the top, it is critical to understand how these direction-setting creative activities are going to occur. Some of these activities will come from the tool set that we are calling *Aha creativity*, which focuses on that which did not exist before. Some creative tools are things like meditation, taking a walk, having a nap, always having a blank piece of paper with you, or carrying a tape recorder. For instance, Brian Wilson of Beach Boys had a sandbox in his living room with a piano in the middle. He used this alternative of playing in the sand and playing the piano as a free unstructured way of creating some of the music he wrote.

We are not necessarily talking about empty rooms and open space. Aha creativity, typically, is an individual experience. It rarely occurs in groups or teams. The typical result is something new—something that did not exist before. Brian Wilson's assignment to himself was to create music and lyrics that never existed before. He had no assignment to write a specific kind of music for a specific kind of audience. Rather, he created the music that he wanted to create. When did he do it? His structure was completely at random. Typically, Aha creativity could occur at 2:00 a.m. or at 2:00 p.m. Aha creativity is hard to plan, hard to schedule, and extremely hard to make happen on a schedule. It frequently occurs in a formatted workspace. A formatted workspace is a place that is conducive to this kind of creativity and innovative thinking. The space itself often determines the outcome of the effort. It should be a place that allows your thoughts to mature and grow.

This top thinking stratum also frequently uses provoked types of tools. Creativity from provoked tools provides some sort of movement. Provoked creativity uses a catalyst to overcome inertia. Tools provide the power to overcome the block of the blank piece of paper. Classical tools of provoked creativity enable you take a different approach from your accustomed path. For instance, you may choose to take a negative or a positive view. Provoked tools provide a license to change your approach by using toys or widgets, dictionary word searches, or any other catalyst to keep your mind alive and fresh. Typically, teams that are their own boss do provoked creativity in organizations. For instance, they may be a group of senior executives who must decide where the market is going to be in the future. Their work is to develop the direction and value system of the organization. Not only is this a self-directed group of senior executives working on the value system, but also they must identify the core competencies, the mission statements. They are the only group of people positioned to work on the macrosystems that define the organization. The way an organization configures and allocates resources at the broadest dimension is provoked thinking. For example, when Fred Smith, CEO of FedEx, decided to go to China, he was able to bring together his top managers. They decided how best to serve that part of the world. Their answer was to have a major hub in Philippines.

Major development of direction and systems needs an environment conducive to a group of people working outside of their everyday pressures. The world contains many beautiful retreats, conference centers, golf courses, and pleasant environments to provoke creativity. Collectively, senior individuals and senior teams determine the direction and intent of an organization. Without work occurring at this level, organizations go along doing what they have always done and go out of business in today's rapidly changing marketplace. One challenge of any creative initiative is to support senior management, in terms of providing the resources and incentive to do provoked and Aha creativity using provoked and Aha tools.

From an individual viewpoint, every individual must spend some time determining where they are going, their values, and direction. Using these provoked and Aha tools can be equally valuable when we apply them to our own lives.

PLANNING

After management sets the direction, the organizations need to put in place systems and processes that will keep us on track. This is true for individuals and for organizations. Systems and process-style creativity benefit from nonlinear and provoked kinds of thinking. Provoked tools provoke movement against issues.

Teams of people are often formed to collaborate on important or common issues. These teams work on systems and processes, such as an inventory maintenance process, accounts payable process, new product development systems, and so forth. Quite often, these creative initiatives are special projects, process reengineering, reengineering current products, problem-solving, or process improvement. Most often, nonlinear and provoked creativity occurs on demand. It is a very effective approach when processes or products are not meeting minimum requirements. Nonlinear and provoked creativity is designed to focus on issues like dissatisfied customers, loss of market, revenues lost, or resources wasted. This type of creativity tends to revolve around a conference room environment where all the attendees are encouraged to exchange their ideas. These office meetings are typically followed by a period where the group members collect data and/or experiment with alternatives.

Most large organizations have set aside breakout rooms, projectors, flip charts, etc., to provide a creative environment separate from the normal activities.

Nonlinear kinds of tools include tools like brainstorming, flowcharts, storytelling, and PDCA, etc. to help the team focus on the improvement opportunity. The people involved in these teams usually are experts and have a lot to say about the improvement opportunity. These team meetings must create an environment for open honest communication, and the team members should feel comfortable with expressing unpopular positions. Nonlinear tools encourage people to say what is on their mind. Sharing opinions and ideas that already exist in people's mind is a creative use of talents and ideas. It often provides the team with new insight into the root cause and impacts that an individual improvement opportunity has within the organization.

DOING

Once the basic systems and process performance tools and methodologies are functioning, the organization can focus on the use of nonlinear creativity tools and methodologies. At this stage of evolution, cross-functional teams give way to natural work teams. These individuals report to a common manager and often directly support another individual. This type of organization mostly uses structured creativity-type organizational structure. Draftsman, druggist, sales personnel, in-house left drivers, and supporting engineers are typical examples of assignments where structured creativity prevails. These are individuals who have interdependencies on a regular, almost hourly, basis. This is the most use of structured creativity. These individuals are responsible for improving the efficiency, effectiveness, and adaptability of the natural work team operations. Primary responsibility for performance improvement rests directly on the shoulders of an individual performing the task. To accomplish this, responsible team members must focus on improving their performance by the use of structured and nonsense linear tools. Structured and nonlinear creativity are the most common and fundamental types of creativity used in the natural work team environment in a very structured approach.

Structured and non-linear creativity usually follow a problem-solving model such as PDCA, which is a set of basic creative tools that everyone in the organization should be familiar with and capable of using effectively. In addition, there are many other creativity tools that are designed to take advantage of specific types of improvement opportunities. Typically, this will require special training based upon the specific opportunity that is being addressed. We have heard people saying that you cannot train your employees too much. We disagree with that statement. Too many organizations try to train other employees on all the problem-solving methodologies. As a result, most employees cannot effectively use any one of them.

EVALUATING

Next, the organization must evaluate how effective the plan was in meeting its objectives and goals. All planning activity is only as good as the results from implementing the project. All too often, results reported are not in keeping with the impact upon the stakeholders.

The 30 Impact Results

When you are evaluating results, you must look at the project's impact upon all the stakeholders, not just the customers or the organization. Typically, what is viewed as positive results for each of the major stakeholders are as follows:

Management's Positive Results
- Return on assets
- Value-added per employee
- Stock prices
- Market share
- Reduced operating expenses

Investors' Positive Results
- Return on investment
- Stock prices
- Return on assets
- Market share
- Successful new products

Customers' Positive Results
- Reduced costs
- New or expanded capabilities
- Improved performance
- Ease of use
- Improved responsiveness

Suppliers' Positive Results
- Increased return on investment (suppliers investment)
- Improved communication/fewer interfaces
- Simplified requirements/fewer changes
- Longer contracts
- Longer cycle times

Employees' Positive Results
- Increased job security
- Increased compensation
- Improved personal growth potential
- Improved job satisfaction
- Improved morale/less stress

Community/Mankind Positive Results
- Increased employment of people
- Increased tax base
- Reduced pollution
- Increased support of community activities
- Safety of employees

Often, it is necessary to evaluate a broad range of scenarios. What if you don't do it? What impact will this have on each of the results? For example, a new product may not gain customers for the organization, but if they don't change to the new product, the organization will lose 25% of its current customers. A correct analysis will always include a comparison of "What if we don't do it?" to "What if we do it?" This turns out to be the most positive way you can evaluate the results of an improvement activity. In evaluating value added, you should look at the thirty positive results and determine whether the impact of the project was positive, negative, or had no effect related to each of the results. Positive and negative impacts should be evaluated, quantified, and combined before a decision can be made if the results were value added. Time after time, executive managers complain that they spent a lot of money on improvement processes that reported big savings but had no impact on the bottom line. Great care should be taken in evaluating conflicting results. For example, change in the design may make an item easier to assemble, reducing the assembly time from 3.6 h to 3.2 h per unit. From the management standpoint, it represents added value per employee. From the employee's standpoint, it indicates a loss of three people's jobs, reducing job security. In reality, what typically happens is that individuals are assigned to do something that was not being done before, because it could not be cost justified. True value within an organization only occurs when the results increase the bottom line or it has a direct financial impact on the organization's future outputs. If you couldn't justify doing it before the productivity improvement, how can you justify doing it after? A typical example is an improvement that saves ten people twenty minutes a day at a cost of $35 per hour. That's a savings of $117 per day times three hundred days per year, which is a savings of $35,000 per year. Frequently, what really happens as a result of the change is no increase in productivity, but it does allow the workers to spend more time at the coffee machine and talking in the morning or they are reassigned to do a job that didn't need to be done before. This is the reason there are very little performance improvement results and impact on the bottom line.

All too often, we streamline our processes by reducing the effort required to produce output. These people are often put to work doing a job that didn't need to be done before and, in reality, doesn't need to be done now. Another way that reported laborsaving is false is when the savings is fifteen minutes per day per employee. So the employee takes a little longer and/or spends more time talking to other workers so that the headcount in the organization remains constant. Every time there is a reported value added, this savings should be reflected in the organization's budget. If three people's workload is truly eliminated, three people should be identified as surplus and added to the organization's surplus pool of employees. People removed from the surplus pool of employees' list only when they leave the organization or are set aside to perform an application that generates value-added content to the organization is greater than direct and indirect costs.

Key Points to Developing Aha Solutions

Many believe that structured creativity can save them from themselves. This may be true in some cases, usually when a small group of people are the only ones impacted by the change. Structured creativity is particularly effective in self-centered improvement opportunities when all the individuals impacted by the improvement opportunity take part in preparing a structured improvement plan. The night guard may realize that leaving the lights on wastes the organization's money. The analysis may indicate that they don't need the lights because each of the guards has flashlights, and they know where the master switch is for the electrical power. What they may not know is that by turning the power off, the product that is in the deep freeze waiting to be shipped in the morning will thaw out and, thus, get ruined.

Keep in mind the following three key points:

- Using the tools for structured and nonlinear types of creativity will never produce the Aha type of creativity. Even using the tools from provoked creativity does not do that.
- Aha creativity does not result from following standard well-known approaches to create a significantly new and unique improvement. It is the result of mankind's ability to connect different points of view and experiences to form a unique improvement opportunity. It comes from our creative thought patterns that link previously independent variables together forming a new and unique improvement action plan.
- Usually, Aha ideas are personal, rather than team oriented. It is the individual who comes up with truly Aha ideas, and then it occurs very solemnly. Frequently, Aha ideas are the result of accidents, rather than targeted action planning. It is the individual who creates the tools that help the individual structure his or her thinking. This book can help you think, but we cannot do the thinking for you. Only mankind has the unique ability to carve out improvement strategies that continue to better mankind's environment.

Individuals who are successful are those who can look and see the long-term ramifications of their creative ideas and then also have the power and structure within their own environment to move that idea forward.

THINKING OUTSIDE THE BOX

A very common saying around the world is, "You must think outside the box." That's a good thought pattern, but it doesn't go far enough.

FIGURE 2.14
Thinking outside the box.

Everyone has to smash down the walls that keep them boxed into a specific knowledge group and be willing to share their information with anyone throughout the organization (see Figure 2.14). Just too many managers get their security by having information that the employees don't have. Many believe that much of this type of information should not be shared with the employees for fear that the competition will soon have access too. This is a fallacy in thinking, because you can almost be certain that your competitor already knows about these deep dark secrets, and the only people you're hiding this from is your employees.

I used to think that tearing down the walls around me was adequate. I quickly found out that this just opens my knowledge base to looking at the four sides I come in contact with. All too often, the information that you need is located on the other side of the organization, i.e., parts of the organization I would never come in contact with, unless I went out of my way to penetrate their domain (see Figure 2.15).

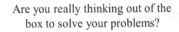

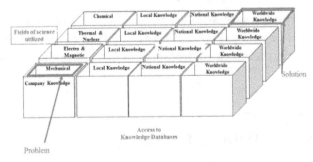

FIGURE 2.15
All the walls within the typical organization.

THE WORLD IS CHANGING RAPIDLY

The world is changing rapidly, and we either need to change with it or be put aside in the mailroom for the rest of our careers. The work environment and culture are evolving very rapidly, and you will have to run very hard just to keep up with it. For example, I call upon my eight-year-old granddaughter when my computer is acting up and I don't know how to fix it, but she does.

Just look at how work has evolved within the United States (see Figure 2.16). In the 1700s and 1800s, farm workers accounted for the biggest percentage of the working population. During the last part of the 19th century, the work population shifted to unskilled jobs in the new factories opening up throughout the United States. Slavery was abolished by President Lincoln, but a high demand for a new type of slavery was created, tying man to machine. These new types of slave laborers were called factory workers. They worked long hours under extreme environmental conditions at low wages and with little or no benefits.

The next step in the worker evolution was the office workers. These assignments were directed at processes required to operate a complex large organization and the layers of management that were required to keep the organization functioning and moving large quantities of output to the consumers. As the mountains of paperwork grew and grew, individuals got ahead based upon their personal knowledge. Computers started turning out tons of paper, and the knowledge worker became a key player in the organization and the pathway to more responsible positions.

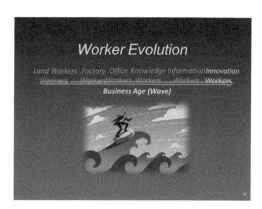

FIGURE 2.16
Worker evolution cycle.

With the mountains of paper growing, these organizations got bogged down just keeping up with the paperwork related to their activity. There was a need to have someone or something that could digest and consolidate all the information that was available. Computer software and the advancing computer technology absorbed large quantities of people in writing software programs. The consolidation of these vast quantities of data into condensed reports spurred on an increased focus on computer technology. These programmers then focused on major computer projects like Customer Relationship Management (CRM) and supply chain management software packages. Every individual was given the ability to search throughout the database, and as a result, the information worker was established. The development of the Internet opened up knowledge and information that had never been made available to management or to the workers. As a result, the information worker became the frontier of organizational changes. With everybody having large amounts of information available to them, it was easy for any organization in any part of the world to compete with developed nations. To add to the problem, many of the underdeveloped countries' labor and benefits were only a small percentage of what it is in the United States. The answer to maintaining our competitive position is to be more creative and innovative.

WORKER EVOLUTION

The old statement that "the early bird gets the worm" was never truer than it is today. In today's environment, organizations depend upon every employee to search for ways to make the organization more competitive and to come up with creative ideas that can be turned into profitable products and services. As a result, the organization that is most innovative (creative ideas that are marketable to external customers) finds itself in a position where it can compete even though its wages and benefits are much higher than its competitors.

The 6 Parts of the Value Chain

Figure 2.17 provides an overview of the innovative process and its supporting activities.

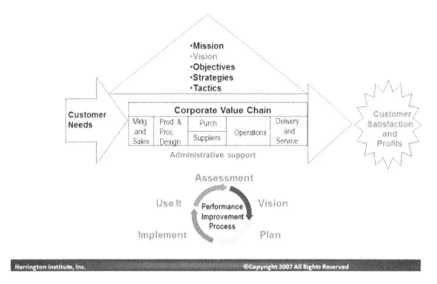

FIGURE 2.17
From mission to results.

You will note that Figure 2.17 starts with the customer needs entering the corporate value chain. The input can also be called opportunity identification or new-product development. At the far right-hand side of the figure, the arrow points to customer satisfaction and profit. Here again, we're trying to satisfy the two major stakeholders—the customer/consumer and the investor. All innovation, corrective action, redesign, and restructuring should be focused on making a profit for the investor and increasing customer satisfaction, for without a positive effect for both of these stakeholders, it's difficult, if not impossible, to have a successful organization. Without a high level of value added to the investor and the consumer, it is difficult for an organization to survive. There are basic things such as mission, vision, objectives, strategies, and tactics that need to be addressed. These are stable platforms that the executive team uses to accomplish the goals set forth in order to provide the investor with adequate return on their investment. Remember, the investor opens his wallet and invests money in the company because he or she believes they will get better return on their investment at a lower risk than they could get by investing in another organization. (This excludes your mother and father investing in your new and growing business.)

In Figure 2.17, the corporate value chain is made up of the following:

1. Marketing and sales
2. Product and process design
3. Purchasing
4. Suppliers
5. Operations
6. Delivery and service

The 5-Phase Process Cycle

The 5-phase process cycle shown in Figure 2.17 takes you all the way from doing a marketing study, so that a prepared marketing specification is defined when the completed item is delivered to the customer/consumer and that services are available and operated to handle any problem that arises related to the product. The circle at the bottom of the figure is one of the many performance improvement process cycles. It is a five-phase process cycle based upon Shewhart's PDCA.

- Phase 1. Assessment—An assessment is conducted to identify problem areas and improvement opportunities. The team then prioritizes the problems and improvement opportunities to select the ones that have the highest value content.
- Phase 2. Vision—The team develops a vision statement that defines how the product/process will look and function when the improvements have been incorporated.
- Phase 3. Plan—The team develops a project management plan using one of the many creative approaches to define a number of potential solutions to the problem and/or ways to take advantage of the improvement opportunities. The value-added benefits analysis is then completed for each of the potential changes, and a minimum of two alternative changes are presented to the executive team. When the executive team accepts a solution, the performance improvement process is ready to move on to the next phase implementation.
- Phase 4. Implementation—The project management plan, which includes a change management plan, is updated to include the implementation plan. Individuals are assigned to relevant parts of the plan, and then the plan is implemented. People are trained to

use the new process, and data collection points are installed in the process.

- Phase 5. Use it—At the beginning of Phase 5, the changes have been fully implemented, and people have been adequately trained to operate the new process. During this phase, the value-added content of the changes are measured, which includes feedback from the customer/consumer. As a result of these measurements, the project is classified as a failure (does not meet the value-added level as committed to the executives) or as a successful innovation if the idea is new and unique.

The team is now ready to go back to Phase 1 to select a new problem or improvement opportunity to work on. Occasionally, they go back to Phase 1 to continue defining alternate approaches for the project that did not meet requirements. As you can see, this is an ongoing never-ending circle designed to represent the continuous improvement activities within an organization. With no beginning or end, the organization is continuously striving to improve.

> There is no saturation point to organizational improvement.
>
> **H. James Harrington**

We have had some interesting discussions related to how Figure 2.17 can be applied to government and not-for-profit organizations. Most of these discussions have focused on the legitimacy of requiring the output to add value to the investors and the customer/consumer. The argument is that, often in government and not-for-profit organization, the investor (citizen/member) does not plan on getting a return on their investment as it is a donation or tax. Often, moral issues are the only compensation that had a tax or donation provided by an investor. At the other end of the spectrum, many of our laws have a negative impact on the individual they are being applied to (for example, a person being put in jail for stealing). But it does have a positive impact upon the safety and security of the total population. We will agree it is a little harder to define inputs and outputs for the government and not-for-profit making organization, but the effort is well worthwhile. Even if you cannot quantify the attached value, you should be able to determine whether it has a positive or negative impact upon the two major stakeholders. I often feel that many of our laws would not get through congress if its value-added content was analyzed and qualified.

INNOVATIVE PACKAGING

You have identified a need and created a unique design. The business proposition was favorable enough to include the idea in the organization's portfolio of projects. Production facilities were constructed, debugged, certified, and you have completed product at the line end. All that is now needed is to get the customer's signature on the bottom line. Now that the sales force has been trained, all we need to do is to go down to Federal Express and buy some light brown cardboard boxes to ship out the product. This would be a big mistake because attractively packaged products will frequently be favored even though the latter's performance may be worse and their price may be more.

Recently, I went to Costco and one of the items on my list was adhesive bandages (see Figure 2.18). One brand of bandages, Assured, was in a very conservative package. I was going to buy two of them when I saw the adhesive bandages in Figure 2.19, which were very attractively packaged. Closer inspection revealed to me that I could buy three boxes of the brand in Figure 2.18 for much less money and get a larger quality than buying one box of Band-Aid. Guess which one I bought?

In the end I bought both of them, only because I wanted to show you what a different set of packaging can make under normal conditions. This bandage example is a little extreme, but if you really want to see differences in

FIGURE 2.18
Packaging of assured brand.

FIGURE 2.19
Packaging of Band-Aid brand.

packaging, walk down the perfume aisle, and there you will find bottles of all different sizes and shapes and advertisement you could possibly ever think of.

We've seen products that had more money, creativity, and innovation put in the packaging than was invested in the design process. Never underestimate the importance of packaging design.

SUMMARY OF CHAPTER 2

America was built on the back of the production worker who could produce more products at better quality and at less cost than anyone else in the world. The middle class was born when Henry Ford Senior started paying his factory workers twice as much as they could get any place else. The marvels of the US production system was demonstrated during World War II with the massive amounts of planes, tanks, bullets, and rifles produced in American factories, giving a military advantage to the allied troops. Since World War II, the US production system has slowly declined as it was based upon old equipment that was obsoleted with new designs. Countries like Germany, Japan, and England had their production capabilities destroyed. These were replaced with factories using the latest and best equipment. When you start out fresh, you get the best. When you have something that is working, you do everything you can to keep it running rather than replacing with expensive new equipment. As a result, the middle class workers in the United States slowly disappeared in favor of just two working classes—the poor and the rich. With our vastly improved communication systems, it made it relatively easy to transfer the production activity from one country to another, providing significant advantage to the organization and its stockholders. As a result, the best, most sought after, jobs go to the individual who has the best ability to think and create new innovative products and services. The following are the 20 best jobs in America according to Quality Progress, April 2018 issue.

The 20 Best Jobs in America
1. Data scientist
2. DevOps engineer
3. Marketing manager
4. Occupational therapist
5. Human Resource (HR) manager
6. Electrical engineer
7. Strategy manager
8. Mobile developer
9. Project manager
10. Manufacturing engineer
11. Compliance manager
12. Finance manager
13. Risk manager
14. Business development manager
15. Front-end manager
16. Site reliability engineer
17. Mechanical engineer
18. Analytics manager
19. Tax manager
20. Creative manager

As a result, our colleges are full of individuals who, in the past years, would be out generating additional revenue. Many jobs that can easily be done by people with a grade-school education have college graduates performing them. Unfortunately it is very difficult for college graduates today to get the jobs they were promised upon graduation. Our society has misled these young people to believe that they must have a college education to succeed in life. This is just not true. There is a growing demand for technical people and we should be inspiring our young adults to attend technical schools if that is their passion. Some of the biggest manufacturing contracts have gone overseas, not because of differences in wages, but because US does not have enough manufacturing engineers to support new products. Almost every store window has a big sign saying "we are hiring." With so many jobs available, why is it we have homeless people standing on almost every corner? Is it because they don't want to work or is it because welfare provides them with a better life than they would get working at minimum wages? I'm an old man, and I remember when Franklin Delanor Roosevelt implemented the Works Progress Administration (WPA), which was the largest part of an ambitious American New Deal agency, employing millions of people (mostly unskilled men) to carry out public work projects, including the construction of public buildings, national parks, and roads. The WPA provided useful meaningful work for the people who were unemployed, thereby maintaining their dignity and enthusiasm to better themselves. Maybe it's time for another WPA-type program.

I recently took a taxi home from the airport, and the taxidriver had a master's degree but was unable to find work in his field. Is it any wonder that he was disappointed with his life and that he had little hope of paying off the debt he accumulated to put him through college. Trade school after trade school has been shut down in favor of MBA classes.

> Work (in the physical labor context) is looked at as a dirty four-letter word.
> There is no doubt about it today–thinking is in and working is out.

The 3 Ways to Improve Our Middle Class

The challenge that the organizations in both private and public sectors face is how to increase the creativity and innovation abilities of their present staff. Our education system needs to focus upon changing their curriculum to graduate students that the workforce is anxious to employ. There are currently three potential ways the US industry has to go about implementing an innovation explosion initiative. How can we rebuild the middle class of individuals who can afford the products we produce, a comfortable home to live in, with a job that generates sufficient income that allows them to save for the future? The most obvious ways to accomplish this is to focus on innovation in one or more of the following ways:

1. Cultural Change—Initiating an initiative to change the culture of the entire organization.
2. Function Change—Select a function (for example, development engineering, sales and marketing, manufacturing, etc.) to be used as a pilot for an innovation explosion initiative.
3. Product Change—Select a product that is in the early development stages as a pilot to apply the innovation explosion initiative to.

Things to Remember

You should remember the following points:

- Using the tools for structured and nonlinear types of creativity will never produce the Aha type of creativity that most people are looking for. Even using the tools from provoked creativity does not do that.
- Major Aha creativity does not follow a standard pattern. It often occurs when the standard pattern is accidentally upset, causing new and unique reactions. It's what we get when combining some standard patterns together in a different order from what we expected.
- Individuals produce creativity; it is not done by methods, processes, tools, or methodologies. The mother of creativity is individuals, not teams or tools. Those individuals who have had a large number of Aha ideas are very small. Seldom will an individual have more than one Aha idea in a lifetime. But if you had your one Aha idea, don't give up. Go ahead and try for two; you may be the lucky exception that distorts the distribution.
- Successful individuals are not the ones who have an improvement idea, but they are the ones who took an idea and turn it into reality.

The 10 Typical Creativity Tools

There are lots of tools to choose from. The difficulty in creativity is not the lack of tools, but the lack of appropriate application of tools.

- Eighty percent of the creative breakthroughs is a result of 20% of tools.
- You must pick the method that is correct for you.
- Creativity methodologies can be used in any order.
- Creative methods can be used more than once to address a given issue.
- Working on a given issue may, indeed, require several different approaches and methods.
- Simple methods are the best.
- Efforts from both groups and individuals can be fruitful in achieving creativity. The determining factor is the context in which the method is being applied.

- This book has been designed so that you do not have to read it entirely to use its content.
- Each tool and method stands alone.
- If you don't have time to use the creative/innovative tools, don't wait and lose the opportunity. Give it your very best guess; frequently, it is the right answer.
- The team approach does not always give you the best answer. Too often, the best solution to an opportunity is compromised in order to achieve consensus. It's a matter of $1 + 1 = 0.5$ not 3.0.

MIND EXPANDER'S EXERCISE

At the end of most of the chapters, we will present a Mind Expander's Exercise. Take a few minutes and develop a solution for each one as you encounter it. There may be more than one solution for some of the exercises. Keep track of how many you answer correctly, and at the end of this book, we will provide you with your personal analysis of your creative abilities.

Answer to Chapter 1. Mind Expander's Exercise

Exercise: There is a clerk at the butcher shop. He is 5 feet 10 inches tall, and he wears size 13 sneakers. What does he weigh?

Answer: Meat!

Chapter 2. Mind Expander's Exercise

How do you put a giraffe into a refrigerator?

RECOGNITION AND COMMENTS

The following books and/or PowerPoint presentations of H. James Harrington were used as references, and information from them was included in many of the chapters.

Presentations on innovation

- *Innovation*—IAOIP (International Association of Innovation Professionals) annual conference presentation by H. James Harrington (Boston 2016)
- *Hmmm—Creativity* presentation by H. James Harrington conference (Jamaica 2008)
- *The Innovation Process* presentation by H. James Harrington at American Society for Quality (ASQ) Section Meeting (Sacramento 2017)
- *Creating a Creative Culture* presentation by H. James Harrington (UAE 2012)
- *Status of Innovation* presentation by H. James Harrington (Mexico 2017)
- *Using TRIZ* presentation by H. James Harrington (Dubai 2016)
- *Innovate or Evaporate* presentation given by H. James Harrington (Abu Dhabi UAE 2010)
- *Organizational Excellence* given by H. James Harrington (Shanghai China 2003).
- *The Innovation Works* given by H. James Harrington (UAE 2014)
- *Innovation with TRIZ*—IAOIP (International Association of Innovation Professionals) annual conference presentation by H. James Harrington (New York 2016)

Books authored or coauthored by H. James Harrington that were used in this chapter

H. James Harrington is a prolific author, publishing hundreds of technical reports and magazine articles. He has authored or coauthored over fifty-five books. The following books were written or coauthored by H. James Harrington and were used as reference with parts of them.

- *Innovative Change Management (ICM): Preparing Your Organization for the New Innovative Culture* (2018)
- *The Innovation Tools Handbook, Volume I—Organizational and Operational Tools, Methods, and Techniques*—(2016)
- *The Innovation Tools Handbook, Volume II—Evolutionary and Improvement Tools*—(2016)
- *The Innovation Tools Handbook, Volume III—Creative Tools, Methods, and Techniques*—(2016)

- *Maximizing Value Propositions to Increase Project Success Rate*—(2016)
- *Effective Portfolio Management Systems*—(2014)
- *Making the Case for Change—Using Effective Business Cases to Minimize Project and Innovation Failures*—(2018)
- *The Framework for Innovation: A Guide to the Body of Innovation Knowledge* (2018)
- *Project Management for Performance Improvement Teams* (2018)
- *Creativity, Innovation and Entrepreneurship* (2018)
- *Innovation Black Belt Handbook*—classes being taught (technical paper 2018)
- *Total Innovative Management Excellence (TIME)*—Technical report released in Quality Progress Magazine 2019
- *Innovative Medal Handbook*—classes being taught/manuscript being prepared/released 1st quarter 2019. Technical paper published 1st quarter 2018.
- *Total Improvement Management—The Generation in Performance Improvement*—(1995)
- *Creativity Toolkit—Provoking Creativity in Individuals and Organizations*—(1998)

3

Setting the Stage

INTRODUCTION

Most of the large, profitable, and successful organizations are the result of a creative individual who believed in a concept so strongly that he brought it to market. For example,

- David Sarnoff—RCA
- The Johnson brothers—Johnson and Johnson
- Alexander Bell—AT&T
- Thomas Edison—General Electric
- J. Rockefeller—Exxon Mobil
- J. Campbell—Campbell's
- G. W. Merck—MERCK
- Henry Ford—Ford Motor Company

This list could go on and on, but by now, you should see the point I'm trying to make. There are many excellent ideas out there just waiting to make millions for any of us who come up with a creative unique product. A unique idea is worthless, unless it adds value to the organization and its stakeholders; then, it is priceless. Ideas that are new, unique, and creative have the ability to be transformed into an output that the customer wants to buy and remain a real challenge to the innovative process.

INDIVIDUAL CREATIVITY AND ORGANIZATIONAL CREATIVITY

There is a difference between individual creativity and organizational creativity. See definition of each below:

- Individual creativity is directed at finding solutions to personal problems, improving financial and/or living standards, and providing a level of personal satisfaction. There are two types of creativity—good and bad plus all of the derivations in between. A single idea can be good or bad based upon how it's used. If you define an original and unique way to kill someone in a children's book, it probably would be a bad idea. But if you're writing a mystery novel, it may be a good idea. (Individual innovation is a creative idea that the originator can transfer to increase value added for himself and/or his family.)
- Organizational creativity is originating a new and unique idea that may or may not be value added to himself/herself and the organization's stakeholders. Organizations need to be innovative to provide increased value-added content to all of their stakeholders (stakeholders include management, investors, customers, suppliers, employees, the employees' families, and the community). Unfortunately, far too many executives only consider three of these stakeholders when they are making decisions. I'll leave the choice up to you. Who are the three stakeholders that the executive team primarily considers? Well, that was an easy question. I'll bet 99.9% of people will come up with the same three stakeholders.

The 15 Typical *What If* Questions

The "What If—?" is the key to innovation. The key to creativity and innovation is the same for big companies or small companies. I will share it with you if you promise to keep it between you and me. It is simply these two words: "What If—?" The key to opportunity identification and creativity is simply to ask yourself "What if—?"

- What if—it was not necessary?
- What if—it was running faster?

- What if—it was half the size?
- What if—it had fewer calories?
- What if—we could grow hair on my head?
- What if—we could reduce the cost by 25%?
- What if—the new technology was applied?
- What if—we had to do it with fewer people?
- What if—we had to do it in half the time?
- What if—it broke down?
- What if—our line loss was half of what it is today?
- What if—we could provide pure water for everyone?
- What if—a car could drive itself?
- What if—I could do my work from home?
- What if—cars could run on saltwater in place of gasoline?

The "What if—?" list for all intents and purposes is a never-ending list? Stop doing what you are doing and look around you. I'll bet you will find more than five items that would provide value added to one of your stakeholders if the situation was addressed. This "What if—?" list provided you with many interesting creative opportunities? Just as there is no end to the list, there is no end to the contributions you can make to add value to your organization and mankind. Enlarge your creative thinking by selecting a minimum of five items per day and ask yourself what if this was better? What added value can be derived for yourself, your family, the organization, its employees, and its customers? You'd be surprised at how much more enjoyable your life will be when you our thinking about how you can improve the things you are complaining about. Now is a good time to start. If you want more money, originate more good ideas—you'd be surprised how fast you move ahead in the organization when you are contributing to its success.

THE 5 PROBLEMS WITH MOST DATABASES

With so much technology available to us today, you would think there was no need for creativity or innovation. No matter what the opportunity is, no matter how big the problem is, someone someplace should already have come up with a solution. All you need to do is go to the Internet and ask the question, "How do you solve the specific issue you're interested in?"

Unfortunately, that doesn't always work for a number of reasons. Consider the following:

1. More than 90% are out of date (five years or older). They do not reflect the present situation because things are changing so rapidly. All too often, these answers present only one side of the situation and do not highlight the negative results from the action that was taken.
2. Most of the data are based upon a statistically unsound sample. Decisions are made based upon data, where statistically, the probability of success or failure is 50% on both sides. You might as well flip a coin and not look at the data. Obtaining reliable data that can actually project future performance as a result of implementing a solution is extremely hard to come by and is usually not readily visible to the person that is making the go or no-go decision.
3. The data is misused by teachers and so-called experts who present concepts that are statistically unsound and/or unproven. Often, concepts are presented as being based on sound factual data that can be used to make decisions. Frequently, this is not the case. You might even say, usually, this is not the case.
4. The recommendation frequently does not represent optimum solutions. It may be a new approach to taking advantage of the opportunity, but frequently it is not the best approach. All too often, implemented recommendations reflect the product and/or technology in the organization that inputted data was selling. (For example, quality professionals would solve most problems by using Total Quality Management or Six Sigma, where the optimum correction would be a software package.)

   If you have a hammer, everything looks like a nail.

5. Occasionally, an individual using the Internet to address a situation does not know all of the conditions an individual providing the potential solution was facing at the time they developed a solution.

For these reasons and many more, we find Internet as an excellent source of information that should be considered as we develop unique and different solutions to the situation we are facing. But before you blindly accept these inputs, be sure that you thoroughly understand all the conditions that were relevant to impacting the data. I spent a number of years taking people on tours of the IBM quality system. I took great pains in explaining all the good things, but purposely stayed away from the negative things.

People as a whole have a tendency to tell an individual what the individual wants to hear. As an example, a CEO may brag about the money their Six Sigma program has saved them, but completely avoids any mention during that period of time about their customer satisfaction index being dropped to 10%. The CEO may tell you that their automated system has increased productivity by 30%, but forgot to mention or didn't know that their new robot was broken down and not working 50% of the time. One of the Japanese auto firms removed all of the automation out of their final painting operations, because humans could do the job better and faster.

The 8 Questions to Evaluate a Solution

For every improvement opportunity, there are a number of potential solutions. All too often, the team will find one solution and then spend the rest of their time trying to justify why that solution is the best answer. You should never be satisfied with one solution. Two or three solutions at a minimum should be developed and analyzed so that an optimum solution is implemented. All too often, year after year, people work on fixing exactly the same problem that was already fixed by another part of the organization. Typically, these problems are manifested in a slightly different manner. The following eight questions should be answered in a positive manner before you select a final solution.

1. Do you know the results you want? We are always surprised at the number of times teams will come up with a solution, but who never considered the impact the solution will have on the total system.
2. Will it work? Can it be implemented? You often have time constraints, money constraints, software constraints, environmental constraints, equipment constraints, etc.
3. Will it get the results you want? At the very beginning of the project, the results that the project should produce should be defined in very specific terms. Will the solution provide results that meet the projected impact when the project was approved? This requires that before- and after-type measurements are made preferably with the two running in parallel.
4. What negative results will it cause? Newton's Law tells us that, for every positive force created, there is a negative and offsetting force created. You need to make a list of all the potential negative impacts and develop contingency factors for the major and midrange exposures.

5. Is it better than any other solution and why? A comparison value-added analysis should be made for all potential solutions that are being recommended by the team.

6. Will it be accepted and is it in line with the organization's culture? Recommended solutions that are not in line with the organization's culture and strategic plan have a high probability of failing. Cultural change requires a great deal of effort and a long period of time to make it effective. You can implement changes very quickly, but it takes years to transform that change into a habit. Culture is driven by habits, not by directives.

7. Is this the right time? Timing is everything. Change that takes place during a very busy season will not be taken seriously and have a high probability of not producing the desired results. Study the workflow within the affected area and timing your changes so that it will not interfere with the normal workflow.

8. Is it worth the effort? What is the probability of failing? What is the probability of being successful? What is the probability of the results needing additional requirements? How long will it take to break even considering the added value to the organization? Is the projected return on investment adequate to implement the change? What unplanned for situation could arise that needs to be considered in making a final decision?

The 10 S's of Improvement Drivers

Successful growing companies have found that the answer to many of their problems is to become more creative and innovative. Of course, that's easier to say than to do. As a result, we have focused on defining the *innovation drivers*. We started out by focusing on the tried and proven McKinsey 7 S's, which are as follows:

1. Shared vision
2. Strategy
3. Systems
4. Structure
5. Skills
6. Styles
7. Staffing

Now I will admit that I am not a fan of "McKinsey," but after working for more than ten years with Ernst & Young, I got to really know the McKinsey organization, which was our competitor. I have to admit that McKinsey had some brilliant creative people working for it. When we started comparing these 7 S's, which we will refer to as *performance drivers*, to the activities going on in some of best known innovative organizations, we found that all seven were relevant and important performance drivers that must be considered and addressed in establishing an innovative organization.

As we gained more experience in innovation transformation, we found that there were three other performance drivers that needed attention to keep pace with the fast changing technology environment/competition organizations face today. They are as follows:

- Specialized technology—information technology systems
- Systematic change management
- Strategic knowledge management

Adding these 3 S's to McKinsey 7 S's makes up a new grouping called *10 S's*. These are subdivided into hard drivers and soft drivers. Hard drivers are easy to define, and the organization can directly influence them. The hard drivers are as follows:

- Strategy
- Structure
- Systems
- Specialized technology

The soft drivers are less tangible and more influenced by culture. Both the soft and hard drivers have a major impact upon an organization's performance. The soft drivers are as follows:

- Shared vision
- Styles
- Staff
- Systematic change management
- Strategic knowledge management
- Skills

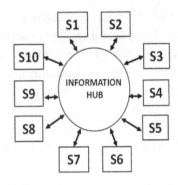

FIGURE 3.1
The hub for the 10 S's.

As you will notice, the 10 S's foundation is a very holistic view of the total organization and the habit patterns with management and employees. To accommodate this and take advantage of the synergy between each of the 10 S's, their output flows into an information hub. This combination of the ten organizational drivers and the information hub makes up a key part of the organization's Knowledge Management System (KMS) (see Figure 3.1).

KNOWLEDGE MANAGEMENT SYSTEM

One of the most crucial tools of innovation is an effective KMS. It supports both solving a problem and taking advantage of opportunities. It is even effective in helping to recognize potential innovative projects. An effective KMS is a proactive, systematic process by which value is generated from intellectual or knowledge-based assets and disseminated to the organization. KMS captures both explicit and tacit data.

Explicit (hard) knowledge is knowledge that is stored as semistructured content, such as documents, emails, voicemails, or video media. It can be articulated in formal language and can be readily transmitted to other people. It is also called as hard or tangible knowledge, and it is conveyed from one person to another in a systematic way. Explicit knowledge represents a small percentage of overall organization knowledge.

Tacit (soft) knowledge is knowledge that is formed around intangible factors embedded in an individual's experience. It often takes the form of beliefs, values, principles, and morals. It guides the individual's actions. It is embedded in the individual's ideas, insights, value, and judgment. It is only accessible through direct corroboration and communication with the individual that has the knowledge. Tacit knowledge comprises the majority of organizational knowledge and must be factored into the KMS.

It's easy to see why an effective KMS is essential in designing an innovative organization structure. Care should be taken in designing an organization's system to maximize the accumulation and details related to the organization's intellectual capital.

> Already an estimated two thirds of US employees work in the services sector, and "knowledge" is becoming the most important product. This trend calls for different organizations as well as different kinds of workers.

Peter Drucker, Author and consultant

Based upon Drucker's input, it's obvious that an innovation process has to be directed primarily at ideas and concepts that are directly delivered to the customer rather than being produced and then delivered to the customer. Improvement should begin with organizations that are concept developers instead of relying on other organizations to develop the concept and take it to market. We could be developing concepts that other organizations produce and take it to market. This is much the same as the grant money some universities get to develop concepts and turn the developed concept over to production and distribution throughout the organization that provided the grant money. This allows organizations to focus only on doing the things that they do best and farming out things that are not part of the core competency and capabilities. We have seen some trends recently to even farm out the quality function activities to an organization that specializes in performance management methodologies and applying them to processes. This is very similar to the action many organizations have implemented, where they farmed out the information technology activities.

THE 20 A's OF CREATIVE BEHAVIOR PATTERNS

Production is driven by machines, processes, and assembly activities. Innovation is driven by an individual with creative abilities. More and more organizations are becoming increasingly effective at identifying people within their organization and hiring people that have the personal desire to be creative and get maximum personal satisfaction out of having a creative idea that transformed into reality. To accomplish this, we have identified "The 20 A's" that are the abilities that are commonly found in creative people and in the behavioral patterns of these innovative individuals. They are as follows.

1. The ability to wander, to be curious. Those who want to see over the next hill around the next bend.
2. The ability to be enthusiastic, spontaneous, and flexible. Individuals who can quickly react and accept another person's idea that is better than their own.
3. The ability to be open to new experiences, to see the familiar from the uncertainty point of view. Those who would jump out of an airplane using a parachute so that they can look at the world from a different point of view.
4. The ability to make desirable, but unsought, discoveries by accident. This is called *serendipity*. Those individuals who would eat chocolate grasshoppers.
5. The ability to make one more thing out of another by shifting functions. Those individuals who use a coat hanger to open their car door locks.
6. The ability to generalize and to see universal application of ideas. Those who can see a fly and think of it as a meal for frog.
7. The ability to find disorder, synthesize, and integrate. A mother who goes into her twelve-year-old daughter's bedroom without becoming shocked at the clutter.
8. The ability to be intensely conscious, yet in touch with subconscious sources. In person when you're meditating.
9. The ability to visualize or imagine new possibilities. Your first blind date.
10. The ability to be analytical and critical. When you're driving and someone cuts in front of you.
11. The ability to know oneself and have the courage to be oneself in the face of opposition. A boy wearing a white shirt and tie to high school.
12. The ability to be persistent and to work hard for long periods in pursuit of a goal without guaranteed results. A boy with acne trying to get a date with the prettiest girl in high school.

13. The ability to take a risk for something you believe in. Writing this book about innovation.

14. The ability to put two or more known things together in a unique way, thus creating a new thing and an unknown thing. Driving my Model A Ford as fast as it will go out onto the ice and slamming on the brakes.

15. The ability to transform dreams into reality. Spending my life with my wife.

16. The ability to make new opportunities what others view as normal. Buying a rundown home, fixing it up, and selling it for a profit.

17. The ability to learn from failing and come back running. Not getting the promotion you thought you deserved. So you go out and take evening classes to make you a better candidate.

18. The ability to do more. Individuals who never say no to an interesting assignment even when they are already doing more than most employees.

19. The ability to ?????????????? (#19 allows the reader to add one more ability based upon their environment).

20. The ability to ???????????? (#20 allows the reader to add another ability based upon their environment).

MEET OSCAR AND FELIX

We all have two personalities that live inside of us, as much as Oscar and Felix of the movies and TV Show, "The Odd Couple," that lived together (see Figure 3.2).

The Felix-side of our personality resides in the left-hand hemisphere of our brain. Felix is a well-organized, highly literate individual who loves lists, plans everything he does, and never deviates from the plan. He is driven by rules and the clock. If rules have not been developed, he develops them to define what is expected of him. He likes to have goals, either set for him or by himself. He tries to please others and is very disappointed if others do not recognize his efforts (see Figure 3.3).

The Oscar-side of our personality, on the other hand, rests in the right-hand hemisphere of our brain, the creative side. Oscar's personality is unstructured, reactive, and driven by whims. He drinks beer for breakfast that was left opened the night before. He challenges authority and

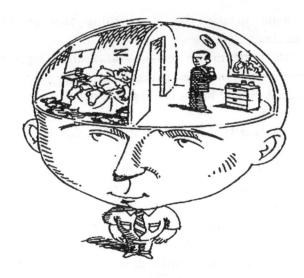

We all have an Oscar and a Felix inside our heads

FIGURE 3.2
The Oscar and Felix sides of the brain.

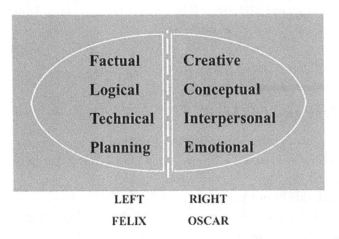

Factual	Creative
Logical	Conceptual
Technical	Interpersonal
Planning	Emotional
LEFT	**RIGHT**
FELIX	**OSCAR**

FIGURE 3.3
Building an Oscar's personality.

rejects conformity. He feels best when he is working on many items, all at the same time. He believes that rules are made to be broken. He works to his own drummer and relies on self-gratification to keep him going.

Felix had a 4.0 average in college. He loves exams because it proves to his teacher that he did the assignments and learned his lessons. Oscar had a 2.0 average. He created problems in class. He told jokes. He was more interested in making friends than in making grades. Felix works to accomplish something. Oscar functions for the joy of doing it.

We go to school and study to satisfy Felix's needs, to define more rules, to define how things are done, and how to plan to accomplish a desired goal. From the time we are born, our parents, teachers, and organizations train us to conform to some predetermined norm. Felix is held up as the example of good. Oscar is the example of bad. Felix always wears a tie, knows what time it is, and always knows what needs to be done next based upon past experience or training. Oscar—oh well, he is out to lunch.

Felix uses new rules and regulations to establish a creative idea screen so that he can concentrate his efforts on "getting the job done." The more rules that he can establish, the finer the filter of the screen, keeping more and more of the creative thoughts from getting through for Felix to consider (see Figure 3.4). The first step in increasing an individual's creativity is to start eliminating rules that screen out creative thoughts.

As a result of the feedback we receive throughout our lives, we push our Oscar personality into the shadows, only allowing it to emerge when we relax. Things would work fine if Oscar or Felix lived in the house

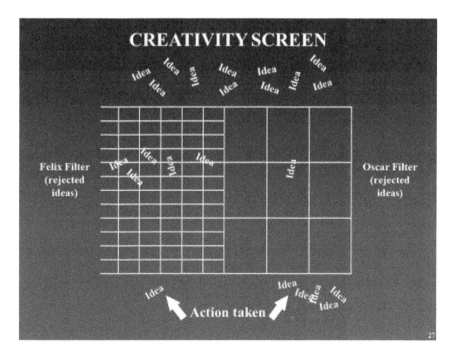

FIGURE 3.4
Felix's creative ideas filter.

(our mind) by themselves. But this is not the case. At night when we sleep, Oscar rules with no conflict with Felix because our thoughts do not normally result in accomplishing anything.

During the day, both Oscar and Felix live in the same house and must coexist. But Felix rules. Oscar operates like a child, emotionally reacting to outside circumstances. Oscar's outputs are radical and reactive. As a result, they are processed by Felix before we can put them into action. Felix takes these inputs and tries to put them in order, reshaping and boxing them into Felix's acceptable performance rules. This often results in Felix rejecting the idea and chastising Oscar for even suggesting it.

> Watch your thoughts; they become words. Watch your words; they become actions. Watch your actions; they become habits. Watch your habits; they become character. Watch your character; it becomes your destiny.
>
> **Frank Outlaw**

Oscar suggests that we should smell the socks, and if they don't smell too bad, put them on. Felix reacts by saying, "No way. Rule 1593 states, 'Put clean socks on every day.' How sloppy can you be?" Of course, Felix could wind up like the young boy at camp, whose mom said to put on clean socks every day. After a week, the boy called his mom and said he could not get his shoes on because wearing all the pairs of socks made his feet too big to get his shoes on. He followed the rules but did not get good results.

In other cases, Felix reshapes the idea so drastically that Oscar cannot recognize it. After years of rejection, Oscar just gives up and stops submitting ideas, being content to slip back into the shadow of the individual's dreams. The problem that we face today is how we get Felix to encourage Oscar to submit ideas and get Felix to react to these ideas in a positive manner as perceived by Oscar. How do we encourage the creative side of our personality to participate more actively in our day-to-day activities? That, simply put, is one of the objectives of this book.

INNOVATION'S MAGIC WAND

Innovation and creativity are not like Amazon's Alexa—you can't turn it on whenever you want to become more creative. There are things that you can do to help yourself become more innovative and creative, but they are just helpers that can make those great ideas emerge into the real world. The mind is like a muscle, and, like any muscle, it must be exercised regularly to keep it in good working order. Earlier in this book, we talked about mind expanders. These are a group of exercises designed to stimulate both sides of brain and help you think more creatively. These mind expanders help you to address the creative challenges that you face at work and in your personal life. Although you can be inventive or creative at any time and any place, there are particular times and places that vary from individual to individual that are more conducive to creative thinking. Everyone has a "when" and "where" they are most creative.

THE 6 CREATIVE FUNDAMENTALS

There are some fundamental activities related to when people are most creative that apply to almost everyone. Six of them are as follows:

1. When you break the rules by looking for different ways of doing the same old thing.
2. When you learn something that you have not been taught before.
3. When you take a risk by taking an unpopular position.
4. When what you have been taught does not apply to a specific condition.
5. When you look for more than one solution to an opportunity.
6. When you stop and think, "There must be a better way and I can find it."

Creativity is a random, unscheduled reaction to a situation that varies based upon the environment, personality, and makeup of the individual. In a team environment, one individual may be extremely creative while another individual will find it confusing and distracting. It's up to you define your personal creativity corner. I personally have two.

1. I have a small cluttered room that was converted from a bedroom into a man's cave. It is over 80 feet away from the big sixty-inch TV screen in the family room. Sitting in this room trying to ignore my stiff joints, I feel I can accomplish anything. However, on the other side of the coin, it is a room where I can come and relax.

It is the only room in the house where the maid does not clean or pick up anything. A Baby Ruth candy bar wrapper can lay on the floor for weeks. I have a huge window in front of my desk where I can look over Silicon Valley and see San Francisco sixty miles away (on a clear day). In the center of the window, two Argentine boleros with a snake wrapped around each hang reminding me of the wonderful conferences I had with Marcos Bertin in South America. On the wall I have the hide of a kangaroo and antelope I shot. In between them is a large set of horns from Africa. The rest of the wall is covered with masks from different countries in Africa that I visited over the years. At the very top of all of this is an African feathered headdress and the blowgun that were used when I was in Africa. The third wall has my collection of model cars I have owned over the years or wanted to own. Also in my thinking room, there are four 6-foot bookcases and two smaller ones. There are three file cabinets, two desks, two computers, a forty-inch TV, and a twenty-two-inch monitor. I could go on describe the room, but by now you've got the idea. My man cave is customized to make me think about things that I have done in the past, things I promised myself I would do in future, things I need to do now, and new things I would like to do soon. When the doors close to my man's cave, no one would knock on its door unless it was a major emergency.

2. As I mentioned earlier, there are two places that are my thinking spots. The second place is at 6 o'clock in the morning as I am lying in bed knowing I should be getting up and getting dressed. There is something about 6 o'clock in the morning that makes the bed much softer than any other time. I stick my toes out and quickly bring them back under the covers where it is warm and comfortable. I justify just lying there in bed, not thinking about going fishing, getting the car, or even pretty girls. I lay there thinking about what I would be doing if I had to get up and go to work. Thinking about what I should writing in the next chapter of the book, the curriculum of the class, or about how I am going to respond to the request for quote received the day before. This is how I just justify lying in that warm cozy bed instead of challenging the colder rest of the room. That works until I come up with so many answers and/or so many action items that I am afraid I will forget some of these so I jump out of that warm cozy bed to write down my thoughts.

Everyone should have their special thinking spot. For you, it may be in the middle of a team meeting. It may be while you're talking with the person next to you at work. It may be when you're on the golf course. It may be when you're swimming in the pool. It may be when you're doing meditation exercises. Everyone has an environment that stimulates them to be more creative and more willing to take a risk. Companies like Apple have quiet areas for employees to lay down in hooded couches with soft music transforming them into a state of relaxation.

Creativity can occur anytime and at anyplace. Sometimes, we are very creative. Other times, it is just impossible to pluck out an original thought. I've sat in front of my computer for hours pecking at one key at a time to capture a few unimportant thoughts that I erased at the end of the session. At other times, the ideas flow out of my mind so rapidly that I lose them because I cannot record them fast enough. There is a lot that we can do to prepare ourselves to become more creative. We can position and train the right-hand side (Oscar side) of our brain to speak out more often and the left-hand side (Felix side) of our brain to listen more intently and openly to Oscar's ideas. For this to occur, three conditions need to be present:

- Time. Extra time is often required to develop and sell a creative solution that is not in line with the individual's or organization's culture.
- Environment. It is difficult to be truly creative when you are continuously being interrupted with phone calls, questions, or have children climbing on your lap.
- Success. Nothing gets Felix's attention better than when we are recognized because we came up with creative new solutions.

CREATIVITY WORKSPACE

Our emotions and actions are directed by our preconceived notions about the environment we find ourselves in. We enter the library and we talk softly and move carefully. We go to a party and we laugh and smile more. We pick up a baby and we coo and gurgle like we have no mind at all. We go to work and we become more conservative, reserved, and formal. We go to a movie and sit beside a friend for hours without talking. This behavior is not only acceptable, but expected. We have been trained from birth to conform to the expectations related to the environment in which we find ourselves.

The 6 Creative Time Rules

We like to set aside a specific location where we exercise our creativity. For some, it is a desk in a small back bedroom. For one of my friends, Bob Reed, it is a beach. We discovered this when we developed an earlier book while we were conducting a class in Curacao. We spent each evening on the beach working on our new book. It does not have to be a grand place. It could be a workbench in the garage or an old desk in the cellar behind the furnace. The important thing is that, in your mind and in your family or business associate's mind, it is your space, and there are specific rules associated with it.

Rule 1. No interruptions are tolerated unless it is an emergency.

Rule 2. The clean-desk policy does not apply. Do not take time to organize the work area, and it is out of bounds to your spouse and/or your coworkers. Remember, the world of Oscar is one of clutter and disorganization. Just think of the time you will save by not having to pick up, put away, and get out the same materials later.

Rule 3. Make your creativity place very visual. Use lots of post-its. Write down good ideas on them and stick them up around your creativity area. Make sketches and flow diagrams, and put them on the walls also. Put up very different, interesting pictures and change them often. Your creativity place is to stimulate ideas, not to impress others.

Rule 4. Have a relaxed atmosphere. Have a comfortable chair, one that you can lean back in and rest your head while your mind goes blank and opens to creative thoughts. Have furniture that you can put your feet on. Choose a spot that is not too hot or cold.

Rule 5. Have the right equipment. Be prepared to be flooded with new ideas, and when they come, you need to be able to capture them rapidly. Things that can be useful are as follows:
- a good lighting
- a computer
- lots of paper
- colored markers
- a tape recorder
- a CD or tape player (for restful music)
- a filing system
- a corkboard
- a bookcase

Rule 6. Have a focal point. This is something that relaxes you when you look at it. It could be a window that you look out of or a small aquarium. Other people find that an ocean scene or an abstract painting does the job for them. Use whatever relaxes you.

Each person's creativity place is very unique to them, since it must fit into their individual personality and output expectations. We are not telling you that you must have a creativity place, but we strongly suggest that you should consider using a creativity place as a tool to help turn on your creative juices. Does this mean that this is the only place where you will be creative? The answer is a resounding no. It is a lot like the treadmill that you buy and put in your house to jog on. When you get on the treadmill, you don't start eating a sandwich, you start to jog, and because you have a treadmill, it does not mean that you cannot run around the block in front of your house.

PROACTIVE CREATIVITY

Far too often, people only call on their creative powers when they are faced with a problem. This is truly unfortunate because they underutilize this gift by not applying it fully. As a result, they develop a reactive, rather than a proactive approach, to creation. In reality, we believe that individuals need to develop and use both their proactive and reactive creative powers in order to make maximum use of their creative potential.

The 4 Drivers of Creativity and Innovation

There are a variety of factors that drive individuals or groups to become creative. The most common are the following four reasons that drive innovation and creativity:

1. A significant personal experience. (Example: you back into someone's car.)
2. Seeing a void that could be filled. (Example: a typical ice cream falls out of the cone onto the ground.)
3. Internal need to be creative. (Example: writing a book.)

4. Using Mind Expander's Exercise. (Example: Using exercises that help the brain looking things in a different way than they had been looked at before. Serve a hotdog like serving the hotdog on a waffle.)

To sharpen your creative powers, you need to establish a workout program and exercise your creative selves at least three times a week. Individual workout sessions can vary from five to sixty minutes, depending on the exercises you select and your personal interest in the outcome.

THE 6 TECHNIQUES FOR MANAGING CREATIVE PEOPLE

As we roll out our innovative system, we are expecting a lot of changes from everyone in the organization, but the individuals who will need to change the most is our management team. Job descriptions will have to be rewritten for almost all levels of management. Managers need to be trained on how to evaluate the performance of a creative/innovative individual. In some organizations, taking a nap in the middle of the day on company time invigorates the individual so that they are far more creative and productive for the remainder of the day. If you measure an individual's activities based upon their results, many organizations are finding that a nap pays big dividends in output and originality of the output.

The following techniques have proven helpful for getting quality results from imaginative people:

1. Allow people to make "intelligent" mistakes. Mistakes are the steps forward in the innovative process.
2. Establish desired goals and milestones, and then let creative people approach them in their own way and on their own timetable.
3. Let them personalize their work areas.
4. Hold them accountable for the results of their work, instead of for their actions or the time spent.
5. Define their jobs in terms of "key results" rather than with specific activities. Define the target and try to aim the gun.
6. Don't try to be more technically competent so that your employees become more creative than you are.

The Burning Platform

To have a successful transformation, it is imperative that everyone in the organization realizes that innovation is not an option. It is a necessity. Everyone needs to feel that they have a portion of the innovation workload to carry and that it is urgent that they accept the responsibility to improve their creativity and innovation. Change is going to happen; it is not an option. You can be part of the change parade or an onlooker. It is up to you. You can be the bandleader or you can sweep up the horse droppings after the parade has passed by.

The board of directors and the executive team need to develop a sense of urgency so obvious that everyone will see change as the desirable way to go (see Figure 3.5). Employees need to believe that tomorrow will be better if they are just more creative in the way they do things. Today is already yesterday and tomorrow is here. I will call this sense of urgency, the burning platform (see Figure 3.6).

Target Plus–Minus Analysis

As we have previously discussed, change is a process. For individuals to start to move through this process, they must feel that they will benefit from the change. One of the major challenges that an Innovation Team (INT) faces is to surface the benefits of making the change. This, in reality, is a pain management process. It is surfacing the pain related to the current process, or what we call, "establishing the burning platform."

FIGURE 3.5
Creating a sense of urgency.

FIGURE 3.6
Creating a sense of urgency, the burning platform.

The term "Establishing a Burning Platform" (i.e., a term related to getting people who will be effected by change to move out of the current state and accept the change) was originated by Daryl Conner, based upon the following story:

The Burning-Platform Story

At nine-thirty on a July evening in 1988, a disastrous explosion and fire occurred on an oil-drilling platform in the North Sea, off the coast of Scotland. One hundred and sixty-six crew members and two rescuers lost their lives in the worst catastrophe in the twenty-five-year history of North Sea oil exportation. One of the sixty-three crew members who survived was a superintendent on the rig, Andy Mochan. His interview helped me find a way to describe the resolve that change winners manifest.

From the hospital bed, he told of being awakened by the explosion and alarms. He said that he ran from his quarters to the platform edge and jumped and jumped fifteen stories from the platform to the water. Because of the water's temperature, he knew that he could live a maximum of only twenty minutes if he were not rescued. Also, oil had surfaced and ignited. Yet Andy jumped one hundred and fifty feet in the middle of the night into an ocean of burning oil and debris.

When asked why he took that potentially fatal leap, he did not hesitate. He said, "It was either jump or die." He chose possible death over certain death...

He jumped because he had no choice—the price of staying on the platform, of maintaining the status quo, was too high. This is the same type of situation in which many business, social, and political leaders find themselves every day. We sometimes *have* to make some changes, no matter how uncertain and frightening they are. We, like Andy Mochan, would face a price too high for not doing so.

An organizational burning platform exists when maintaining the status quo becomes prohibitively expensive. Major change is always costly, but when the present course of action is even more expensive, a burning-platform situation erupts.

The key characteristic that distinguishes a decision made in a burning-platform situation from all other decisions is not the degree of reason or emotion involved, but the *level of resolve*. When an organization is on a burning platform, the decision to make a major change is not just a good idea—it is a business imperative.

From *Management at the Speed of Change*

Pain Management

People are willing to pay the price for solving a problem or capturing an opportunity. Both problems and opportunities can be subdivided into current and anticipated. We will discuss both problems and opportunities in detail later on in this book.

The employees normally understand the problems related to the current process as they directly relate to them, but not as they relate to the total organization. Most employees do not have the information available to understand the pain related to lost opportunity and anticipated pain. Management and the project team need to define and communicate this pain to all the targets. This is called establishing "the burning platform."

Then, the project team needs to provide a clear vision of the future-state process so that the employees can assess the pain that is related to the future state. (In the Project Change Management [PCM] methodology, the proposed future-state solution is often called the remedy.) In addition, management must provide the employees with an understanding of what pain they will be subjected to during the transitional period. (Example: working overtime to make up for lost productivity as a result of the training program or having to learn a new system.) If the current-state pain is not greater than the combined anticipated pain after the best-value future-state solution has been implemented plus the anticipated pain that may occur during the transition period, the only way that management will be able to get the employees to accept the change is by dragging them along, kicking and fighting (see Figure 3.7).

You will note in Figure 3.7 that there are two ingredients of pain related to the current process (the left-hand side of Figure 3.7). The employees probably have an excellent understanding of the current (AS/IS) pain. The other factor related to the current model is lost-opportunity pain. This is pain that will be created if the process is not changed. The employees, in this case, have no way of assessing the magnitude of lost-opportunity

FIGURE 3.7
The pain management teeter-totter.

pain. Therefore, management must help the employees understand and quantify lost-opportunity pain.

At the other end of this fulcrum (the right-hand side of Figure 3.7) is the pain related to the future-state solution. Of course, all processes have some advantages and disadvantages. No process is perfect. Because of this, management and employees must realize that even the best-value future-state solution will still have some pain associated with it. In addition to that, the B end of the fulcrum is weighted down by the pain that occurs during the transitional state. When starting out on the change process, management and employees anticipate what the pain will be during the transitional state and the future state. For this reason, this pain is called anticipated pain.

Transformation Management

Very simply put, you can think of transformation management as the conversion of resistance to the project to commitment to the project. We need to change the attitude of everyone from "it can't be done" to "we will get it done." That's what is meant by changing resistance into commitment. To make this transformation, we need to

- Define the pain related to the current state
- Define an achievable remedy
- Prepare a future-state vision statement
- Define what's-in-it-for-me scenario (for the target, the organization, and the team)
- Understand the reasons for resistance
- Respect those who put up resistance
- Be truthful with the targets
- Listen intently to the targets
- Develop win–win scenarios
- Align the change to the organizational culture
- Don't move so fast that we overstress the system
- Set up reward systems that encourage people to change
- Maintain open communications
- Stop talking and start listening
- Look at the situation from the eyes of the person who is putting up the resistance
- Recognize that resistance is normal

- Understand the emotional cycles related to change and specific bailout points related to how the individual perceives the individual change
- Help targets over the bailout points
- Provide everyone with required change training
- Build models where the targets can observe the change and gain hands-on experience with the change before it is implemented
- Involve as many of the targets as possible in the change decisions

Too many people who are implementing a project take resistance to the project personally. In truth, resistance is good and normal. Resistance to change is just human. We are trained to question everything that can impact us from the beginning. Our mothers warn us not to touch the stove because we may get burned, and put on our coats in the winter because it is cold outside. We are taught to question everything, every change before we accept it, to be sure that it is good for us. I would like to buy a new car every year, but I resist that transformation, after doing a cost-benefit analysis. Mentally, every change that comes down the road meets resistance. Individuals stop to ask the question: "What's there in it for me?" Each person performs a cost-benefit analysis of the change and either accepts or rejects the change. The degree of resistance to the change varies from individual to individual based upon their past experience, age, and culture. In general, the more bad experiences an individual has had related to changes that impact him or her or the older the person is, the more resistant the individual is to change. The way people express their resistance to change could be classified into two categories:

1. Covert Resistance is a marked, hidden, or concealed reaction to the change.
2. Overt Resistance is the expression of open and honest opposition to the change.

Although the individual resistance classification approach is not part of the Managing Organizational Change (MOC) methodology, we have found that individuals' resistance to change can be classified into six categories.

- Arbitrary Resistance—This is characterized by individuals who are just against everything. It does not make any difference if it is good or bad; they are against it.

- Justified Resistance—These are individuals who realize that the change is going to hurt them, and as a result, they are going to do everything possible to keep it from occurring. For example, a change that will cause these individuals to be released from the organization.
- Informed Resistance—In this case, the individuals understand the change that is going to impact them and have an idea that will lessen that impact on them or will improve the effectiveness of the change. These are individuals who are not against the change but have a strong feeling that the proposed change should be restructured to improve the benefits to the organization's stakeholders.
- Mistaken Resistance—There are individuals who are reacting to gossip or false information that has turned them against the change, but have the potential to change their opinion when provided with the correct information.
- Uninformed Resistance—These are individuals who have not been provided with enough information about the change. Everyone is against changes that they don't understand.
- Fearful Resistance—These are individuals who can imagine all sorts of bad things happening to them if there is any change in the comfortable environment they exist in. These individuals are against any progress.

It is extremely important that the project team recognizes the type of resistance that it faces and then provides communication systems to the target that offset the various types of resistance. Usually, by providing sound information, good vision statements, and future-state models, everyone that does not fall into the arbitrary or justified classification can be converted from resistance to commitment.

THE 5 TYPES OF INNOVATION

- Product Innovation, which primarily leads to producing a competitive advantage through differentiation.
- Process Innovation, which primarily leads to producing a competitive advantage through lower prices or reduced cycle time or improved reliability or a combination of all three.

- Sales & Marketing Innovation, which primarily leads to producing a competitive advantage or a marketing mix (target market, distribution, product, price, and promotion).
- Management Innovation, which primarily leads to producing a competitive advantage through better organizational ways of achieving the organization's goal and better use of the organization's resources.
- Service Innovation, which applies to servicing the customer after they have purchased the item and services to internal organizations. This basically drives improved responsiveness, understanding of the consumer's environment, and improved relationships.

For each of these types of innovation, there are three subcategories. They are as follows:

- Breakthrough Innovation—This is when a radical new design and/or approach is created and implemented. It's often referred to as Aha innovation.
- Evolutionary Innovation—This is a logical expansion of an existing product, process, or strategy. It typically does things like making it smaller and faster and adding additional capabilities.
- Gradual Innovation—This means small improvement activities that are implemented throughout the organization. This is commonly called continuous improvement in the product and employees performance. It can be as simple as a janitor finding a new broom or the project engineer finding a new design that uses the next-generation technology to perform the same or similar function as the present one.

THE 5 LEVELS OF IMPROVEMENT

Many of our experts argue continuously about whether an activity is continuous improvement or is it an innovation? If you look at it in the broadest sense for any change that adds value to the organization and/or the customer, it is a form of innovation. The improvement opportunities can be broken down into five levels. On the basis of a massive study of thousands of patents and technology systems, Genrich Altshuller divided the improvement opportunity as follows (see Table 3.1):

TABLE 3.1

The 5 Levels of Improvement

Level 1—Apparent solutions (gradual innovation) = 68.3% of the changes
Level 2—Minor improvements (gradual innovation) = 27.1% of the changes
Level 3—Major improvements (evolutionary innovation) = 04.3% of the changes
Level 4—New paradigm (breakthrough innovation) = 00.24% of the changes
Level 5—Discovery's (breakthrough innovation) = 00.06%

Figure 3.8 displays the five levels of improvement in a graphic format. I found this knowledge on the shocking side, but it was very interesting.

- Level 1—Apparent Solutions: Is apparent solutions more continuous improvement or is it new and unique so that it can be classified as innovative? I personally would estimate that the three Sigma of this population would be classified as continuous improvement.
- Level 2—Minor Improvements: What percentage of minor improvements is continuous improvement and what percentage is innovative? Based upon looking at a small sample of data, I would estimate that 80%–85% of the minor improvements are continuous improvement and only 15% could be classified as innovative.

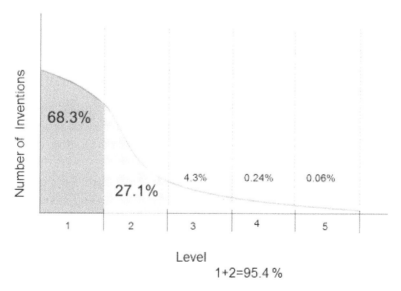

FIGURE 3.8
The 5 levels of improvement.

- Level 3—Major Improvements: What percent of major improvements is continuous improvement and what percent is innovative? My estimate is as little as 20%–30% are continuous improvement and as much as 70%–80% are innovative.
- Level 4—New Paradigm: What percent of the new paradigms is continuous improvement and what percent is innovative? Here, the biggest percentage of innovative concepts and ideas are a whopping 95% in only 5% continuous improvement.
- Level 5—Discovery's: What percentage of the discoveries is continuous improvement and what percentage is innovation? Again, this ratio is 98% for innovative and 2% for continuous improvement.

You may not agree with the exact ratio that I am estimating, but it should give you an idea of the magnitude between continuous improvement and innovation for each of the five categories. More important is to point out that approximately 93% of all improvements that are new and creative fall in the categories of apparent solutions and minor improvements. This would indicate that the innovative system needs to focus upon 7% of the total improvements that have made up of Levels 3, 4, and 5. It's important to point out that these are the types of changes that give an organization a very significant competitive position and reputation. Often, a Level 4 change will be the trigger that promotes many of the Levels 1 and 2 changes.

INNOVATION IS NOT FREE—IT IS PRICELESS

The innovation impact is a lot like an Olympic runner practicing for the hundred-yard dash. They are investing today's effort, sweat, energy, and tears on the practice court, to be the first to receive the Gold medal at the Olympics.

Innovation is difficult to describe because it accomplishes so many positive things. The following is a list of some of the things that innovation means:

- Innovation means process
- Innovation means market
- Innovation means productivity
- Innovation means progress

- Innovation means more customers
- Innovation means freedom for all
- Innovation means perspective
- Innovation means profit
- Innovation means leadership
- Innovation means pride
- Innovation means security

The organization is a reflection of the CEO and its management team. Management needs to measure their performance based upon creating value for the customer based upon the price the customer is paying, while generating a better-than-average return on investment for their stockholders.

Management is the problem and the solution, not technology or the employees' ho-hum attitude about innovation.

- Management hires people
- Management defines processes
- Management defines job assignments
- Management defines priorities
- Management defines training
- Management sets an example

Winning is not a sometimes thing. It is an all the time thing. You don't win once in a while, you don't do anything right once in a while, you do things right all the time. There is no room for second place. There is only room for one place and that's first place.

Vincent Lombardi—Green Bay Packers

Summary

We need to ask ourselves the following questions:

1. How did US lose its leadership role?
2. Why has innovation become an advertising thing when it is used to be taken for granted?
3. Are we doomed to become a second-class industrial power?
4. What can US companies do to reverse the trend in lost market and reputation?

There was a time when creativity and innovation passports were only associated with writers, musicians, artists, etc. Today, 97% of professionals feel it is important to be creative in his or her life (Bayt.com poll February 2015).

THE STEPPING-STONES TO INNOVATION

1. **Management innovation**: Executives must set an example by demonstrating their personal creativity and innovation in the way they operate, strategically plan, and measure the organization. They should be more innovative than the products they sell to the consumer. They need to learn how to be Angel advocates, rather than devils' advocates. Rather than trying to find something wrong with the employee's suggestion, management needs to help the employee turn a good idea into a great idea.
2. **Training your employees**: Everyone from the board room to the boiler room should be trained to have a basic creative and innovative skill set. A common fundamental set of basic creative tools and methodology should be provided across the organization with more complex training related to specific assignments like marketing, sales, research and development, management, etc. The Bayt.com February 2015 poll reported that only 69% of the employees are kept up-to-date related to best practices in their area of expertise.
3. **Make innovation an important priority**: The three-legged stool that has been used in the past to support most organizations consists of quality, cost, and schedule. Unfortunately, this is an unstable situation that can quickly lead to bankruptcy even though each of the three measurements is performing well. Today, our three-legged stool has turned into a four-legged with the fourth leg—innovation. Without innovation, you can have Six Sigma plus quality at no cost to produce and you will end up with warehouses of surplus stock. Today, you need a pull-delivery process in place of the push-delivery process many organizations are using. You want the system where customers are clamoring for more output rather than debating if they should buy it from someone else.
4. **Employee involvement**: You need to have a culture where every individual feels that innovation is part of their job assignment.

Management should restrain their natural tendency to talk and develop their ability to listen. Involve everybody in the planning session, particularly, as it relates to them or impacts them. Make it a *we* organization, not a *me* organization. Develop internal career paths for all employees, making the organization something they are investing in, rather than working for. Ask the employee if they have any good ideas to improve the processes. We all go out for dinner and the waiter asks us, "How did you like your meal?" And we answer saying, "It was good or it was okay." But what if the waiter had asked, "Do you have any suggestions on how we can improve?" Then we could tell him the truth—"Actually, the soup was cold and steak was so tough I couldn't cut through it." Be proactive in employee involvement, not reactive.

5. **Hire innovative employees**: You can train your present employees to be more innovative, but it is the new employee who brings a breath of fresh air and unpolluted creativity to the organization. These new employees challenge the regular staff to try something new, different, and risky. It is often better to hire an engineer with a 3.5-grade point average than one with a 4.0. You want the freethinkers, not the individuals who can regurgitate something they read or have been told.

6. **Innovative rewards and recognition systems**: If you want to get something done, we set up a system that rewards people for doing it. You need a system where innovation is recognized and rewarded. The system has to be broad enough to meet the needs of a broad range of people as everyone should be innovative. As a result, there is a need for a reward and recognition system that gives a pat on the wallet and at other times a pat on the back. Only 44% of the companies surveyed had systems designed to reward creativity and innovation.

7. **Measurement of innovation**: There's an old saying, "What management wants done, they measure it." If you want to improve innovation, you have to have some way of measuring progress or lack thereof. Many organizations have not actively measured innovation and/or creativity in the past. As a result, they find themselves in a difficult position in coming up with an innovation measurement system. Typical measures are percent of income generated by product that was not in existence two years ago, number of patents generated, comparison to competitive products, percentage of projects

that generate real-value added, etc. One measurement that covers everyone in the organization is to set targets for each natural work team, related to the number of suggestions per month that were made and implemented. We have seen organizations that, on an average, receive two implemented suggestions per month per employee and other companies that are averaging two implemented suggestions per hundred employees per year.

8. **Risk taking**: An innovative organization is one that encourages its employees to stick out their necks and take a prudent risk. They encourage their employees to sail in uncharted waters, greatly increasing the risk of potential failure. Innovative organizations turn the other cheek with employees who failed when they're trying to meet stretch goals. Failures are looked at as a learning experience, at least the first time.

9. **Thinking time**: Design work schedules and workload so that everyone is given a regularly scheduled opportunity to be creative and come up with innovative ideas. In some situations, this time needs to be coordinated through organized team meetings that make effective use of brainstorming techniques to create new and unique ideas. With other groups, it is better to give the individual time by themselves to identify improvement opportunities.

10. **Turn the world upside down**: It's imperative that everyone within the organization looks for new ways of doing things and different products that will attract customers. Yes, okay, we need to stop thinking that's good enough; it worked last time so it is good enough. In today's environment, we need to question all we do to understand if it could be done better. Be careful if you're content with your job, you probably should've been moved to a different job some time ago. Often, changing jobs turn your world upside down.

11. **Don't say it if you're not going to do it**: An innovative organization is a *doing* organization. It believes it is better to do something wrong, rather than to sit and do nothing. Creativity is good, but innovation is great. The best ideas that stay within your mind are worthless. Ideas must be converted into action to have a positive impact upon the organization, its customers and stakeholders. The best way to demoralize an innovation initiative is to not follow through on your commitments. I just looked at the strategic plan for the organization I joined back in the 1970s and compared it with the 1987

strategic plan. It looks like they just changed the heading on the front cover of the 1987 strategic plan and released it as the 2018 strategic plan. You have no strategy without a plan and no plan without action. If the results are bad, you can learn from the mistakes you made; if the results are good, you have an innovative idea.

MIND EXPANDER'S EXERCISE

To improve your innovative and creative ability, you need to think outside the box. These exercises are designed to challenge the way you think about a situation. Keep track of how many you answer correctly, and at the end of this book, we will provide you with your personal analysis of your creative abilities.

Answer to Chapter 2. Mind Expander's Exercise

Exercise: How do you put a giraffe into a refrigerator?
   Answer: You open the door and put the giraffe in it.

Chapter 3. Mind Expander's Exercise

Before Mt. Everest was discovered, what was the highest mountain in the world?

RECOGNITION AND COMMENTS

The following books and/or PowerPoint presentations of H. James Harrington were used as references, and information from them was included in many of the chapters.

Presentations on innovation

- *Innovation*—IAOIP annual conference by H. James Harrington (Boston 2016)
- *Hmmm—Creativity* presentation by H. James Harrington conference (Jamaica 2008)

- *The Innovation Process* presentation by H. James Harrington at ASQ Section Meeting (Sacramento 2017)
- *Creating a Creative Culture* presentation by H. James Harrington (UAE 2012)
- *Status of Innovation* presentation by H. James Harrington (Mexico 2017)
- *Using TRIZ* presentation by H. James Harrington (Dubai 2016)
- *Organizational Excellence* given by H. James Harrington (Shanghai China 2003)
- *Innovation with TRIZ* presentation by H. James Harrington at annual conference (New York 2016)

Books authored or coauthored by H. James Harrington that were used in this chapter

H. James Harrington is a prolific author, publishing hundreds of technical reports and magazine articles. He has authored or coauthored over fifty-five books. The following books were written or coauthored by H. James Harrington and were used as reference with parts of them included in the narrative within this chapter.

- Innovative Change Management (ICM): Preparing Your Organization for the New Innovative Culture (2018)
- The Framework for Innovation: A Guide to the Body of Innovation Knowledge (2018)
- Project Management for Performance Improvement Teams (2018)
- Creativity, Innovation and Entrepreneurship (2018)
- Total Innovative Management Excellence (TIME)—Technical report released in Quality Progress Magazine 2019
- Innovative Medal Handbook—classes being taught/manuscript being prepared released 1st quarter 2019. Technical paper published 1st quarter 2018.
- Total Improvement Management—The Generation in Performance Improvement—1995
- Creativity Toolkit—Provoking Creativity in Individuals and Organizations—1998

4

Overview of the 76 Most Used Innovation Tools, Methods, and Techniques

INTRODUCTION

We debated whether we should present the Innovation Systems Cycle (ISC) first and then present the tools and methodologies. We decided to do the tools and methodologies first so that you can see how they fit into the ISC.

A working group made up of individuals from the International Association for Quality, the Asian-Pacific Quality Organization, and the International Association of Innovation Professionals (IAOIP) studied the literature that was currently available to define tools and methodologies that were proposed for being used. Then, they contacted numerous universities offering classes on innovation for entrepreneurship to determine what tools and methodologies were promoted. In addition, they contacted individual consultants who were providing advice and guidance to organizations to identify tools and methodologies that were recommended. As a result of this research, more than 250 tools and methodologies were identified as being potential candidates for an innovative professional.

The group then sent surveys out to leading innovative lecturers, universities, consultants, and individual companies that are well known for their innovation, asking them to classify each tool or a methodology into one of the following categories:

- This tool or methodology is used in almost all innovation projects = 4 points
- This tool or methodology is used in a minimum of two of five innovation projects = 1 point

- This tool or methodology is installed in every used innovation project = 0 points
- Not familiar with the tool or methodology = −1 point
- Never used or recommended this tool or methodology in doing innovation projects = −4 point

The group then calculated the priority for each of the tools/methodologies by assigning a point value for each answer. The goal was to define fifty of the most effective or most frequently used tool/methodology by the innovative practitioner. They ended up with the 76 tools/methodologies that are the most effective or the most frequently used tool/methodology by the innovative practitioner/professional (see Table 4.1).

TABLE 4.1

List of the Most Used and/or Most Effective Innovative Tools and Methodologies in Alphabetical Order

	IT&M	Book III	Book II	Book I
1	The 5 why questions	S	P	S
2	The 76 standard solutions	P	S	
3	Absence thinking	P		
4	Affinity diagram	S	P	S
5	Agile innovation	S		P
6	Attribute listing	S	P	
7	Benchmarking		S	P
8	Biomimicry	P	S	
9	Brain-writing 6-3-5	S	P	S
10	Business case development		S	P
11	Business plan	S	S	P
12	Cause and effect diagrams		P	S
13	Combination methods	P	S	
14	Comparative analysis	S	S	P
15	Competitive analysis	S	S	P
16	Competitive shopping		S	P
17	Concept tree (concept map)	P	S	
18	Consumer cocreation	P		
19	Contingency planning		S	P
20	Costar	S	S	P
21	Cost analysis	S	S	P

(Continued)

TABLE 4.1 (*Continued*)

List of the Most Used and/or Most Effective Innovative Tools and Methodologies in Alphabetical Order

	IT&M	Book III	Book II	Book I
22	Creative problem-solving model	S	P	
23	Creative thinking	P	S	
24	Design for tools		P	
	Subtotal number of points	7	7	10
25	Directed/focused/structure innovation	P	S	
26	Elevator speech	P	S	S
27	Ethnography	P		
28	Financial reporting	S	S	P
29	Flowcharting		P	S
30	Focus groups	S	S	P
31	Force field analysis	S	P	
32	Generic creativity tools	P	S	
33	Harmful/useful diagrams	P		
34	I-TRIZ	P		
35	Identifying and engaging stakeholders	S	S	P
36	Imaginary brainstorming	P	S	S
37	Innovation blueprint	P		S
38	Innovation master plan	S	S	P
39	Kano analysis	S	P	S
40	Knowledge management systems	S	S	P
41	Lead user analysis	P	S	
42	Lotus blossom	P	S	
43	Market research and surveys	S		P
44	Matrix diagram	P	S	
45	Mind mapping	P	S	S
46	Nominal group technique	S	P	
47	Online innovation platforms	P	S	S
48	Open innovation	P	S	S
49	Organizational change mgt	S	S	P
50	Outcome-driven innovation	P		
	Subtotal number of points	15	4	7
51	Plan–do–check–act	S	P	
52	Potential investor present	S		P
53	Proactive creativity	P	S	S

(*Continued*)

TABLE 4.1 (*Continued*)

List of the Most Used and/or Most Effective Innovative Tools and Methodologies in Alphabetical Order

	IT&M	Book III	Book II	Book I
54	Project management	S	S	P
55	Proof of concept	P	S	
56	Quick score creativity test	P		
57	Reengineering/redesign		P	
58	Reverse engineering	S	P	
59	Robust design	S	P	
60	S-curve model		S	P
61	Safeguarding intellectual properties			P
62	Scamper	S	P	
63	Scenario analysis	P	S	
64	Simulations	S	P	S
65	Six thinking hats	S	P	S
66	Social networks	S	P	
67	Solution analysis diagrams	S	P	
68	Statistical analysis	S	P	S
69	Storyboarding	P	S	
70	Systems thinking	S	S	P
71	Synetics	P		
72	Tree diagram	S	P	S
73	TRIZ	P	S	
74	Value analysis	S	P	S
75	Value propositions	S		P
76	Visioning	S	S	P
	Subtotal—number of points	7	12	7

Book I—Organizational and/or Operational IT&M.
Book II—Evolutionary and/or Improvement IT&M.
Book III—Creative IT&M.
Note: IT&M, innovative tools and/or methodologies.
P = primary usage; S = secondary usage; Blank = not used or little used.

(P) Priority Rating	Creative	Evolutionary	Organizational
Total	29	23	24

IT&M in creativity book: 29.
IT&M in evolutionary book: 23.
IT&M in organizational book: 24.

The group then had twenty-eight practicing innovators write one or more chapters on each of the 76 tools, methods, and techniques. They then decided to divide the tools/methodologies into the following three categories (see the following bullet points). The following three volumes were then published by CRC Press.

- *The Innovation Tools Handbook, Volume 1: Organizational and Operational Tools, Methods, and Technologies that Every Innovator Must Know.* (Chapter 5 is based upon this book.)
- *The Innovation Tools Handbook, Volume 2: Evolutionary and Improvement Tools, Methods, and Technologies that Every Innovator Must Know.* (Chapter 6 is based upon this book.)
- *The Innovation Tools Handbook, Volume 3: Creative Tools, Methods, and Techniques that Every Innovation Must Know.* (Chapter 7 is based upon this book.)

Now I'm sure we all will agree that 76 tools/methodologies are too many for an individual to absorb at one time. As a result, we are highlighting over twenty-five of the simpler tools and methodologies in this book. Even for these twenty-five tools, we have room to only introduce them to you without going into details and giving examples. For a detailed explanation of each of the tools along with examples and suggested software, we recommend that you refer to the books pictured below (see Figure 4.1).

FIGURE 4.1
The book covers of the three-book series: *The Innovation Tools Handbooks—Volume 1, Volume 2, and Volume 3.*

TABLE 4.2

List of Tools That Are Covered in This Book

Volume 1	Volume 2	Volume 3
Benchmarking	The 5 why questions	Concept tree
Business case development	Attribute listing	Elevator speech
Business plan	Cause-and-effect diagrams	Lotus blossom
Comparative analysis	Flowcharting	Matrix diagram
Contingency planning	Nominal group technique	Mind mapping
Costs analysis	Plan–do–check–act	Proof of concept
Focus groups	Reengineering/redesign	Storyboarding
Identifying and engaging stakeholders	Statistical analysis	TRIZ
Market research and surveys	Tree diagram	
Organizational change management	Value analysis	
Project management		
Value propositioning		
Visioning		

Table 4.2 is not a complete list of all available tools and methodologies; these are only the basic tools and methodologies that are required to support 85% of the innovative initiatives. You will find that these limited tools and methodologies will handle almost all of the situations that will be discussed in Chapters 5–7.

MIND EXPANDER'S EXERCISE

To improve your innovative and creative ability, you need to think outside the box. These riddles are designed to challenge the way you think about a situation. Keep track of how many you answer correctly, and at the end of this book we will provide you with your personal analysis of your creative abilities.

Answer to Chapter 3. Mind Expander's Exercise

Exercise: Before Mt Everest was discovered, what was the highest mountain in the world?

Answer:

Mt Everest! It just wasn't discovered yet. (You aren't very good at this, are you?)

Chapter 4. Mind Expander's Exercise

How do you put an elephant in a refrigerator?

5

Organizational and Operational Tools, Methods, and Techniques

INTRODUCTION

This chapter provides an overview of some of the tools, methods, and techniques listed in the book, *Volume I—The Innovation Tools Handbook: Organizational Tools, Methods, and Technologies That Every Innovator Must Know* (published by CRC Press) See Figure 5.1.

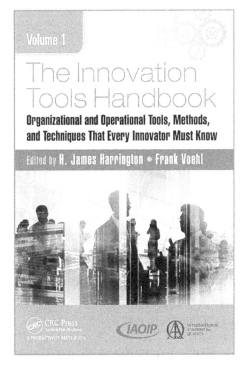

FIGURE 5.1
Volume I—The innovation tools handbook.

ORGANIZATIONAL AND OPERATIONAL TOOLS/METHODS	
Agile Innovation	
Benchmarking	X
Business Case Development	X
Business Plan	X
Comparative Analysis	X
Competitive Analysis	
Competitive Shopping	
Contingency Planning	X
Co-Start	
Costs Analysis	X
Financial Reporting	
Focus Groups	X
Identifying and Engaging Stakeholders	X
Innovation Master Plan	
Knowledge Management System	
Market Research and Surveys	X
Organizational Change Management	X
Potential Investor Presentation	
Project Management	X
S-Curve Model	
Safeguarding Intellectual Properties	
Systems Thinking	
Value Propositioning	X
Visioning	X

FIGURE 5.2
List of Organizational and Operational tools/methodologies frequently used in innovation.

The tools with an X following its name are the ones that are required for an individual to reach the Silver Innovation Medal proficiency level. Knowledge of all the tools and methodologies listed are required for an individual to reach the Gold Innovation Medal proficiency level (see Figure 5.2).

OVERVIEW OF THE ORGANIZATIONAL AND OPERATIONAL TOOLS, METHODS, AND TECHNIQUES

The following is a detailed description of the thirteen organizational tools and/or methodologies that must be understood to reach the Silver Innovation Medal proficiency level.

Benchmarking

Definition

- Benchmark (BMK)—A standard by which an item can be measured or judged.
- Benchmarking (BMKG)—A systematic way to identify, understand, and creatively evolve superior products, services, designs, equipment, processes, and practices to improve your organization's real performance.

User

This tool can be used by an individual, but its best use is with a group of four to eight people. Cross functional teams usually yield the best results from this activity.

Often Used in the Following Phases of the Innovation Systems Cycle (ISC)

The following are the three phases of the ISC. Those phases noted with an "X" indicate that the tool/methodology is used during that specific phase.

- Phase I. Creation X
- Phase II. Preparation and Production
- Phase III. Delivery X

Tool Activity by Phase

- Creation Phase—During this phase, BMKG is used to provide a BMK for the criteria that a new product/process should be able to equal or beat in order to be competitive.

  Also during this phase, BMKG is often used to understand and estimate the market potential for new product or service.
- Delivery Phase—In this phase, BMKG is used to compare the performance and value added of a product or service compared with the competition. The information is used to help direct future product development cycles.

Business Case Development

Definition

A business case captures the reason for initiating a project or program. It is most often presented in a well-structured written document, but in some cases, it may also come in the form of a short verbal agreement or presentation. The logic of the business case is: whatever resources, such as money or effort, are consumed, they should be in support of a specific business needs or opportunity.

User

This tool can be used by an individual, but its best use is with a group of four to eight people. Cross functional teams usually yield the best results from this activity. It is best if this activity is led by an individual who is not the one that originated the business opportunity.

Often Used in the Following Phases of the ISC

The following are the three phases of the ISC. Those phases noted with an "X" indicate that the tool/methodology is used during that specific phase.

- Phase I. Creation
- Phase II. Preparation and Production X
- Phase III. Delivery X

Tool Activity by Phase

- Preparation and Production Phase—The business case is developed as part of the knowledge base that is used during the resourcing phase to determine whether a project/program should have resources assigned to it. This decision is based upon the projected requirements for resource consumption and the benefits the project/program are projected to accomplish compared with other ways that the resources could be utilized. This comparison is typically used to determine whether the project will be included in the organization's portfolio of projects/programs, put on hold, or dropped.
- Preparation and Production Phase—The projected resources that will be consumed, and the benefits derived from the

project/program become key measurements that are included in the documentation.

- Delivery Phase—During this phase, the resources consumed and the benefits gained from the completed project/program are compared with the equivalent figures included in the business case to determine whether the business case objectives were met and if the project/program was successful.

Business Plan

Definition

A business plan is a formal statement of a set of business goals, the reason they are believed to be obtainable, and the plan for reaching these goals. It also contains background information about the organization or team attempting to reach these goals.

User

This tool is usually developed by a subset of the executive team chaired by the highest ranking member of the organization. It is presented to the total executive team before it is formalized. It serves as the basis for all future planning and goal setting.

Often Used in the Following Phases of the ISC

The following are the three phases of the ISC. Those phases noted with an "X" indicate that the tool/methodology is used during that specific phase.

- Phase I. Creation X
- Phase II. Preparation and Production X
- Phase III. Delivery

Tool Activity by Phase

- Creation Phase—The end result of preparing the value proposition is to decide whether the new concept has the potential of meeting the organization's requirements to become a committed-to activity. For those concepts that meet these requirements, the last step in the value proposition phase is preparing the initial business plan.

- Preparation and Production Phase—There are two documents that drive the phase. They are as follows:
  - New Concept Performance Specifications
  - Business Plan

  The New Concept Performance Specification must result in an output that fulfills the unmet needs of the potential consumer of the output. If this condition is not met, the concept could not be funded.

  The Business Plan is analyzed to determine whether the value-added content and the associated risk are in line with the expectations of the stakeholders. A negative or inadequate value-added content related to the concept should result in the project not being approved. An analysis of the key organizational managers/executives is done to determine the organization's probability of implementing the project successfully, based upon their education and past experience. Again, projects that an organization does not have a high probability of implementing the project successfully should not be funded.
- Remaining Four Phases of the Innovation Process

  Throughout the remaining four phases of the innovation process, the business plan is used as a foundation for all the goal setting and planning activities. The remaining four phases are all designed to implement the concept and meet the goals and schedules as defined in the Business Plan. A formal Business Plan serves as the fundamental requirements and objectives that the innovative processes' success and/or failure is measured against.

Comparative Analysis

Definition

Comparative analysis is a detailed study/comparison of an organization's product and/or service to the competitors' comparable product and/or service.

User

This tool can be used by individuals, but its best use is with a group of 4–6 people. Cross functional teams usually yield the best results from this activity.

The following are the three phases of the ISC. Those phases noted with an "X" indicate that the tool/methodology is used during that specific phase.

- Phase I. Creation X
- Phase II. Preparation and Production
- Phase III. Delivery X

Tool Activity by Phase

- During the creation phase, the concept is compared with the competitors' products or services to make a business decision if the concept is going to be value added to the organization. Projects are frequently dropped at this point when the comparison is not favorable to the organization.
- Delivery Phase—During this phase, both sales price and marketing strategy are compared with the competition and effort to maximize the value to the organization.

Contingency Planning

Definition

Contingency planning is a process that primarily delivers a risk management strategy for a business to deal with the unexpected events effectively and the strategy for the business recovery to the normal position. The output of this process is called "contingency plan" or "business continuity and recovery plan."

User

A cross functional team of four to eight people led by a senior management leader and facilitated by a contingency planning professional gives the best results.

Often Used in the Following Phases of the ISC

The following are the three phases of the ISC. Those phases noted with an "X" indicate that the tool/methodology is used during that specific phase.

- Phase I. Creation X
- Phase II. Preparation and Production X
- Phase III. Delivery X

Tool Activity by Phase

Undesirable changes or unexpected problems can occur during all phases of the innovation cycle. In each phase, the innovator should assess the activities and define potential negative things that could occur. Once the potential negatives have been identified, contingency planning should be developed to minimize the time to react to the negative shifts in a minimal amount of time.

Cost-Benefit Analysis

Definition

- **Cost-Benefit Analysis (CBA)**—A financial analysis where the cost of providing (producing) a benefit is compared with the expected value of benefit to the customer, stakeholder, etc.
- **Confirmation Bias**—The tendency of people to include or exclude data that does not fit a preconceived position.

User

A CBA can be used by an individual or a team and is often part of a value proposition and/or business plan. The tool can be used by an individual, but most often requires a team with sufficient knowledge of the end product, its proposed features, how customer value those features, as well as the current or potential cost of the component parts.

Often Used in the Following Phases of the ISC

The following are the three phases of the ISC. Those phases noted with an "X" indicate that the tool/methodology is used during that specific phase.

- Phase I. Creation X
- Phase II. Preparation and Production X
- Phase III. Delivery

Tool Activity by Phase

- Creation Phase—The CBA is tailor-made for this phase. During this phase, one or more value propositions are clearly identified. As these are identified, it is useful to quantify these benefits. In this process, the innovator might find that the benefit is not what they originally thought. If the data supports the low-benefit valuation, then data has been collected that will feed the subsequent CBA. A quick CBA during this phase can often redirect the innovator to focus on different, a different mix, or perhaps even fewer, proposed new benefits.

- Production Phase—The financial output of the CBA is often a requirement for completing this phase. The innovator must be able to show that their selected idea is well thought out and that it justifies the amount of financing being requested. The CBA should demonstrate the value proposition to the company as well as to the customer, and the resulting analysis from this phase is often used to review the actual outcome of the project with the forecast made in the original CBA.

- Production Phase—The cost analysis in this phase is more often the straightforward type of capital investment analysis in production machinery, for which many companies have their own tailor-made spreadsheets and/or software programs. However, if the value proposition includes innovations to the production process, perhaps creating a process new to the company, then this will need to be considered in earlier phases and, if necessary, updated during this phase.

Focus Group

Definition

A focus group is a structured group interview of typically seven to ten individuals who are brought together to discuss their views related to a specific business issue. The group is brought together so that the organizer can gain information and insight into a specific subject or the reaction to a proposed product. The information gained from focus groups provides the organization conducting the interview to make better educated decisions regarding the topic being discussed.

User

The focus group is made up of a group of individuals who are knowledgeable of and/or would make use of the subject being discussed. The facilitator is used to lead the discussions and record key information related to the discussion.

Often Used in the Following Phases of the ISC

The following are the three phases of the ISC. Those phases noted with an "X" indicate that the tool/methodology is used during that specific phase.

- Phase I. Creation X
- Phase II. Preparation and Production
- Phase III. Delivery X

Tool Activity by Phase

- Creation Phase—During this phase, focus groups are often used to help identify unfulfilled needs and to evaluate how different alternatives will be viewed by external customers.

  Also during this phase, focus groups are often used to define the value added to the individuals who will be receiving the output from the innovative concept.
- Delivery Phase—Focus groups provide an excellent way to predetermine how the output from the innovative concept should be advertised and delivered to the external consumer.

  Also during this phase, focus groups can be used to determine how the customer perceives the output from the innovative process. For example, when they recommend the product to their friends, will they come back and deal with the organization again based upon their experience?

Identifying and Engaging Stakeholders

Definition

A "Stakeholder" of an organization or enterprise is someone who potentially or really impacts on that organization, and who is likely to be impacted by that organization's activities and processes. Or, even more significantly, perceives that they will be impacted (usually negatively).

User

The user of stakeholder mapping can be anyone in the organization who makes decisions on products, processes, and services that may have an impact outside their immediate work area or team. For more senior corporate players, the potential value to the business or organization of doing stakeholder mapping is incalculable. This may be used as a personal and professional learning tool or as a part of team activities in business development, marketing, strategy formulation, and operational strategy (see Table 5.1).

Often Used in the Following Phases of the ISC

The following are the three phases of the ISC. Those phases noted with an "X" indicate that the tool/methodology is used during that specific phase.

- Phase I. Creation X
- Phase II. Production
- Phase III. Delivery X

Tool Activity by Phase

Although focusing on and considering the stakeholders is important in all the three phases of the innovative process, the primary focus and involvement take place during the Creation Phase, with the product or service being designed, and the customers are invited to participate in the design activities. It also plays a very important role in evaluating the impact a proposed change will have when preparing the value proposition and acquiring resources to support the change initiative. During the Delivery Phase, a great deal of focus is placed upon identifying external stakeholders and modifying the sales and marketing strategies to be in line with the external stakeholder's specific needs.

TABLE 5.1

Mapping Matrix

User Level/Type and Mapping Used	Mapping Matrix: User Type and Level x Mapping Tool					
	Mapping Tool Used and Possible Applications/Purposes					
	Competition	Community Impact	Innovation Evaluation	Stakeholder Communications	Change Programs	Political Support
Type of mapping used	Interest (A)	Interest (A)	Interest (A) Tracking (B)	Tracking (B)	Interest (A) Tracking (B)	Interest (A)
Purpose of mapping	Market research	EIA SIA	Market testing	Community profile/ status	For/against change	For/against champion
External consultancy	Yes	Yes				
Board and chair of board	Yes	Yes				May be a personal tool, not to share?
CEO and executive	Yes	Yes	Yes	Yes	Yes	May be a personal tool, not to share?
Innovator	Yes	Yes	Yes, in business plan	May be	May be	May be a personal tool, not to share?
Implementer/ manager				Yes, as part of process/ project management	Yes, a core responsibility	
Operatives/contact staff		Yes, in engagement work		Yes, in engagement work and feedback	Yes, in engagement work and feedback	

(A) Power/interest quadrant matrix outlined below.

(B) Communications tracking stakeholder mapping tool outlined below.

EIA = Environmental impact assessment.

SIA = Social impact assessment.

Market Research and Surveys

Definition

Marketing research can be defined as the systematic and objective identification, collection, analysis dissemination, and use of information that is undertaken to improve decision-making related to products and services that are provided to external customers.

User

This tool can be used by individuals, but its best use is with a group of four to eight people. Cross functional teams usually yield best results from this activity.

Often Used in the Following Phases of the ISC

The following are the three phases of the ISC. Those phases noted with an "X" indicate that the tool/methodology is used during that specific phase.

- Phase I. Creation X
- Phase II. Preparation and Production
- Phase III. Delivery X

Tool Activity by Phase

- Creation Phase—Market studies are usually used during this phase to define customer needs and expectations and also to define the size of the market.
- Also, market studies are used here to validate the assumptions related to customer requirements and value-added considerations. Size of the market, customer expectations, and price point are the major considerations in preparing the value proposition. The best way to acquire this type of information is through a statistically sound market study.
- Delivery Phase—Market studies are frequently used to define the best sales and marketing strategy.

Organizational Change Management

Definition

Organizational change management (OCM) is a comprehensive set of structured procedures for decision-making, planning, executing, and evaluation activities. It is designed to minimize the resistance and cycle time to implementing a change.

User

This tool is usually used by a project management team when working on a complex or important project.

Often Used in the Following Phases of the ISC

The following are the three phases of the ISC. Those phases noted with an "X" indicate that the tool/methodology is used during that specific phase.

- Phase I. Creation X
- Phase II. Preparation and Production X
- Phase III. Delivery

Tool Activity by Phase

- Creation Phase—During this phase, the plan for organizational change activities plays a key role in estimating project implementation time, impact, and risk.
- Preparation and Production Phase—During this phase, OCM activities are directed at communicating a vision related to the change and impact that the change will have on the individuals who will be using the changed process.
- The primary impact OCM will be recognized during the production implementation phase of the proposed project and during the months following implementation, where the change is being internalized.

Project Management

Definition

Project management is the application of knowledge, skills, tools, and techniques to project activities in order to meet or exceed stakeholders' needs and expectations from a project (source: PMBOK Guide).

Users

Project management is most effectively used with groups and teams across different functions. Key members from each function involved in a project should be a part of the project management team.

Often Used in the Following Phases of the ISC

The following are the three phases of the ISC. Those phases noted with an "X" indicate that the tool/methodology is used during that specific phase.

- Phase I. Creation X
- Phase II. Preparation and Production X
- Phase III. Delivery X

Tool Activity by Phase

- All Phases—Project management is used in all phases of the innovation process. In some initiatives, a project is formed as soon as a potential unfulfilled need is identified. By the time the value proposition phase is completed, a formal project plan with all of its elements is often documented and approved.

Value Proposition

Definition

A value proposition is a document that defines the benefits that will result from the implementation of a change or the use of an output as viewed by one or more of the organization's stakeholders. A value proposition can apply to an entire organization, parts thereof, customers, products, services, or internal processes.

A business case captures the reasoning for initiating a project or task. It is most often presented in a well-structured written document, but in some cases may come in the form of a short verbal agreement or presentation. A business case is preferably prepared by an independent group after the project concept has been approved by the executive management.

User

This tool can be used by an individual, but its best use is with a group of 4–8 people. Usually, the best results from preparing a value proposition are realized when the group is made up of members from cross functional units.

Often Used in the Following Phases of the ISC

The following are the three phases of the ISC. Those phases noted with an "X" indicate that the tool/methodology is used during that specific phase.

- Phase I. Creation X
- Phase II. Preparation and Production X
- Phase III. Delivery

Tool Activity by Phase

- Creation Phase—During this phase, the value proposition is prepared and presented to the executive committee or the organization assigned the responsibility for approving new projects.
- Production Phase—During this phase, the value proposition is used to prepare the business case that is used to justify financing the project. Also during this phase, other resources like staffing, facilities, and equipment are acquired.

Vision/Goals

Definition

- **Vision**—A documented or mental description or picture of a desired future state of an organization, product, process, team, a key business driver, activity, or individual.
- **Vision Statements**—A group of words that paint a clear picture of the desired business environment at a specific time in the future. Short-term vision statements usually are between 3 and 5 years. Long-term vision statements usually are between 10 and 25 years. A vision statement should not exceed four sentences.
- **Goal**—The end toward which effort is directed: the terminal point in a race. These are always specified in time and magnitude so that

they are easy to measure. Goals have key ingredients. First, they specifically state the target for the future state, and second, they give the time interval in which the future state will be accomplished. These are the key inputs to every strategic plan.

User

One of the primary responsibilities of the innovator is to ensure that aggressive but realistic organizational/product vision and goals are established and communicated throughout the organization. In finalizing vision and goals, the innovator should involve as many of the top management team as possible so that they will have their support.

Often Used in the Following Phases of the ISC

The following are the three phases of the ISC. Those phases noted with an "X" indicate that the tool/methodology is used during that specific phase.

- Phase I. Creation X
- Phase II. Preparation and Production X
- Phase III. Delivery X

Tool Activity by Phase

- Creation Phase—During the creation phase, the innovator and/or the creative team will develop value statements that define how the innovative product, service, or situation will impact the customer/receiver of the innovative activity. Goals are established to quantify expected impact, timing, and value added to the innovative organization as a result of implementing the innovative concept.
- Preparation and Production Phase—During the analysis and preparation activities related to preparing value proposition, the vision of who will be impacted and how they will be impacted are refined and updated. The goals are also evaluated and updated to reflect the information that has been collected. These visions and goals are one of the primary inputs to the value proposition.
- The comparison of the financial plan and the vision and goals for the innovation concept must be supportive of each other. Often, the

optimism that is reflected in the vision and goals is completely out of line with the actual financial requirements to implement the innovation concept. This is a critical phase where many of the innovative concepts are abandoned because adequate funds cannot be obtained internally or externally. Investors can become very enthusiastic about a vision, and a supporting set of goals quickly become disillusioned when the actual financial impacts are defined.

- As the organization documents the innovation implementation plan and requirements, it must consider the vision and goals established for the innovation concept. The formal documentation and the vision and goals must be in harmony in order to eliminate confusion and to have any hope of having a successful program.
- The goals set related to output performance, costs, and delivery schedules is a primary input in defining how the production activities are organized, the quality of the production process, and the timing of delivery to external customers.
- Delivery Phase—The sales and marketing strategy/activities must be based upon the vision statement that defines the potential receivers of the outputs from the innovative process. Sales quotas, market segments, pricing, and quantity targets are derived from the goals set related to the outputs created by the innovative process.
- The performance analysis activities compare actual results to the established vision and goals for the innovative concept. Success or failure is measured by the degree the visions and goals established for the innovative activity met or exceeded when the actual results are analyzed. Having realistic and attainable visions and goals is absolutely essential for successful innovative activity.

SUMMARY

This chapter provided an overview of the tools, methods, and techniques covered in the book, *Volume 1: Innovation Tools Handbook— Organizational and Operational Tools, Methods, and Techniques* that Every Innovator Must Know (CRC Press). We described in detail the thirteen organizational and operational tools, methods and techniques that must be understood to reach the Silver Innovation Medal proficiency level. We did not have the opportunity to explain how to use all the tools, as it would make this an extremely large book. We strongly recommend that you obtain a copy of this CRC Press book, which will provide you with instructions on how to use all the tools, examples of how it has been used, and the list of software that will aid you in using the tool/methodology for each of the tools described in this chapter.

MIND EXPANDER'S EXERCISE

To improve your innovative and creative ability, you need to think outside the box. These riddles are designed to challenge the way you think about a situation. Keep track of how many you answer correctly, and at the end of this book, we will provide you with your personal analysis of your creative abilities.

Answer to Chapter 4. Mind Expander's Exercise

Exercise: How do you put an elephant in a refrigerator?

Answer: Open the door, take the giraffe out, and put the elephant in the refrigerator.

Chapter 5. Mind Expander's Exercise

How much dirt is there in a hole that measures two feet by three feet by four feet?

RECOGNITION AND COMMENTS

Note—The following people contributed to this chapter.

- Bauer, Julian
- Bokhari, S. Ali, PhD
- Friedman, Lisa
- Goodstadt, Paul
- Harrington, H. James
- Landry, Dana J. PhD

- Morris, Langdon
- Parmelee, Steven G.
- Rundi, Achmad
- Schweitzer, Fiona
- Speller, Simon
- Voehl, Frank

6

Evolutionary and Improvement Tools, Methods, and Techniques

INTRODUCTION

This chapter provides an overview of the tools, methods, and techniques listed in the book, *Volume 2: The Innovation Tools Handbook—Evolutionary and Improvement Tools that Every Innovator Must Know* (published by CRC Press) (see Figure 6.1).

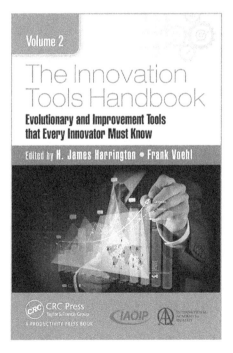

FIGURE 6.1
Volume 2—Innovation tools handbook.

EVOLUTIONARY AND IMPROVEMENT TOOLS/METHODS	
5 Why Questions	X
Attribute Listing	X
Brain-Writing 6-3-5	
Cause and Effect Diagrams	X
Creative Problems Solving Model	
Design for Tools	
Flowcharting	X
Force Field Analysis	
Kano Analysis	
Nominal Group Technique	X
Plan-Do-Check-Act	X
Reengineering /Redesign	X
Reverse Engineering	
Robust Design	
Scamper	
Simulation	
Six Thinking Hats	
Social Networks	
Solution Analysis Diagrams	
Statistical Analysis	X
Tree Diagram	X
Value Analysis	X

FIGURE 6.2

List of Evolutionary and Improvement Tools/Methods frequently used in innovation.

The tools with an X following its name are the ones that are required for an individual to reach the Silver Innovation Medal proficiency level. Knowledge of all the tools and methodologies listed are required for an individual to reach the Gold Innovation Medal proficiency level (see Figure 6.2).

There are twenty three tools, methods, and/or techniques that have been classified as preferred evolutionary and improvement tools, methods, and techniques for developing continuous improvement opportunities. This does not mean that they cannot be used in one of the other categories; it only indicates that this is the primary category they relate to.

OVERVIEW OF THE EVOLUTIONARY AND IMPROVEMENT TOOLS, METHODS, AND TECHNIQUES

The following is a detailed description of the ten evolutionary and improvement tools and/or methodologies that must be understood to reach the Silver Innovation Medal proficiency level.

The 5 Whys

Definition

The 5 Whys is a technique to get to the root cause of the problem. It is the practice of asking five times or more why the failure has occurred in order to get to the root cause. Each time an answer is given, you ask why that particular condition occurred. As outlined in the 5 Whys' Overview, it is recommended that the 5 Whys be used with Risk Assessment in order to strengthen the use of the tool for innovation- and creativity-enhancing purpose.

User

This tool can be used by an individual, but its best use is with a group of four to eight people. Cross functional teams usually yield the best results from this activity.

Often Used in the Following Phases of the ISC

The following are the three phases of the ISC. Those phases noted with an "X" indicate that the tool/methodology is used during that specific phase.

- Phase I. Creation
- Phase II. Preparation and Production
- Phase III. Delivery

Tool Activity by Phase

- Creation Phase—During this phase, the 5 Whys technique is used to get to the root cause of questions like, "Why does the customer want that?"
- Preparation and Production Phase—During this phase, the 5 Whys is used to get to the root cause of questions related to problems that are defined and in implementing a proposed initiative.
- Delivery Phase—During this phase, the 5 Whys tool is used to get to the root cause of problems like, "Why aren't the customers buying this product?"
- During this phase, this tool is used to answer questions like, "Why was the return on investment so low?" or "Why was this product so profitable?"

Attribute Listing, Morphological Analysis, and Matrix Analysis

Definition

Attribute Listing, Morphological Analysis, and Matrix Analysis techniques are good for finding new combinations of products or services. We use attribute listing and morphological analysis to generate new products and services. Matrix analysis focuses on businesses. It is used to generate new approaches, using attributes such as market sectors, customer needs, products, promotional methods, etc.

User

This tool can be used by individuals or groups, but its best use is with a group of four to eight people. Cross functional teams usually yield the best results from this activity. Since attribute listing is a creative method to find new ideas to solve problems and to find innovative products and services, this method can be usefully combined with a brainstorming session. The core idea is for a team to forget everything they have learned and retained when thinking about a possible solution, i.e., wipe the slate clean.

Often Used in the Following Phases of the ISC

The following are the three phases of the ISC. Those phases noted with an "X" indicate that the tool/methodology is used during that specific phase.

- Phase I. Creation X
- Phase II. Preparation and Production X
- Phase III. Delivery X

Tool Activity by Phase

- Creation Phase—During this phase, this tool is used to generate ideas that will lead to new and unforeseen products and services.
- During this phase, the tool is used to define potential markets and marketing approaches in order to improve the accuracy of potential revenue and risks related to the product or service.
- Preparation and Production Phase—During this phase, the tool is primarily used in the problem-solving mode.
- Delivery Phase—During this phase, the tool is used for defining marketing and sales approaches and to help define market segments.

Cause-and-Effect Diagram

Definition

Cause-and-Effect diagram is a visual representation of possible causes of a specific problem or condition. The effect is listed on the right-hand side and the causes take the shape of fish bones. This is the reason it is sometimes called a "Fishbone Diagram" or an "Ishikawa Diagram."

User

This tool can be used by an individual, but its best use is with a group of 4–8 people. Cross functional teams usually yield the best results from this activity.

Often Used in the Following Phases of the ISC

The following are the three phases of the ISC. Those phases noted with an "X" indicate that the tool/methodology is used during that specific phase.

- Phase I. Creation X
- Phase II. Preparation and Production X
- Phase III. Delivery

Tool Activity by Phase

Cause-and-effect diagrams can be used whenever a problem is identified and, as a result, could be used in all the phases. It is primarily used during the production phase and creation phase.

Flowcharting

Definition

Flowcharting is a method of graphically describing an existing or proposed process by using simple symbols, lines, and words to pictorially display the sequence of activities. Flowcharts are used to understand, analyze, and communicate the activities that make up major processes throughout an organization. It can be used to graphically display movement of product, communications, and knowledge related to anything, takes an input and adds value to it, and produces an output.

User

This tool can be effectively used by an individual to document an activity or process. It can be equally effective when used by a team to gain common understanding or to document an activity, process, and/or system.

Often Used in the Following Phases of the ISC

The following are the three phases of the ISC. Those phases noted with an "X" indicate that the tool/methodology is used during that specific phase.

- Phase I. Creation X
- Phase II. Preparation and Production X
- Phase III. Delivery

Tool Activity by Phase

- Creation Phase—During this stage, flowcharting is frequently used to identify and characterize the present process and/or system. They are also used to study a proposed solution to defiance weaknesses, improve upon it, and document the final solution.
- Also, flowcharting is frequently used to analyze and understand the proposed process. It is then used to calculate key parameters like cost, cycle time, and risk.
- Preparation and Production Phase—During this phase, the flowchart is an effective tool of doing activity-based costing and cost-benefit analysis. During the Production Phase, flowcharts are frequently used to communicate the sequence of operations that are required to produce the end output and to communicate key information to the individuals performing the activities within a complex process.
- During this phase, flowcharting is often used as a key part of the operating instructions and workflow diagrams.

Nominal Group Technique

Definition

Nominal Group Technique (NGT) is a technique for prioritizing a list of problems, ideas, or issues that give everyone in the group or team equal voice in the priority setting process.

User

NGT is a powerful and time-tested group ideation and problem-solving technique involving the so-called triple crown of problem identification, creative solution generation, and decision-making. It can easily and consistently be used in groups of many types and sizes—groups or teams who want to make their decision quickly by voting—but who want at the same time everyone's input and opinions to be taken into account.

Often Used in the Following Phases of the ISC

The following are the three phases of the ISC. Those phases noted with an "X" indicate that the tool/methodology is used during that specific phase.

- Phase I. Creation X
- Phase II. Production X
- Phase III. Delivery X

Tool Activity by Phase

- Creation Phase—As a result of a typical brainstorming session, a long list of options/problems is created. After discussing the list, the brainstorming team will need to prioritize the ideas that they will focus their initial effort on. This is where the NGT provides an effective approach to getting a common agreement from the team.
- Preparation and Production Phase—Frequently, during the production phase, there are a number of alternatives that need to be considered. For example, what would be produced, what parts will be farmed out, which suppliers should be used, where should the product be stored, etc. The NGT is frequently used in cases where there are differences of opinion about what option is the best for the organization.

- Delivery Phase—During this phase, an innovative team will come up with many different options relating to the marketing sales and delivery approaches. The NGT is frequently used to help gain a common agreement on which of the alternatives is the one that will be pursued.

Plan–Do–Check–Act (Shewhart Cycle)

Definition

Plan–Do–Check–Act is a structured approach for the improvement of services, products, and/or processes. It is also sometimes referred to as plan–do–check–adjust. Another version of this PDCA cycle is OPDCA. The added "O" stands for observation or as some versions say "Grasp the current condition."

User

This tool can be used by individuals or groups, but its best use is with a group of four to eight people. Cross functional teams usually yield the best results from this activity.

Often Used in the Following Phases of the ISC

The following are the three phases of the ISC. Those phases noted with an "X" indicate that the tool/methodology is used during that specific phase.

- Phase I. Creation X
- Phase II. Preparation and Production X
- Phase III. Delivery X

Tool Activity by Phase

- Creation, Production, Delivery Phases—The Plan-Do-Check-Act methodology is extensively used in each of these phases to address problems or opportunities that arise to develop a corrective action plan to eliminate the problem or to take advantage of an opportunity.

Reengineering/Redesign

Definition

- Process—A series of interrelated activities or tasks that take an input and produce an output.
- Process Redesign—A methodology used to streamline a current process, with the objective of reducing cost and cycle time by 30%–60% while improving output quality from 20% to 200%.
- Process Reengineering—A methodology used to radically change the way a process is designed by developing an aggressive vision of how it should perform and using a group of enablers to prepare a new process design that is not hampered by the present processes paradigms. Used when a 60%–80% reduction in cost or cycle time is required. Process reengineering is sometimes referred to as New Process Design and/or Process Innovation.

User

This tool can be used by a group of 4–12 people. Cross functional teams usually yield the best results from this activity.

Often Used in the Following Phases of the ISC

The following are the three phases of the ISC. Those phases noted with an "X" indicate that the tool/methodology is used during that specific phase.

- Phase I. Creation X
- Phase II. Preparation and Production X
- Phase III. Delivery

Tool Activity by Phase

As indicated earlier, reengineering/redesign methodologies are primarily used during creation and production phases.

- Creation Phase—During this phase, the methodology is used to create the future-state definition of the process being studied.
- Production Phase—During this phase, the future-state definition is documented in operating procedures and flowcharts. Also during

this phase, the future-state solution is implemented and adjustments are made to optimize overall performance.

Statistical Analysis

Definition

Statistical analysis is a collection, examination, summarization, manipulation, and interpretation of quantitative data to discover its underlying causes, patterns, relationships, and trends.

User

This tool is best used by an individual but it can be used by small groups of 2–3 people.

Often Used in the Following Phases of the ISC

The following are the three phases of the ISC. Those phases noted with an "X" indicate that the tool/methodology is used during that specific phase.

- Phase I. Creation X
- Phase II. Preparation and Production X
- Phase III. Delivery

Tool Activity by Phase

- Creation Phase—During this phase, it is used to conduct design experiments and to analyze data to make engineering decisions.
- During this phase, this tool is used to evaluate options and to predict results so that decisions can be made whether to continue or terminate a project or program.
- Preparation and Production Phase—During this phase, the tool is used to evaluate different production alternatives, maintain process control, and to solve problems.

Tree Diagrams

Definition

Tree Diagram Breakdown (Drilldown) is a technique for breaking complex opportunities and problems into progressively smaller parts. Start by writing the opportunity statement or problem under investigation down on the left-hand side of a large sheet of paper. Next, write down the points that make up the next level of detail a little to the right of this. These may be factors contributing to the issue or opportunity, information relating to it, or questions raised by it. For each of these points, repeat the process. This process of breaking the issue under investigation into its component part is called drilling down.

User

This tool can be used by an individual, but its best use is with a group of 4–8 people.

Often Used in the Following Phases of the ISC

The following are the three phases of the ISC. Those phases noted with an "X" indicate that the tool/methodology is used during that specific phase.

- Phase I. Creation X
- Phase II. Preparation and Production X
- Phase III. Delivery X

Tool Activity by Phase

- Creation, Production, Delivery Phases—For complex problems, highly creative solutions are needed, and tree diagrams are frequently used to divide complex problems into smaller units that can be addressed directly.

Value Analysis (Value-Added Analysis)

Definition

Value Analysis is the analysis of a system, process, or activity to determine which parts of it are classified as Real-Value Added (RVA), Business-Value Added (BVA), or No-Value Added (NVA).

User

This tool can be used by an individual, but its best use is with a group of 4–8 people.

Often Used in the Following Phases of the ISC

The following are the three phases of the ISC. Those phases noted with an "X" indicate that the tool/methodology is used during that specific phase.

- Phase I. Creation X
- Phase II. Preparation and Production X
- Phase III. Delivery

Tool Activity by Phase

- Creation Phase—During this phase, the costs related to the individual projects are analyzed to determine what percentage of them is RVA and what percentage is BVA or NVA.
- Preparation and Production Phase—During the production phase, it is often necessary to expend effort to reduce costs that are not related to RVA.

SUMMARY

This chapter provided an overview of the tools, methods, and techniques covered in the book, *Volume 2: Innovation Tools Handbook—Evolutionary and Improvement Tools, Methods, and Techniques That Every Innovator Must Know* (CRC Press). We only described in detail the ten tools that must be understood to reach the Silver Innovation Medal proficiency level. We did not have the opportunity to explain how to use all the tools as it would make this an extremely large book. We strongly recommend that you obtain a copy of this CRC Press book which will provide you with instructions on how to use all the tools etc., examples of how it has been used, and list of software that will aid you in using the tool/methodology for each of the tools etc. described in this chapter.

MIND EXPANDER'S EXERCISE

To improve your innovative and creative ability, you need to think outside the box. These exercises are designed to challenge the way you think about a situation. Keep track of how many you answer correctly, and at the end of this book, we will provide you with your personal analysis of your creative abilities.

Answer to Chapter 5. Mind Expander's Exercise

Exercise: How much dirt is there in a hole that measures two feet by three feet by four feet?

Answer: There is no dirt in a hole.

Chapter 6. Mind Expander's Exercise

They are having a party in the jungle. All the animals, including the baboons, giraffes, gazelles, etc., showed up, except one animal. Which animal was missing?

RECOGNITION AND COMMENTS

Note: The following people contributed to this chapter.

- Burge, Dr Stuart
- Farmer, Neil
- Harrington, H. James
- Michaelides, Dimis
- Mignosa, Charles
- Nelson, Doug
- Rundi, Achmad
- Voehl, Frank
- Westbrook, Peter

7

Creative Tools, Methods, and Techniques That Every Innovator Must Know

INTRODUCTION

This chapter provides an overview of the tools, methods, and techniques listed in the book, *Volume 3—The Innovator Tools Handbook: Creative Tools, Methods, and Technologies that Every Innovation Must Know* (published by CRC Press) (see Figure 7.1).

FIGURE 7.1
The Innovation Tools Handbook—Volume 3.

The tools with an X following its name are the ones that are required for an individual to reach the Silver Innovation Medal proficiency level. Knowledge of all the tools and methodologies listed are required for an individual to reach the Gold Innovation Medal proficiency level (see Figure 7.2).

There are twenty-nine tools, methodologies, and/or techniques that have been classified as preferred tools, methods, and techniques used in support of creative innovation. This does not mean that they cannot be used in one of the other categories. It only indicates that this is the primary category they relate to.

CREATIVE TOOLS, METHODS, AND TECHNIQUES	
76 Standards	
Absence Thinking	
Biomimicry	
Combination Methods	
Concept Tree	X
Consumer Co-Creation	
Creative Thinking	
Directed Focus Structured Innovation	
Elevator Speech	X
Ethnography	
Generic Creativity Tools	
HU Diagrams	
I-TRIZ	
Imaginary Brainstorming	
Innovation Blueprint	
Lead User Analysis	
Lotus Blossom	X
Matrix Diagram	X
Mind Mapping	X
Online Innovation Platforms	
Open Innovation	
Outcome Driven Innovation	
Proactive Creativity	
Proof of Concept	X
Quickscore Creativity Test	
Scenario Analysis	
Storyboarding	X
Synetics	
TRIZ	X

FIGURE 7.2
List of creative tools/methodologies frequently used in innovation.

OVERVIEW OF THE CREATIVE TOOLS, METHODS, AND TECHNIQUES

The following is a detailed description of the eight tools and/or methodologies that must be understood to obtain Silver Innovation Medal certification.

Concept Tree (Clustering)

Definition

Conceptual Clustering is an inherent structure of the data (concepts) that drives cluster formation. Since this technique is dependent on language, it is open to interpretation, and consensus is required.

User

This tool is best used by multidisciplinary teams who are in a constant dialog that requires access and transparency to information from both sides or with a private online community managed through a platform or software.

Often Used in the Following Phases of the ISC

The following are the three phases of the ISC. Those phases noted with an "X" indicate that the tool/methodology is used during that specific phase.

- Phase I. Creation X
- Phase II. Preparation and Production X
- Phase III. Delivery

Tool Activity by Phase

This tool is primarily used during the creative and preparation/production phases. Because it is used to help analyze problems, it could be used in any phase when a problem occurred.

Elevator Speech/Coffee Clutch Opportunity

Definition

- Elevator speech: An elevator speech is a clear, brief message or a "commercial" about an innovative idea you are in the process of implementing. It communicates what it is, what you're looking for, and how it can benefit a company or organization. It's typically no more than two minutes, or the time it takes people to ride from the top to the bottom of a building in an elevator.
- The Coffee Clutch Opportunity: The coffee clutch presentation is used primarily in a relaxed environment and consists of a very short discussion that lasts between 90 and 120 s. It typically takes place around the water fountain, walking to or from a meeting, or during a coffee break.

User

This tool can be used by individuals who are trying to convince an individual or group to become supportive and/or actively involved in their part of the innovative process. A variety of people, including *project managers*, sales people, evangelists, and policy makers, commonly rehearse and use elevator pitches to get their point across quickly.

Often Used in the Following Phases of the ISC

The following are the three phases of the ISC. Those phases noted with an "X" indicate that the tool/methodology is used during that specific phase.

- Phase I. Creation X
- Phase II. Preparation and Production X
- Phase III. Delivery X

Tool Activity by Phase

- Creation Phase—The elevator speech is used during the value proposition phase to provide management with an overall understanding about the innovative concept and how it will impact the organization. The elevator speech is used to acquaint management with an understanding of why they should invest resources into the proposed innovative concept.

- Preparation and Production Phase—The elevator speech is used to get the impacted people to participate in the changes necessary to implement the innovative concepts.
- Delivery Phase—The elevator speech is used to capture the attention of potential customers/consumers. It is also used to gain the enthusiasm of the sales force related to the innovative concept.

Lotus Blossom

Definition

Lotus Blossom: This technique is based on the use of analytical capacities and helps to generate a great number of ideas that will possibly provide the best solution to the problem to be addressed by the group. It uses a six-step process.

User

This tool can be used by individuals or groups, but its best use is with a group of 4–8 people. Cross functional teams usually yield the best results from this activity.

Often Used in the Following Phases of the ISC

The following are the three phases of the ISC. Those phases noted with an "X" indicate that the tool/methodology is used during that specific phase.

- Phase I. Creation X
- Phase II. Preparation and Production X
- Phase III. Delivery X

Tool Activity by Phase

The Lotus Blossom is a tool that can be effectively used whenever an individual or group is having problems when coming up with a creative solution to a problem or a new product or service. It is particularly effectively used during the creation, production, sales, and delivery phases.

Matrix Diagram (Decision Matrix)

Definition

Matrix Diagram, also called Decision Matrix, is a systematic way of selecting from larger lists of alternatives. They can be used to select a problem from a list of potential problems, select primary root causes from a larger list, or to select a solution from a list of alternatives.

User

This tool can be used by an individual, but its best use is with a group of four to eight people. Cross functional teams usually yield the best results from this activity.

Often Used in the Following Phases of the ISC

The following are the three phases of the ISC. Those phases noted with an "X" indicate that the tool/methodology is used during that specific phase.

- Phase I. Creation X
- Phase II. Preparation and Production X
- Phase III. Delivery X

Tool Activity by Phase

- Creation Phase—Frequently, during this phase, there are a number of alternative potential approaches to address an opportunity or problem. In these cases, the decision matrix provides insight into the one alternative that should be pursued first.
- Preparation and Production Phase—There are often a number of different financing alternatives that need to be evaluated. The decision matrix helps the group to come to a common agreement on prioritizing the financing alternatives.
- Delivery Phase—There are often many different marketing and sales approaches that need to be considered before the final delivery process is put in place. Alternatives are as follows: Should we market it ourselves? Should we set up our own stores? Should we run through major wholesalers? Do we want to get in the retail business? Do we want to use outside marketing representatives? Do we need different

marketing approaches for Europe, etc.? The decision matrix provides an excellent way to help the sales team define the options they would like to implement.

Mind Mapping (Spider Diagrams)

Definition

Mind Mapping is an innovation tool and method that starts with a main idea or goal in the middle, and then flows diagrams or ideas out from this one main subject. By using mind maps, you can quickly identify and understand the structure of a subject. You can see the way that pieces of information fit together in a format that your mind finds easy to recall and quick to review. They are also called Spider Diagrams.

User

This tool is best used by individuals, but it can also be used with a group of almost any size up to 10.

Often Used in the Following Phases of the ISC

The following are the three phases of the ISC. Those phases noted with an "X" indicate that the tool/methodology is used during that specific phase.

- Phase I. Creation X
- Phase II. Preparation and Production X
- Phase III. Delivery X

Tool Activity by Phase

- Creation Phase—Mind Maps and Spider Diagrams are often used during the creative phase to analyze a problem and create a list of potential solutions. They are also used to pictorially show the different aspects of the situation to be sure that all of them are addressed when the solution is prepared.
- Production Phase—Mind Maps and Spider Diagrams are used to visibly depict the different aspects of a problem to be sure that all of them are addressed.

- Delivery Phase—Mind Maps and Spider diagrams are frequently used to visibly depict all approaches to marketing and sales campaigns and the advantages and disadvantages of each.

Proof of Concept

Definition

A Proof of Concept (POC) is a demonstration, the purpose of which is to verify that certain concepts or theories have the potential for real-world application. A POC is a test of an idea made by building a prototype of the application. It is an innovative, scaled-down version of the system you intend to develop. The POC provides an evidence to demonstrate that a business model, product, service, system, or idea is feasible and will function as intended.

User

This tool can be used by an individual, but its best use is with a group of 4–8 people. Cross functional teams often yield the best results from this activity.

Often Used in the Following Phases of the ISC

The following are the three phases of the ISC. Those phases noted with an "X" indicate that the tool/methodology is used during that specific phase.

- Phase I. Creation X
- Phase II. Preparation and Production
- Phase III. Delivery

Tool Activity by Phase

- Creation Phase—The POC methodology is principally used during the Creation Phase. During this phase, the innovator and/or the creative team develops value statements that define how the innovative product, service, or situation will impact the customer/receiver of the innovative activity. The POC may be used in refining and validating value statements.

- During the analysis and preparation activities related to preparing value proposition, the vision of who will be impacted and how they will be impacted are refined and updated. The goals are also evaluated and updated to reflect the information that has been collected. The POC model is useful in working with potential customers and users to evaluate these value propositions.
- Preparation and Production Phase—Sometimes, POC is used to make a comparison of the financial plan, and the vision and goals for the innovation concept must be supportive of each other. The POC is an important requirement in seeking investment from outside parties.

    As the organization documents the innovation implementation plan and requirements, it must consider the vision and goals established for the innovation concept. The formal documentation of the vision and goals is occasionally validated through the use of POC methodologies.

    The goals set related to output performance, costs, and delivery schedules is a primary input in defining the organization of production activities, the quality of the production process, and the timing of delivery to external customers. These goals may be further refined and validated through the use of POC methodologies such as pilot production.
- Delivery Phase—Sales delivery systems may be refined and validated through POC tools, such as implementation of a test marketing program.

Storyboarding

Definition

Storyboarding physically structures the output into a logical arrangement. The ideas, observations, or solutions may be grouped visually according to shared characteristics, dependencies upon one another or similar means. These groupings show relationships between ideas and provide a starting point for action plans and implementation sequences.

User

This tool can be used by individuals or groups, but its best use is with a group of four to eight people. Cross functional teams usually yield the best results from this activity.

Often Used in the Following Phases of the ISC

The following are the three phases of the ISC. Those phases noted with an "X" indicate that the tool/methodology is used during that specific phase.

- Phase I. Creation X
- Phase II. Preparation and Production X
- Phase III. Delivery X

Tool Activity by Phase

- Creation Phase—During the creation phase, a storyboard is often used to transform an innovative idea into vivid focus. It helps to clarify and refine the original concept into a series of pictures that provide significantly more detail than was originally defined in the creative idea. It is used to clarify detail and to communicate the original concept.

  The storyboard provides a great deal of detail related to the original concept, allowing the team to better define the resources that are required to support the original concept.
- Preparation and Production Phase—The storyboard is often used as the blueprint for constructing the product or service. It provides a picture of what the finished output should look like.
- Delivery Process—Storyboarding is often used as the outline for a marketing campaign and is sometimes used to provide a potential customer/consumer with an understanding of how the product or service will benefit them.

TRIZ

Definition

TRIZ (pronounced "treesz") is a Russian acronym for "Teoriya Resheniya Izobretatelskikh Zadatch," the Theory of Inventive Problem Solving, which was originated by Genrich Altshuller in 1946. It is a broad title representing methodologies, toolsets, knowledge bases, and model-based technologies for generating innovative ideas and solutions. It aims to create an algorithm to the innovation of new systems and the refinement of existing systems and is based on the study of patents of technological evolution of systems, scientific theory, organizations, and work of arts.

User

This tool can be used by individuals or groups, but its best use is with a group of four to eight people. Primarily, it was originally applied to new product design, product evolution improvement, and technical problem-solving, and as a result, it was used in an engineering environment. Over the recent years, it has been expanded to cover processes and systems improvement and development, expanding its usage to cross functional teams.

Often Used in the Following Phases of the ISC

The following are the three phases of the ISC. Those phases noted with an "X" indicate that the tool/methodology is used during that specific phase.

- Phase I. Creation X
- Phase II. Preparation and Production X
- Phase III. Delivery

Tool Activity by Phase

- Creation Phase—TRIZ is most effectively used as a tool to help design new products and/or to improve existing products or services.
- Preparation and Production Phase—During this phase, TRIZ is frequently used to solve manufacturing problems and to improve manufacturing procedures.

THE REALITY OF TOOLS AND METHODOLOGIES

I know of no one who uses all of the seventy-six different tools/ methodologies as part of their innovation activities. They choose tools they like to use and feel the most comfortable with, although, as a certified innovator, you need to understand the seventy-six preferred tools plus some others that are unique to the organizations' products and activities. Individuals who reach the Gold Innovation Medal proficiency level must have at least an understanding of how to use all seventy-six tools. Those who reach the Silver Innovation Medal proficiency level must have a thorough understanding of a selection of the seventy-six tools as we noted in each chapter. This is necessary, as frequently experienced and knowledgeable innovators change jobs to promote their personal income, growth, and personal challenges. We recommend that you select and work with a small group of tools/methodologies and use them until they become as natural as breathing. As you work with the innovation system, you will find that frequently another tool becomes useful, so you add them to the list of tools/methods you are using. The following is a list of my personal twenty-three favorite tools/methodologies.

1. Brainstorming
2. Benchmarking
3. Project management
4. Supply chain management
5. Plan–do–check–act
6. What if's
7. Business process improvement
8. Flowcharting
9. Survey
10. Organizational change management
11. Business plan development
12. Elevator speech
13. Knowledge management systems
14. Statistical analysis
15. S-curve model
16. Business case development
17. Contingency planning
18. Cost analysis
19. Design for tools
20. Innovative master plan
21. Market research and surveys
22. Nominal group technique
23. Rewards and recognition

You will note that there are a number of tools/methodologies that I frequently use that are not on the list of seventy-six of the most used and/or the most effective ones. This is because I focus on the total innovation from creation to transformation. Most people tend to think of innovation as it applies to developing new products and services, rather than considering the total innovation cycle. In reality, having a potentially innovative design does not ensure that you will have an innovative product unless everyone involved in the innovative cycle is very creative related to how they perform their assigned tasks.

Other people include continuous improvement as part of the innovation cycle. In these cases, a number of additional tools are valuable like Lean, Six Sigma, Business Process Improvement, Sampling, etc.

There are far too many innovative tools and methodologies for all, but very few people to learn and understand. We recommend selecting no more than fifteen tools to learn and become effective and in using and expanding your database based upon tools/methodologies that you need related to your work environment.

Call it what you will. Innovation is just constructive thinking.

H. James Harrington

SUMMARY

This chapter provided an overview of the tools, methods, and techniques covered in the book, *Volume 3: Innovation Tools Handbook—Creative Tools, Methods, and Techniques* (CRC Press). We only described in detail the eight tools that must be understood to reach the Silver Innovation Medal proficiency level. We did not have the opportunity to explain how to use all the tools as it would make this an extremely large book. We strongly recommend that you obtain a copy of this CRC Press book which will provide you with instructions on how to use all the tools etc., examples of how it has been used, and list of software that will aid you in using the tool/methodology for each of the tools etc. described in this chapter.

MIND EXPANDER'S EXERCISE

To improve your innovative and creative ability, you need to think outside the box. These riddles are designed to challenge the way you think about a situation. Keep track of how many you answer correctly, and at the end of this book, we will provide you with your personal analysis of your creative abilities.

Answer to Chapter 6. Mind Expander's Exercise

Exercise: They are having a party in the jungle. All the animals, including the baboons, giraffes, gazelles, etc., showed up except one animal. Which animal was missing?

Answer: The animal that didn't show up at the party was the elephant. He was still in the refrigerator.

Chapter 7. Mind Expander's Exercise

What word in the English language is always spelled incorrectly?

RECOGNITION AND COMMENTS

Note: The following people contributed to this chapter.

- Benjamin, Scott
- Damci, Gul Aslan
- Friedman, Lisa
- Harrington, H. James
- Landry, Dana J.
- Mignosa, Charles
- Nelson, Doug
- Rioboo, Jose Carlos
- Smith, Larry R.
- Thompson, Maria B.
- Trusko, Brett
- Voehl, Frank
- Walsh, Stephen P.
- Zusman, Alla

8

Now the Honeymoon Is Over

INTRODUCTION

Up to this point in this book we have focused on the requirements for innovation and Phase I. Creation of the ISC. This is the phase that everyone likes to write and talk about. It includes four process groupings. They are as follows:

- Process Grouping 1. Opportunity Identification
- Process Grouping 2. Opportunity Development
- Process Grouping 3. Value Proposition
- Process Grouping 4. Concept Validation

Completing these four process groupings should result in the individual or team feeling a sense of accomplishment for originating a potentially innovative opportunity. It's a lot like the feeling a fullback experience on the football team when he crashes the opposition's line breaking through to make a touchdown. He receives a strong sense of accomplishment, self-satisfaction, and recognition by his team. On the other hand, when the fullback hits the line and fumbles the ball, there is a sense of failure and shame that the individual has let the team down.

No matter what anyone says, we all know that every individual has a real sense of accomplishment when they come up with a new and original concept that has a large potential of adding value to some, if not all, of the stakeholders. The organization has a potential innovation project when

1. Opportunity Identification Process Grouping—Identifying an opportunity that can bring about improvement within the organization and planning for outside of the organization is a very positive experience. At this point, an individual thinks to himself that this is an opportunity for me to do something that no one else has taken advantage of. It's my chance to be a white knight fighting to improve performance.

2. Opportunity Development Process Grouping—At this point, you define ways to take advantage of the opportunity and then assign individuals or a team to look at many different ways the opportunity can be addressed. It calls upon an individual to step away from his or her daily activities and use his or her mental capabilities to come up with new and unique solutions. Again, there is a great deal of self-satisfaction and pride when an individual or team defines one or more ways to take advantage of an opportunity that no one else was able to take advantage of.

3. Value Proposition Process Grouping—Once you have developed a potential solution, the next question you have to ask yourself, "Is this potential solution value added to the stakeholders?" If you come up with a number of potential solutions, you need to evaluate which solution creates the most value added per investment. Again, this process grouping requires a great deal of imagination, estimation, and research. It relies heavily on the judgment of the individual defining the potential solution. This process evaluates the creativity of the individuals developing the potential solution. Failure at this point in the system often results in reevaluating of the opportunity to see if it is real or at a minimum sending it back to develop a new and more comprehensive potential solution.

4. Concept Validation Process Grouping—By now, you have identified an improvement opportunity, defined ways to take advantage of this opportunity, and evaluated the potential solution to determine whether it is value added to the stakeholders. Now the big question is, "Will it work?" "Will the solution bring about the potential savings as defined in the value proposition?" Failure at this point in the ISC results in considerable loss of money, time, and human resources. It usually means that the potential project is dropped or at a minimum redirected back to the beginning of the cycle.

THE START OF PHASE II. PREPARATION AND PRODUCTION

With Phase I. Creation successfully completed, Phase II. Preparation and Production begins. The initiative becomes an approved project for the organization. Large complex and mission-critical projects are assigned to a project manager and become part of the organization's active project portfolio. The hundreds of minor improvement activities usually referred to as continuous improvement do not have the luxury of being managed by a trained and experienced project manager.

Phase II. Preparation and Production consists of the following four process groupings:

- Process Grouping 5. Business Case Analysis
- Process Grouping 6. Resource Management
- Process Grouping 7. Documentation
- Process Grouping 8. Production

As the names imply, these four process groupings are very much standard activities. None of them require a great deal of imagination and/or creativity. This doesn't mean that there isn't a continuous flow of improvement concepts being developed and implemented in these four process groupings. Usually, these changes are far less visible than the activities that take place during the four process groupings in Phase 1. Creation. Typically, the projects that are considered major in nature and receive high levels of attention are process reengineering projects and/or new software packages that are being applied to one or more of the four process groupings.

Many people feel that the creative/innovative cycle is over when they complete Phase I. Creation. This is far from the truth as less than 20% of the total ISC cost is normally expended during all of Phase I. All of Phase II is an investment in future that may or may not pay off. Phase I should have put us in a position where we have a high degree of confidence that continuing the project into Phase II will result in real-value added to the organization and/or the customer. Here are the activities that typically occur in the four process groupings under Phase II. Preparation and Production. They are as follows:

- Process Grouping 5—Business Case Analysis

  This is where you get approval, financing, budget, performance specifications, human resources, schedules, and executive support to an individual project/concept. It is usually a go or no-go decision activity.

- Process Grouping 6—Resource Management

  This is where you transform a budget into money, people, facilities, and materials required to develop the concept so that it can be produced in large quantities. This is typically the point where an official project manager is assigned, and additional staff is added to the Innovative Project Team (INT).

- Process Grouping 7—Documentation

  This is where the rough notes from the engineering notebook are transformed into engineering specifications that are released as product specifications and requirements. These product specs are then used to document the processes and procedures that will be used to produce the output and control its efficiency and effectiveness.

- Process Grouping 8—Production

  This is where manufacturing documentation (routings, training procedures, operating instructions, and test procedures) is collected, decisions are made to build or subcontract, equipment is installed, data collecting systems are installed, and facilities are set up. It includes training of the people who will produce the output and the suppliers who provide input to the process so that the process cost is minimized and the external consumer receives output that meets and preferably exceeds their requirements and at a price they consider reasonable. The object is to maximize the value added for all the stakeholders.

Phase III. Delivery consists of four process groupings. They are as follows:

- Process Grouping 9—Marketing, Sales, and Delivery
- Process Grouping 10—After-Sales Services
- Process Grouping 11—Performance Analysis
- Process Grouping 12—Transformation

We have decided to highlight five of the most important methodologies of Phase III that are designed to pull the four process groupings together. They are as follows:

- Project Management
- Project Change Management

- Risk Management
- Supply Chain Management
- Rewards and Recognition

PROJECT MANAGEMENT

Project Management Drives Innovation

Most small, evolution-type innovation does not require a formal project management system, but all projects need to consider the elements of a comprehensive project management approach. For small, obvious evolutionary-type innovations involving a limited number of people (one to five), a documented comprehensive project mission document, including a work breakdown structure that shows what has to be done and the interrelationships between activities and people, is sufficient. For major and/or mission-critical projects, a formal Project Management System needs to be put in place usually managed by a certified Project Manager. Project Management is one of the fastest-growing career fields in the United States. The Project Management Institute is the largest professional society in United States and is growing rapidly.

According to the Chaos Report compiled by the Standish Group International,

- Only 26% of all projects are successful.
- 40% of all Information Technology (IT) projects fail or are cancelled.

Processes define how organizations function, and projects are the means by which organizations improve their processes or products. By definition, a project is defined as a "temporary endeavor undertaken to create a unique product or service." Basically, innovative projects can be classified into three categories. They are as follows:

1. Defining and implementing new or improved potentially innovative products/services.
2. Defining and implementing new or improved innovative processes or systems.
3. Defining and implementing new or improved innovative managerial concepts and organizational structures.

You will note that I left out continuous improvement projects and activities as they do not represent the level of creativity, enthusiasm, and excitement that naturally innovative concepts generate for the team. (This is contrary to the ISO current position.)

There are endless numbers of examples of poor Project Management. Two examples are as follows:

- NASA's Space Station Freedom was originally budgeted for $8 billion; it is now up to $32 billion and climbing.
- The 2004 Olympic Games that was held in Greece was 300% over budget one year before the opening.

Successfully completing the Business Case Analysis and obtaining management approval upgrade the status of the project from a temporary unfunded project to a committed project. Part of this successful upgrading is an operating budget to cover the project for each of the various functions that will be participating. As a result, a team of individuals is assigned full-time or part-time to the project.

It is important to note that Project Management principles can be applied to any project and not just innovative projects.

The 5 Project-Related Managers

With the approval of a project team arises the need for five kinds of management related to the project. They are as follows:

1. Project Manager—Responsible for the project being completed on time, within budget, and capable of performing all the prescribed functions
2. Project Risk Manager—Part of project management team
3. INT Manager—Daily INT team manager
4. Daily Work Management—Daily management of the personnel in the affected areas
5. Executive Sponsor—The individual who can approve variations to the project

Definitions of Project Management Roles

- Project Manager
  The Project Manager has the application of knowledge, skills, tools, and techniques to project activities in order to meet or exceed

stakeholder's needs and expectations for the project. Frequently, a Project Manager will manage a portfolio of projects.

- Project Risk Management

    Project Risk Management is a subset of Project Management that includes the project concerned with the identification, analyzing, reporting, and developing contingency plans. A list of things that could impact the project from being completed successfully is prepared, and each item is analyzed to determine if it is a critical, business major risk or minus risk. All critical and major risks should have contingency plans prepared for them. Normally, the contingency plans are not included in the budget but require a modification to the project plan and often to the budget in order to implement them. Normally, the Project Risk Management activities are assigned to the project manager.

- INT Manager

    INT stands for the Innovation Team. The INT manager is responsible for the outcome of the project, and people working on the project will report directly to the INT manager. They are responsible for the total success of the project and, as such, will make day-to-day decisions related to work priorities.

- Daily Work Management

    Daily Work Management is managing the way the change is evaluated and phased into the organization's current work environment, without having a negative impact upon the output schedules. This takes into consideration the collection of additional data, employee training, and special handling requirements.

- Executive Sponsor

    The Executive Sponsor is usually an executive within the organization who has been assigned or volunteered to work with the project team to help them overcome any difficulties the INT manager cannot handle. The Executive Sponsor is responsible for ensuring that the functions impacted by the project apply the required resources and have the proper skills and time available to perform in an excellent manner. The Executive Sponsor provides an organizational view of how the project is progressing and determines where additional executive involvement will ensure successful completion of the project. Depending on the project, the INT will get his approval at the key checkpoints without involving the total executive team.

Five different types of management involved in the individual project may seem like a lot of additional bureaucracy built into the process. I agree with you, and for all but the large critical projects that require the involvement of many parts of the organization, the project-related management could be reduced to three and four managers, and very small projects can be reduced to one INT manager.

The Five Things Required to Have a Successful Product/Process Cycle

Let's stop right here and define what makes up a successful innovative product/process cycle. The innovative cycle is successful when it is

- Completed on or ahead of schedule
- Completed within budget
- The change performance is equal to or better than the marketing and engineering specifications
- Its return on investment is high enough to fairly compensate its employees, management, and investors
- Output is seen as value added by the customer in comparison to present conditions and/or performance

Project Management has a direct impact on the first three requirements for a successful innovation cycle and has a secondary impact on all five of them. In this case, we are suggesting that Project Management methodologies and controls need to be implemented as soon as the product is approved to be part of the organization's portfolio or when the project risks are high and there is a high probability that the project will not successfully pass the Business Case Analysis. A formal project management process may be started as early as preparation of the value proposition.

Projects in most organizations are mission-critical activities, and delivering quality products on time is nonnegotiable. Even in IT projects, things have changed. The benchmark organizations are completing 90% of their projects within 10% of budget and schedule. Information systems organizations that establish standards for project management, including a project office, cut their major project cost overruns, delays, and cancellations by 50%.

Project Management Responsibility

Project management is the application of knowledge, skills, tools, and techniques to project activities in order to meet or exceed stakeholder's needs and expectations for the project. It includes the following:

- Project Integration Management
- Project Scope Management
- Project Team Management
- Project Financial/Cost Management
- Project Quality Management
- Project Resource Management
- Project Communications Management
- Project Risk Management
- Project Procurement Management
- Project Change Management
- Project Documentation/Consideration Management
- Project Planning and Estimating Management

Usually, how each of these twelve management responsibilities will be handled is defined in the project plan for the individual project. The project plan is then used as the road map for developing and implementing the project.

> Why are over 70% of your improvement efforts unsuccessful? What would happen to your organization if 70% of your products were scrapped? We need our engineering functions to be as capable as the manufacturing process.

We liken project management to quality management; everyone thinks they know what quality is, so anyone can manage quality. This same thought pattern applies to project management, but just as a quality manager is a special type of professional with very special skills and training, so is a project manager. Project managers require skill, training, and effective leadership specifically related to project management.

Project Management Body of Knowledge

The Project Management Body of Knowledge (PMBOK) defines sixty-nine different tools that a project manager needs to master. Few of the project managers who I have come in contact with over the past fifty years have mastered all of these tools. In today's complex world, most organizations have numerous projects going on at the same time. Many of these projects are interlinked and others are interdependent. Their requirements and schedules are continuously changing, causing a chain reaction through the organization. As a result, the organization cannot afford to manage each project one at a time. They have to manage their portfolio of projects, making a proper trade-off of personnel and priorities.

Within any organization, there are usually a number of projects whose implementations difficulty is low and the probability of successfully being approved during the business case analysis activities is relatively high. In these cases, the INT manager/leader will assume the roles of the Project Manager and be responsible for performing all the requirements that a Project Manager would be responsible for. Of course, the preferable organizational structure is to combine a group of projects into a single portfolio. In these cases, an experienced Project Manager is assigned to support all of the projects that are assigned to the portfolio.

Project Management Excellence—The Art of Excelling in Project Management, which is Book II in the series, *The Five Pillars of Organizational Excellence* (published by Paton Press), focuses on how to use project management tools to effectively manage the organization's projects and to integrate them into the organization's total operations, which means the effective integration of projects, resources, and knowledge to obtain an effective, efficient, and adaptable business intelligence.

> Processes define how organizations function and projects are the means by which organizations improve those processes.

The Reasons Projects Fail

Let's look at why projects fail.

- Failure to adhere to committed schedule is caused by
  - Variances
  - Exceptions
  - Poor planning
  - Delays
  - Scope creep

- Poor resource utilization is caused by
  - Proper skills not available
  - Poor time utilization
  - Misalignment of skills and assignments
- The portfolio of projects was not managed correctly as
  - Wrong projects were selected
  - High-risk projects were not identified
  - Poor control over interdependencies between projects
- Loss of intellectual capital/knowledge capital means
  - Lack of the means to transfer knowledge
  - Not taking proper patent and copyright activities
  - People leave the organization
- Not preparing the people who will use the output from the project (change management)
- Technology changes obsolete in the project

Research confirms that as much as 60 percent of change initiatives and other projects fail as a direct result of a fundamental inability to manage their social implications.

Gartner Group

PROJECT CHANGE MANAGEMENT

Change management is the process, tools, and techniques to manage the people side of change to achieve the required business outcomes. Change management incorporates the organizational tools that can be utilized to help individuals make successful personal transitions, resulting in the adoption and realization of change. There are two basic approaches to Organizational Change Management. They are as follows:

- Project Change Management—this methodology focuses on preparing a group of people to reduce resistance to a specific change and accepted as part of the routine life.
- Cultural Change Management—this methodology focuses upon changing the class culture throughout the organization to make it more resilient in the face of a continuous changing environment.

We all like to think of ourselves as change masters, but in truth, we are change bigots. Everyone in the management team is all for change. They want to see others change, but when it comes to the managers changing, they are reluctant to move away from their past experiences that have proven to be so successful for them. If the organization is going to change, top management has to be the first to change.

Change is inevitable, and we must embrace it if we are going to be successful in this challenging world we live in. The change management system is made up of three distinct elements. They are as follows:

- Defining what will be changed
- Defining how to change
- Making the change happen

We (Japan) will win and you (USA) will lose. You cannot do anything about it because your failure is an internal disease. Your companies are based on Taylor's principles. Worse, your heads are Taylorized, too. We have passed the Taylor stage. We are aware that business has become terribly complex. Survival is very uncertain in an environment filled with risk, the unexpected, and competition.

Konosuke Matsushita, Founder,
Matsushita Electric Industrial Company

PROJECT RISK MANAGEMENT

Unlike standard activities, the probability of failure for innovative projects is often greater than 80%. Because of this high failure rate, risk management has become part of the international standards for quality. Project risk management is a subset of project management that includes the processes concerned with the identification, analyzing, reporting, and developing contingency plans.

We expect a lot – highly motivated people consciously choosing to do whatever is in their power to assure every customer is satisfied...and more.

SUPPLY CHAIN MANAGEMENT

Note: This section of this book was written by Doug Nelson.

> The secret to supply chain management is often referred to as having "the right product, in the right place, at the right time, at the right cost." The secret to enabling supply chain management is having "the right information, in the right place, at the right time, at the right cost."

> **Doug Nelson**

Introduction

The American Production and Inventory Control Society (APICS) dictionary (15th edition) defines supply chain management as, "The design, planning, execution, control, and monitoring of supply chain activities with the objective of creating net value, building a competitive infrastructure, leveraging worldwide logistics, synchronizing supply with demand, and measuring performance globally." Supply Chain Management methodology has grown and has been implemented extensively due to

- Growth in technological capability. Computer hardware and associated software applications have become faster, better, and less expensive.
- Enterprise Resource Planning (ERP) and the ability to link enterprises electronically have allowed organizations to share large amounts of information quickly and easily.
- Rapid growth in global competition.
- Rapid growth in technological capabilities for products and processes.
- Inventory management methodologies have evolved, such that many companies have developed interorganizational relationships as a standard method of operation.
- Many organizations have increased subcontracting and outsourcing, allowing for concentration on their most important core competencies as internal activities.

Supply Chain Management Issues

Two critical issues within Supply Chain Management are as follows:

1. Flow of materials
2. Flow of information

The keys to managing a successful supply chain are rapid flows of accurate information, timely execution, and increased organizational flexibility.

Manufacturing Planning and Control System

An organization involved in manufacturing or assembling products will typically have a Manufacturing Planning and Control System. The system provided for the below is in alignment with the requirements of major ERP systems.

Strategic Business Plan—The strategic plan is a statement of the major goals and objectives the company expects to achieve over the next two to ten years or more. The plan provides general direction as to how the company plans to achieve these goals over the future time period. It is based on long-term forecasting and includes participation from marketing, finance, production, and engineering. The plan provides direction and coordination across the marketing, finance, production, and engineering plans. The strategic business plan integrates the business plans of all the departments within the organization and is updated annually.

Sales and Operations Plan—The Strategic Business Plan must be regularly updated such that the latest forecasts, changing market and economic conditions, and resource availability are taken into account. Sales and Operations Planning does this through a monthly meeting that determines the high-level production plan, based on these changing conditions. The output of the Sales and Operations Planning meeting is a rolling plan over the next twelve to twenty-four months. It is prepared by a cross functional team, led by the senior executive, with Sales and Marketing providing demand requirements, and operations providing supply availability information. The production plan (in dollars, based on product family) is developed in Sales and Operations Planning.

Production Plan—Based on the objectives set forth in the Sales and Operations Plan, production management includes

- Quantities of each product that must be produced in each time period
- Anticipated inventory levels
- Resources requirements including equipment, labor, and materials for each time period
- Availability of resource requirements

Master Schedule—The Master Schedule represents what the company intends to produce, expressed in specific configurations, quantities, and dates. It is used to provide input to the Material Requirements Plan. This schedule is created by the Master Scheduler based on the forecast, production plan, and other considerations such as backlog, availability of material, availability of capacity, and management policies and goals.

Material Requirements Plan—The material requirements plan is a plan for the production and purchase of the components used in assembling or manufacturing the items in the Master Schedule.

Purchasing and Production Activity Control—Purchasing and Production Activity Control provides for the execution and control of operations. Purchasing is responsible for establishing and controlling the flow of raw materials into the operations facility. Production Activity Control is responsible for planning and controlling the flow of materials and availability of resources throughout the operations facility.

Capacity Management—At each level of the Manufacturing Planning and Control System, the plan must be tested against available resources and capacity of the system. These plans must be adjusted based on comparison of demand requirements and availability of resources at each level of the manufacturing plan.

Distribution Requirements Planning—Distribution Requirements Planning is the systematic process for determining which goods, in what quantity, at which location, and when are required in meeting the anticipated demand. Distribution Requirements Planning inventory systems accumulate lower-level item and location demand that has been placed on distribution centers within the system, and this lower-level demand is aggregated up to higher levels within the system. Using the aggregated information, orders are placed with suppliers, and orders are delivered to each distribution center based on demand requirements.

Supply Chain Management Objectives

A well-developed supply chain management strategy should consider the following key objectives:

1. Segment customers by service requirements, regardless of industry, and then tailor services to those particular segments.
2. Customize the logistics network and focus intensively on the service requirements and on the profitability of the preidentified customer segments.
3. Monitor market demand signals and plan accordingly. Planning must span the entire supply chain to detect signals of changing demand.
4. Differentiate products closer to the customer, since companies can no longer afford to hold inventory to compensate for inadequate demand forecasting.
5. Strategically manage sources of supply, by working with key suppliers to reduce overall costs of owning materials and services.
6. Develop a supply chain information technology strategy that supports different levels of decision-making and provides clear visibility of the flow of products, services, and information.
7. Implement performance measures that apply to every link in the supply chain and measure true profitability at every stage.
8. Know and manage supply chain risks. Anticipate and have plans in place to mitigate supply chain disruptions.

George Plossl's Seven Supply Chain Points

1. Satisfy the customer's real needs, not wants.
2. Understand how the real world works.
3. Have a complete, integrated system.
4. Maintain accurate data.
5. Manage cycle time (CT).
6. Eliminate nonvalue added activity.
7. Use full qualified people.

Supply Chain Principles

There are three constants in life… change, choice and principles.

Stephen Covey

Capacity: The output of a system cannot equal or exceed its capacity.

Utilization: CT increases with utilization and does so sharply as utilization approaches 100%.

Little's Law: Over the long term, average work-in-process (WIP), throughput (TH), and CT for any stable process are related according to the following: $WIP = TH \times CT$.

Queuing: At a single station with no limit on the number of entities that can queue up, waiting time (WT) due to queuing is given by $WT = V \times U \times T$, where V represents a variability factor, U represents a utilization factor, and T is the average effective process time for an entity at the station.

Batching: In a simultaneous or sequential batching environment, (1) the smallest batch size that yields a stable system may be greater than one and (2) delay due to batching (eventually) increases proportionally in the batch size.

Best-Case Performance: Any process flow with bottleneck rate BNR, raw process time RPT, and work-in-process level WIP will have TH less than or equal to min {WIP/RPT, BNR} and CT greater or equal to max {RPT, WIP/BNR}.

Worst-Case Performance: Any process flow with bottleneck rate BNR, raw process time RPT, and work-in-process level WIP will have TH greater or equal to I/RPT and CT less than or equal to $WIP \times RPT$.

Variability Buffering: Variability in a production or supply chain system will be buffered by some combination of inventory, capacity, and time.

Buffer Flexibility: Flexibility reduces the amount of buffering required in a production or supply chain system.

Buffer Position: For a flow with a fixed arrival rate, identical nonbottleneck processes and equal WIP buffers in front of all processes:

1. The maximum decrease in WIP and CT from a unit increase in non-bottleneck capacity will come from adding capacity to the process directly before or after the bottleneck.
2. The maximum decrease in WIP and CT from a unit increase in WIP buffer space will come from adding buffer space to the process directly before or after the bottleneck.

Pull Efficiency: A pull system achieves higher TH for the same average WIP level than an equivalent push system.

Pull Robustness: A pull system is less sensitive to errors in WIP level than a push system is to errors in release rate.

Safety Stock: In a base stock system, safety stock increases in both the target fill rate and (for sufficiently high target fill rate) the standard deviation of demand during replenishment lead time.

Variability Pooling: Combining sources of variability so that they can share a common buffer reduces the total amount of buffering required to achieve a given level of performance.

Inventory Location: In a multiproduct, multilevel supply chain with an objective to achieve high customer service with minimal inventory investment, a low-volume, high-demand variability, and/or high-cost parts should be stocked at a central level, while a low-volume, low-demand variability, and/or low-cost parts should be stocked at a low level.

Inventory Order/Interface Position: Long production lead times require the Inventory/Order (I/O) interface to be located close to the customer for responsiveness, while high proliferation requires it to be located close to raw materials for pooling efficiency.

Bullwhip Effect: Demand at the top (manufacturing) level of a supply chain tends to exhibit more variability than demand at the bottom (retail) level due to batch ordering, forecasting errors, promotional pricing, and gaming behavior by customers.

Risk Sharing Contracts: In interfirm supply chains, individual decision makers optimizing their local objectives generally suboptimize the overall system, because risk falls disproportionally on one party. Contracts that share risk can incentivize decision makers to make globally optimal choices.

The 16 Questions to Evaluate Supplier's Processes

The different processes should be evaluated for items like

1. How are suppliers selected?
2. How are suppliers measured?
3. Are good suppliers rewarded?
4. How are suppliers involved in the design process?
5. How much of the purchase budget goes to each major supplier?
6. How well is the system documented?
7. Is the Supply Management Process in keeping with ISO 9000?
8. How good is the performance feedback process to the supplier?
9. How good is the supplier history file?
10. Are poor performing suppliers dropped?
11. Who gets supplier interface training?

12. What percentage of the items goes through receiving inspection?
13. How good is supplied equipment maintained?
14. When and how were the suppliers certified, and how often are they recertified?
15. Does the organization report cost to stock?
16. How many suppliers are there per item?

Supply Chain Metrics

Measurement is the first step that leads to control and eventually to improvement. If you can't measure something, you can't understand it. If you can't understand it, you can't control it. If you can't control it, you can't improve it.

H. James Harrington

Supply Chain Management often requires management of complex interdependencies between teams, departments, and partner companies across international boundaries. Proper management requires a thorough understanding of the system and appropriate metrics.

The use of analytical models to help solve supply chain management problems will continue to grow as the data available becomes richer and computing power to process the data becomes more robust.

Supply Chain Metrics may include measurements for procurement, production, transportation, inventory, warehousing, material handling, packaging, and customer service. There are hundreds of metrics that can be used to evaluate Supply Chain Management performance. The following are some of the most common.

Market Share: The percentage of a market accounted for by a specific company.

Unit Market Share: The units sold by a specific company as a percentage of total market sales, measured in the same units. Unit Market Share (%) = Unit Sales (#)/Total Market Unit Sales (#).

Revenue Market Share: Revenue market share reflects the prices at which goods are sold (expressed in dollars) by a specific company as a percentage of the total market sales (expressed in dollars).

Sales Plan Performance:

Sales Plan Performance by Product Family: Actual units sold for month/Planned sales for month × 100

Sales Plan Performance by Product or Item: Actual units sold for month/Planned sales for month × 100

Customer Delivery Performance: The percentage of items, Stock-Keeping Unit (SKUs) or order value that arrives on or before the requested ship date. The on-time shipping rate is a key to customer satisfaction. A high rate indicates an efficient supply chain.

Quality

Defects per million opportunities (DPMO): Defects × 1,000,000/Number of units in the sample × Opportunities per unit; DPMO is the performance measure of a process. It is represented in opportunities per million units. It can also be termed as the nonconformities per million opportunities (NPMO). It is used for the improvement of a process and is calculated based on the number of defects, number of units, and number of opportunities per unit.

Cost

Manufacturing Cost: Annualized cost of goods sold/Monthly manufacturing expense – material purchases.

Velocity

Measures of Velocity: Value-added time/CT

Schedule Performance

Project Schedule Performance (Product Development): Number of deliverable milestones completed on time (within quality and time tolerance)/Number of deliverable milestones due during the time period × 100

Production Plan Performance

Production Plan Performance: Actual production for product family (this month)/Planned production for the product family (planned last month for this month) × 100

Master Schedule Performance

Master Schedule Performance: Number of orders or schedules completed on time (within quantity and time allowance)/Number of orders or schedules due during the time period × 100

Manufacturing Schedule Performance

Manufacturing Schedule Performance: Number of orders or schedules completed on time (within quantity and time tolerance)/Number of orders or schedules due during the time period × 100

Supplier Delivery Performance

Supplier Delivery Performance: Number of orders or schedules completed on time (within quantity and time tolerance)/Number of orders or schedules due during the time period × 100

Accuracy

Item Master Accuracy: Number of correct item masters/Total number of item masters checked × 100

Supporting Data Accuracy: Number of supporting data records/Total number of supporting data records checked × 100

Inventory Record Accuracy: Number of correct items/quantities/locations (within tolerance limits)/Number of items/quantities/locations checked × 100

Bill of Material Accuracy: Number of correct bills/Total number of bills checked × 100

Routing Accuracy: Number of correct routings/Total number of routings checked × 100

Master Schedule Accuracy: Number of valid master schedules/Number of master schedules checked × 100

Material Plan Accuracy: Number of valid material plans/Number of material plans checked × 100

Capacity Plan Accuracy: Number of valid capacity plans/Number of capacity plans checked × 100

Supplementary Performance Measurements for Planning and Control

Sales and Operations Planning
Sales Planning
Sales Order Entry
Master Production Scheduling
Master Planning and Control
Production Planning and Control

Purchasing
Capacity Planning and Control
Bills of Material
Inventory Records
Routings
Distribution Resource Planning

Supply Chain Risk Management

> Supply Chains cannot tolerate even 24 hours of disruption. So, if you lose your place in the supply chain because of wild behavior you could lose a lot. It would be like pouring cement down one of your oil wells.

> **Thomas Friedman**

Supply chain risk is the variety of possible events and their outcomes that could have a negative effect on the flow of goods, services, funds, or information, resulting in some level of quantitative or qualitative loss for the supply chain (APICS).

Disruptions in the global supply chain can occur anytime and from anywhere. Supply chain professionals are often the first responders when it comes to interruptions of supply. While a rapid response is important, of greater importance is to plan strategically to avoid or mitigate risks to the supply chain on a proactive basis. When disaster strikes, it is critical to have these plans in place and be able to rely upon them for immediate mitigation. Before the crisis: Know your customers; Know your company; Know your suppliers; Study the entire system; Analyze the system; Identify and log risks, Conduct qualitative and quantitative risk analysis; Conduct risk planning; Develop a risk matrix; Develop a risk mitigation plan; Review and update contingency and mitigation plans on a regular basis. When disaster strikes: Act calmly; Check your plans; Review alternatives; Act and stay updated; Revise as conditions change.

Cause–Risk–Effect Examples

- Discrete electronics part problems (cause) may lead to recalls that force rework or retesting of delivered hardware (risk), thus impacting the schedule (effect).
- New equipment fabrication (cause) may continue to slip in schedule (risk), resulting in a delay in integration (effect).

- Improper packaging and handling (cause) may cause damage during shipping (risk), resulting in breakage of equipment, necessitating repair or replacement (effect).

Risk Log Example

			Date					Close
Risk ID	WBS	Rank	Found	Assigned	Description	Strategy	Status	Out Date

Supply Chain Risk Log — Last updated [mm/dd/yy]
Project Manager: [Name]

Description of Fields

Risk Id: A unique identifier.

WBS: WBS number of the task(s) related to this risk.

Rank: How important is this risk relative to others? Rank with 1 = highest. No risks have the same rank.

Date found: Date risk became known. mm/dd/yy.

Assigned to: Person who is assigned to manage this risk.

Description: High-level description of risk event, impact, and probability.

Strategy: What will be done to reduce the probability, impact, or both?

Status: On-going log of changes to risk, in order from most recent to oldest. Format: mm/dd/yy – action/update.

Close out date: When did the risk probability go to zero? Describe in the final status. Remove any rank from this risk.

REWARDS AND RECOGNITION

It is often said, "What management thinks is important gets done." If you want to have an innovative organization, you need to restructure the rewards and recognition system so that it reflects the importance of innovation in every job. Rewards and recognition span all the way from a simple thank you to a fist full of money. It can be as simple as buying someone a cup of coffee because they came to work early or as complex as giving the individual a new car for a truly innovative concept that produces great output value to the organization. The key is everybody hears "thank you" in a different way, and the organization has to have a toolbox full of rewards and recognition options so that management can choose the right tool to keep the individuals' innovative floodgates open and hopefully even open them further. The biggest mistake that any organization makes related to their employees is to recognize or reward them for something that truly is within their job description. When everybody gets an award, nobody gets an award because no one is singled out as doing an outstanding innovative work. The individual's salary is the reward that he or she receives for doing everything that is in their job description.

> If your desired behavior is increased innovation than your rewards and recognition system has to be designed to reinforce these behaviors when they occur.

A good reward process has eleven major objectives, often referred to as "Ingredients of an Organization's Reward Process":

1. To provide recognition to employees that have developed original, creative new ideas that produce added value to the stakeholders.
2. To encourage creativity and innovation of the employees.
3. To provide focus and a sense of urgency for current needs like innovation.
4. To provide recognition to employees who make unusual contributions to the organization to stimulate additional effort for further innovation improvement.
5. To show the organization's appreciation for superior performance.
6. To ensure maximum benefits from the reward process by an effective communication system that highlights the individuals who were recognized.
7. To provide many ways to recognize employees for their efforts, creativity, and innovation.
8. To ensure management understands that variation enhances the impact of the reward process.
9. To improve morale through the proper use of rewards.

10. To reinforce behavioral patterns that management would like to see continuously.

11. To ensure that the employees recognized are perceived as earning the recognition by their fellow employees.

Why does recognition matter? George Blomgren, president of Organizational Psychologists, puts it this way, "Recognition lets people see themselves in a winning identity role. There's a universal need for recognition and most people are starved for it."

Reward Process Hierarchy

In this chapter, the word *reward* is defined as something given or offered for a special service or to compensate for effort expended. Rewards can be subdivided into the following categories:

- Compensation—to financially reimburse for service(s) provided.
- Award—to bestow a gift for performance or quality.
- Recognition—to show appreciation for behaving in a desired way.

Why Reward People?

The single most basic behavior is to perform in ways that we are rewarded for. The first lesson we learn is directly related to being rewarded for crying. A baby cries, and they are fed or their diaper is changed. Later on in life, we learn that if we cry, we get picked up and held. We grow a little older, and we are told to clean our plates, and we will get dessert, or be good, and Santa Claus will bring us a new toy. Later on, we are told that if we clean our room, we can go to the movies.

Yes, all through our lives, we have been rewarded for acting out a desired behavior, and punished when our behaviors are undesirable as defined by someone else or even by our own self. These rewards make eating the asparagus, mowing the lawn, and being good a little more worthwhile. There is no doubt about it, increased creativity and innovation are the desired behaviors for 2020s. It is important to note that all these rewards occur relatively close to the time that the desired behavior occurs. If we didn't get the dessert until the following Sunday or go to the movies until next month, or if mother tells us on February 2 that if we are not good, Santa Claus will not bring us a toy, the asparagus would stay on the plate, the clutter would remain on the floor, and we probably would continue misbehaving.

Three factors affect the degree to which the desired behavior is reinforced. They are as follows:

- Type of reward
- Elapsed time between meets or exceeds the performance standard
- The extent to which the behavior meets or exceeds the performance standard

Up to this point, we have discussed direct, tangible, positive stimuli that reward people for acting in a desired behavior mode. There are two other ways to encourage people to behave in a desired manner. They are as follows:

- Negative stimulation
- Humanistic stimulation (recognition)

Negative stimulation takes the form of physical and mental pain within the individuals(s) who do not perform in the desired manner. For example, telling a child who wants to go outside to play that she will have to stay at the table until her plate is clean, spanking a child because his room is not picked up, or taking away television rights because a child didn't have his homework done are all examples of negative stimulation. A manager applies negative mental stimulation to an individual when the manager explains why the person is not performing at an acceptable level. Often, employees will subject themselves to mental pain. We have all walked out of a meeting thinking, "Why did I say that? How dumb can I be?" Really good, conscientious employees will take themselves to task when they do something wrong far more than their managers will.

Although recognition is an intangible reward, its positive impact on behavior is usually very effective and should never be overlooked. For example, when we put a good report card up on the refrigerator door recognizing that the child has done a good job or when a teacher displays a particularly good drawing in the classroom.

Definitions

Indirect stimulation: This act normally takes the form of nonfinancial recognition. It benefits the organization by instilling pride and degree of satisfaction in the individual. Typical examples are being rewarded with a bigger office, or one with a window, or with a trophy, a plaque or new computer, etc.

Direct stimulation: This normally takes the form of financial compensation or activities that are related to financial compensation like salary increases, paid for trips, pay for education, and/or technical conferences, etc.

Whenever possible, direct and humanistic stimulation should be combined. For example, when someone is promoted, the promotion is indirect stimulation, and the increased salary is direct stimulation. Often, management thinks about rewards and recognition as two separate activities. In truth, recognition is just one element of a total reward structure that is needed to reinforce everyone's desired behavioral patterns. As Don Roux, a Minneapolis-based sales and marketing consultant, states, "They (incentive programs) both motivate people to perform some task or achieve some goal by offering rewards. The desirable performance is rewarded, and rewarded behavior tends to be repeated."

When Xerox won the Malcolm Baldrige Award, The Xerox Business Products and Systems National Quality Award release stated:

> Recognition and Rewards: Ensures that Xerox people are encouraged and motivated to practice the new behaviors and use the tools. Both individuals and groups are recognized for their quality improvements – whether that takes the form of a simple thank-you or a cash bonus.

This highlights a very important point. Up to now, we have been talking about rewarding individuals, but that is not enough. In today's environment, the organization needs to encourage teams of people to work together to provide the most efficient, effective, and adaptable organization. If we reward only individuals, we develop an organization of prima donnas who are only interested in doing things that make them look good. It is for this reason that your reward process must include both individual and group rewards.

The complexity of today's environment and the sophistication of today's employees make it necessary to carefully design a reward process that provides the management team with many ways to say thank you to each employee, because the things that are valued by one individual may have no impact upon another.

Vince Lombardi said, "Winning isn't everything. It's the only thing."

Recognition is something everyone wants, needs, and strives to obtain. Studies have shown that people classify recognition as one of the things they value most.

Types of Rewards

Everyone hears "thank you" in different ways. The reward process must take these different needs into account. Some people want money, some want a pat on the back, others want to get exposure to upper management, while still others want to look good in front of their peers. For example, American Express has an awards program that they call, "Great Performer Award Luncheon." Typical activities that won employees invitations to these luncheons were

- One American Express employee bailed a French tourist out of jail in Columbus, Georgia
- Another took food and blankets to travelers stranded at Kennedy Airport

The earlier are unusual performances for employees to take on their own. However, this is what we need if we want to have empowered employees and a truly world-class organization.

It's easy to see that the reward process is only limited by the creativity of your managers and the individuals who design the process. The National Science Foundation study made this point: "The key to having workers who are both satisfied and productive is motivation; that is, arousing and maintaining the will to work effectively—having workers who are productive not because they are coerced, but because they are committed."

To help structure a reward process, let's divide the rewards into the following categories:

1. Financial Compensation
   a. Salary
   b. Commissions
   c. Piecework
   d. Organizational bonuses
   e. Team bonuses
   f. Gainsharing

    g. Goal sharing
    h. Stock options
    i. Stock purchase plans
    j. Benefit programs

2. Monetary Awards
    a. Suggestion awards
    b. Patent awards
    c. Contribution awards
    d. Best-in-category awards (example: best salesperson, employee of the year, etc.)
    e. Special awards (example: president's award)

3. Group/Team Rewards
4. Public Personal Recognition
5. Private Personal Recognition
6. Peer Rewards
7. Customer Rewards
8. Organizational Awards

Implementation of the Reward Process

To develop an effective reward process, many factors have to be taken into consideration. The following steps will help you avoid most reward processes:

- Reward Fund—The organization should set aside a specific amount of money that the reward process will use. This amount will set the boundaries that the reward process will operate within.
- Reward Task Team (RTT)—This team will be used to design and/or update the reward process.
- Present Reward Process—The RTT should pull together a list of all the formal and informal rewards that are used within the organization today.
- Desired Behaviors—The RTT should prepare a list of desired behaviors.
- Present Reward Process Analysis—The present reward process should be reviewed to identify the rewards that are not keeping up with the organization's present and projected future culture and visions.

- Desired Behavior Analysis—Each desired behavior is now compared to the reward categories to see which category or categories should be used to reinforce the desired behavior. Each behavior should have at least two ways of rewarding people that practice the behavior.
- Reward Usage Guide—When the reward process is defined, a reward usage guide should be prepared. This guide should define the purpose of each of the reward categories and the procedures that are used to formally process the reward. This guide will be used to help management and employees to understand the reward process and to standardize the way rewards are used throughout the organization.
- Management Training—One of the most neglected parts of most management training processes is how to use the reward process. As a result, most managers are far too conservative with their approach to rewards, while others misuse them.

In creating a reward process, consider the following:

- Always have it to reinforce desired behaviors.
- Only reward for exceptional customer service and performance.
- Publish why rewards are given.
- Create a point system that can be used to recognize teams and individuals for small and large contributions. The employee should be able to accumulate points over time to receive a higher level reward.
- Structure the reward process so that 50% of the employees will receive at least a first-level reward each year.
- Structure the reward process so that the managers can exercise their creativity and personal knowledge of the recipient in selecting the reward.
- Provide ways that anyone can recognize a person for their contributions.
- Provide an instant reward mechanism.

In a paper by Shelly Sweet (a Palo Alto, California, quality consultant), titled "Reinforcing Quality," she warns us to avoid the following seven pitfalls:

- Cumbersome procedures are costly to administer.
- Executives or middle managers are not consistently supporting the program.
- Awards are applied inconsistently.
- Unexpected behaviors result.
- Employees perceive that the same employees are rewarded repeatedly.
- Enthusiasm wanes.
- Company's cost cutting curtails the program.

Reward and Recognition: Advantages and Disadvantages

Let's look at some of the advantages and disadvantages of the six reward media

Advantages of Financial (Money) Rewards
- Its value is understood
- It's easy to handle
- The rewardee can select the way it is used

Disadvantages of Financial (Money) Rewards
- Once it is spent, it is gone
- If used too often, it can be perceived as part of the employee's basic compensation
- It is hard to present in a real showmanship manner
- Often, it is not shared with the family

Advantages of Merchandise Rewards
- It can appeal to the total family
- They have a trophy value
- They can be used as progressive reward (for example, the employee is given points that can be redeemed or accumulated for a higher-level merchandise reward)
- They cannot be confused with basic compensation

Disadvantages of Merchandise Rewards
- More administrative time is required
- A choice of merchandise rewards must be kept in stock
- There may be other things the rewardee would prefer

Disadvantages of Merchandise Rewards
- More administrative time is required
- A choice of merchandise rewards must be kept in stock
- There may be other things the rewardee would prefer

Advantages of Plaques/Trophy Rewards
- Directly tied in to the desired behavior
- Lasts a long time and is never used up
- Customized to the employee (name is often engraved on them)

Disadvantages of Plaques/Trophy Rewards
- May not be valued by the recipient
- Usually not useful
- Often not valued by the family

Advantages of Published Communications
- Can be very specific
- Receives wide distribution
- Inexpensive way of rewarding an individual
- Document is long-lasting

Disadvantages of Published Communications
- No tangible value
- Can reduce cooperation and cause envy
- Can be blown out of proportion by the individual in comparison to total contributions over a longer period of time

Advantages of Verbal Communication
- Very personal
- Can be given when the desired behavior occurs
- Least expensive

Disadvantages of Verbal Communication
- Not tangible
- Has no visual reinforcement
- It can be misunderstood

Advantages of Special Privileges
(For example, attend conference, take a business trip, additional vacation days, new equipment, etc.)

- The recipient can be involved in the selection
- Can meet unique employee needs
- Highly valued by the employees
- Can be used to support organizational objectives

Disadvantages of Special Privileges
- Can cause envy
- Can impact the organization's operation when the individual is not available
- Can be expensive

To be the most effective, the reward process should combine different reward media, thereby taking advantage of the positive impacts that each have and offsetting their disadvantages. For example, an individual incident could be reinforced by presenting the recipient with a check and a plaque at a department meeting.

Good Behavior = Rewards and Recognition = Better Behavior

Basically, the following media are used individually or in combination to produce desired behavior (innovation).

1. Money
2. Merchandise
3. Plaques/trophies
4. Published communications
5. Verbal communication
6. Special privileges

A well-designed reward process will use all six, because each has its own advantages and disadvantages. One of the biggest mistakes management makes is to use the same motivating factors for all employees. People are moved by different things because we all want different things. The reward process needs to be designed to meet the following basic classifications of needs:

- Money
- Status (ego)
- Security and respect

People Want Recognition

After the organization has provided the employee with a paycheck and health coverage, what more can or should the organization do for the employee? Management is obligated to do more than just eliminate their financial worries. Employees excel when they are happy, satisfied, and feel that someone else appreciates the efforts they are putting forth. A tangible and intangible reward process can go a long way to fulfilling these needs in stimulating innovation when properly used.

Research has proven that when management rewards employees for adopting desired behaviors, they work harder, are more creative, and provide better customer service. The benchmark service organizations are more likely to have well-defined and well-used approaches for telling their employees that they are important creative individuals. Individuals in the world-class organizations that go beyond expectations are held up as customer heroes and role models for the rest of the organization. This provides a continually more aggressive customer performance standard for the total organization.

MIND EXPANDER'S EXERCISE

To improve your innovative and creative ability, you need to think outside the box. These exercises are designed to challenge the way you think about a situation. Keep track of how many you answer correctly, and at the end of the book, we will provide you with your personal analysis of your creative abilities.

Answer to Chapter 7. Mind Expander's Exercise

Exercise: What word in the English language is always spelled incorrectly?

Answer: Incorrectly!

Chapter 8. Mind Expander's Exercise

Billy was born on December 28th, yet his birthday is always in the summer. How is this possible?

SUMMARY

In Chapter 7, many of the tools and methodologies that are most frequently used are representative. In Chapter 8, we presented an overview of the ISC. We then focused on the major systems that unite Phase I, Phase II, and Phase III together to provide the reader with a better understanding of these critical interrelated systems. The systems that were presented are as follows:

- Project Management
- Project Change Management
- Project Risk Management
- Supply Chain Management
- Rewards and Recognition Systems

These five management systems play a key role in the total ISC. They have a major impact upon the resistance that the change meets as it is being implemented and how effective the change is in taking advantage of the opportunity. Although Phase I is the primary creative part of the cycle, the other systems and activities are absolutely crucial for the organization to produce innovative products. In reality, no organization can claim to be innovative until the customer/consumer recognizes their output as being innovative and value added compared with the previous product or service.

BOOK SUMMARY

This book is designed to break the reader away from the theoretical to the practical implementation activities. It replaces the "what to do" with the "how to do it" approaches. This book takes the reader through a detailed step-by-step on how to improve an organization's creativity and innovation. Our experience indicates that there is a direct relationship between all creative people within the organization and the quality of innovative ideas that are generated. Creativity is a general condition within all people; innovation is a specific directed creative process focusing on generating value for its stakeholders.

This book was divided into eight chapters.

- Chapter 1—Innovation—What Is It? How Do You Do It? Who Does It?
- Chapter 2—The Creative and Innovative Story
- Chapter 3—Setting the Stage
- Chapter 4—Overview of the 76 Most Used Innovation Tools, Methods, and Techniques
- Chapter 5—Organizational and Operational Tools, Methods, and Techniques
- Chapter 6—Evolutionary and Improvement Tools, Methods, and Techniques
- Chapter 7—Creative Tools, Methods, and Techniques
- Chapter 8—Now the Honeymoon Is Over

Typical detailed approaches included in these chapters are as follows:

- The 12 Process Groupings of the Innovation System Cycle
- The 4 Basic Types of People Who Drive Innovation
- The 5 Innovator DNA Skills
- Organizing for Innovation Improvement
- The 50 Innovation Approaches/Concepts
- The 9 Ways to Finding Creative/Innovative Solutions
- The 5 Innovation Proficiency Levels
- The 5 I Do It Statements
- The 6 Must Be Willing to Do
- The 3 Reasons for Lack of Creativity
- The 12 Idea Evaluation Questions
- The 5 Creative Myths
- The 30 Impact Results

At the end of each chapter is a mind expander/experiment designed to help the reader to think out of the box.

We believe that by faithfully following the step-by-step instructions you will establish an organization that is hungry to be more creative. This type of organization is not only competitive, but is among the leaders in the field. It's time to take off your coat, roll up your sleeves, and get to work making your organization more innovative.

Do not wait, start to create!

H. James Harrington

MIND EXPANDER'S EXERCISE ANALYSIS

If you tracked your answers to all the mind expander exercises, use the following to evaluate your responses.

- Correctly answered 1–3 exercises—Poor
- Correctly answered 4–5 exercises—Average
- Correctly answered 6 exercises—Good
- Correctly answered 7 exercises—Outstanding

Appendix A—Glossary

- **5 Whys**—A technique to get to the root cause of the problem. It is the practice of asking five times or more why the failure has occurred in order to get to the root cause. Each time an answer is given, you ask why that particular condition occurred.
- **Attribute Listing**—Morphological Analysis and Matrix Analysis techniques are good for finding new combinations of products or services. We use attribute listing and morphological analysis to generate new products and services. Matrix analysis focuses on businesses. It is used to generate new approaches, using attributes such as market sectors, customer needs, products, promotional methods, etc.
- **Benchmarking (BMKG)**—A systematic way to identify, understand, and creatively evolve superior products, services, designs, equipment, processes, and practices to improve your organization's real performance.
- **Business Case**—A business case captures the reason for initiating a project or program. It is most often presented in a well-structured written document, but in some cases, also may come in the form of a short verbal agreement or presentation. The logic of the business case is: whatever resources, such as money or effort, are consumed, they should be in support of a specific business need or opportunity.
- **Business Plan**—A business plan is a formal statement of a set of business goals, the reason they are believed to be obtainable, and the plan for reaching these goals. It also contains background information about the organization or the team attempting to reach these goals.
- **Cause-and-Effect Diagram**—A visual representation of possible causes of a specific problem or condition. The effect is listed on the right-hand side and the causes take the shape of fish bones. This is the reason it is sometimes called a "Fishbone Diagram" or an "Ishikawa Diagram."
- **Change**—A condition where an individual's expectations are no longer aligned with the environment. Change occurs when expectations are not met.

- **Coffee Clutch Opportunity**—A presentation used primarily in a relaxed environment and consists of a very short discussion that lasts between ninety and one hundred and twenty seconds. It typically takes place around the water fountain, walking to or from a meeting, or during a coffee break.
- **Comparative Analysis**—A detailed study/comparison of an organization's product and/or service to the competitors' comparable product and/or service.
- **Conceptual Clustering**—The inherent structure of the data (concepts) that drives cluster formation. Since this technique is dependent on language, it is open to interpretation and consensus is required. (Also known as Concept Tree.)
- **Confirmation Bias**—The tendency of people to include or exclude data that does not fit a preconceived position.
- **Contingency Planning**—A process that primarily delivers a risk management strategy for a business to deal with the unexpected events effectively and the strategy for the business recovery to the normal position. The output of this process is called "contingency plan" or "business continuity and recovery plan."
- **Cost-Benefit Analysis (CBA)**—A financial analysis where the cost of providing (producing) a benefit is compared with the expected value of the benefit to the customer, stakeholder, etc.
- **Direct Stimulation**—This normally takes the form of financial compensation or activities that are related to financial compensation like salary increases, paid-for-trips, pay for education and/or technical conferences, etc.
- **Elevator Speech**—A clear, brief message or "commercial" about an innovative idea you are in the process of implementing. It communicates what it is, what you're looking for, and how it can benefit a company or organization. It's typically no more than two minutes, or the time it takes people to ride from the top to the bottom of a building in an elevator.
- **Executive Sponsor**—Usually an executive within the organization who has been assigned or volunteered to work with the project team to help them overcome any difficulties the INT manager cannot handle. The Executive Sponsor is responsible for ensuring that the functions impacted by the project apply the required resources and have the proper skills and time available to perform in an excellent manner. The Executive Sponsor provides an organizational view

of how the project is progressing and determines where additional executive involvement will ensure successful completion of the project. Depending on the project, the INT will get his approval at the key checkpoints without involving the total executive team.

- **Flowcharting**—A method of graphically describing an existing or proposed process by using simple symbols, lines, and words to pictorially display the sequence of activities. Flowcharts are used to understand, analyze, and communicate the activities that make up major processes throughout an organization. It can be used to graphically display movement of product, communications, and knowledge related to anything that takes an input and value to it and produces an output.

- **Focus Group**—A structured group interview of typically seven and ten individuals who are brought together to discuss their views related to a specific business issue. The group is brought together so that the organizer can gain information and insight into a specific subject or the reaction to a proposed product. The information gained from focus groups provides the organization conducting the interview to make better educated decisions regarding the topic being discussed.

- **Goal**—The end toward which effort is directed: the terminal point in a race. These are always specified in time and magnitude so that they are easy to measure. Goals have key ingredients. First, they specifically state the target for the future state, and second, they give the time interval in which the future state will be accomplished. These are key inputs to every strategic plan.

- **INT Manager**—Responsible for the outcome of the project, and the people working on the project will report directly to the INT manager. They're responsible for the total success of the project and, as such, will make day-to-day decisions related to work priorities.

- **Indirect Stimulation**—This act normally takes the form of nonfinancial recognition. It benefits the organization by instilling pride and degree of satisfaction in an individual.

- **Individual Creativity** is directed at finding solutions to personal problems, improving financial and/or living standards, and providing a level of personal satisfaction. There are two types of creativity— good and bad plus all of the derivations in between. A single idea can be good or bad based upon how it's used. If you define an original and unique way to kill someone in a children's book, it probably would be a bad idea. But if you're writing a mystery novel, it may be a good idea. (Individual innovation is a creative idea that the originator can transfer into increase value added for himself and/or his family.)

- **Innovation**—Innovation is people creating value through the implementation of new, creative, and unique ideas that generate combined measurable added value to the organization's stakeholders. Innovation is how an organization adds value to the stakeholders from implementing creative ideas.
- **Innovator**—An individual who is capable of creating added value to the organization and its customers by being capable of creating new and unique ideas or concepts all the way through the Innovation Systems Cycle from recognizing an opportunity to evaluating the actual value added.
- **Intrapreneur**—An employee of a large corporation who is given freedom and financial support to create new products, services, systems, etc., and does not have to follow the corporation's usual routines or protocols.
- **Lotus Blossom**—A technique based on the use of analytical capacities and helps to generate a great number of ideas that will possibly provide the best solution to the problem to be addressed by the group. It uses a six-step process.
- **Marketing Research**—The systematic and objective identification, collection, analysis dissemination, and use of information that is undertaken to improve decision-making related to products and services that are provided to external customers.
- **Matrix Diagram**—A systematic way of selecting from larger lists of alternatives. They can be used to select a problem from a list of potential problems, select primary root causes from a larger list, or to select a solution from a list of alternatives.
- **Mind Mapping**—An innovation tool and method that starts with a main idea or goal in the middle and then flows or diagrams ideas out from this one main subject.
- **Natural Work Teams**—A natural work team is any group of individuals that report to the same individual. It could be employees that report to the first-line manager or first-line managers that report to a second-line manager, etc.
- **Nominal Group Technique (NGT)**—A technique for prioritizing a list of problems, ideas, or issues that gives everyone in the group or team equal voice in the priority setting process.

- **Organization**—A company, corporation, firm, enterprise, or association of any part thereof, whether it is incorporated or not, public or private, that has its own function and administration. (Source: ISO 8402—1994.) It can be as small as a first-line department or as large as the government in the United States.
- **Organizational Creativity** is originating a new and unique idea that may or may not be value added to him/herself and the organization's stakeholders.
- **Organizational Change Management (OCM)**—A comprehensive set of structured procedures for the decision-making, planning, executing, and evaluation activities. It is designed to minimize the resistance and cycle time to implementing a change.
- **Organizational Structure**—It is a system used to define a hierarchy within an organization. It identifies each job, its function, and where it reports to within the organization. This structure is developed to establish how an organization operates and assists an organization in obtaining its goals to allow for future growth. The structure is illustrated using an organizational chart.
- **Plan–Do–Check–Act**—A structured approach for the improvement of services, products, and/or processes. It is also sometimes referred to as plan–do–check–adjust. Another version of this PDCA cycle is OPDCA. The added "O" stands for observation or as some versions say, "Grasp the current condition."
- **Process**—A series of interrelated activities or tasks that take an input and produces an output.
- **Process Redesign**—A methodology used to streamline a current process with the objective of reducing cost and cycle time by 30%–60% while improving output quality from 20% to 200%.
- **Process Reengineering**—A methodology used to radically change the way a process is designed by developing an aggressive vision of how it should perform and using a group of enablers to prepare a new process design that is not hampered by the present processes paradigms.
- **Project Management**—The application of knowledge, skills, tools, and techniques to project activities in order to meet or exceed stakeholders' needs and expectations from a project. (Source: PMBOK Guide.)
- **Proof of Concept (POC)**—A demonstration, the purpose of which is to verify that certain concepts or theories have the potential for

232 • *Appendix A*

real-world application. A Proof of Concept is a test of an idea made by building a prototype of the application. It is an innovative, scaled-down version of the system you intend to develop. The Proof of Concept provides evidence that demonstrates that a business model, product, service, system, or idea is feasible and will function as intended.

- **Project Manager**—Someone who has the application of knowledge, skills, tools, and techniques to project activities in order to meet or exceed stakeholder's needs and expectations for the project. Frequently, a Project Manager will manage a portfolio of projects.

- **Project Risk Management**—A subset of Project Management that includes the project concerned with the identification, analyzing, reporting, and developing contingency plans. A list of things that could impact the project from being completed successfully is prepared, and each item is analyzed to determine if it is a critical, business major risk or minus risk. All critical and major risks should have contingency plans prepared for them. Normally, the contingency plans are not included in the budget but require a modification to the project plan and often to the budget in order to implement them. Normally, the Project Risk Management activities are assigned to the project manager.

- **S curve**—A mathematical model, also known as the logistic curve, describes the growth of one variable in terms of another variable over time. S curves are found in fields from biology and physics to business and technology. In business, the S curve is used to describe, and sometimes predict, the performance of a company or a product over a period of time.

- **Situation**—A situation is defined as anything that requires a response. It can be an opportunity to take advantage of, a choice between options, or as simple as a need to make a verbal response.

- **Stakeholder of an organization or enterprise**—Someone who potentially or really impacts on that organization, and who is likely to be impacted by that organization's activities and processes. Or, even more significantly, perceives that they will be impacted (usually negatively).

- **Statistical Analysis**—A collection, examination, summarization, manipulation, and interpretation of quantitative data to discover its underlying causes, patterns, relationships, and trends.

- **Status Quo**—A condition where the environment and the individual's expectations about the environment are in harmony. It does not mean the individual's expectations are being met.
- **Storyboarding**—This technique physically structures the output into a logical arrangement. The ideas, observations, or solutions may be grouped visually according to shared characteristics, dependencies upon one another, or similar means. These groupings show relationships between ideas and provide a starting point for action plans and implementation sequences.
- **Structure**—The arrangement of and relations between the parts or elements of something complex.
- **Tree Diagram Breakdown** (Drilldown)—A technique for breaking complex opportunities and problems down into progressively smaller parts.
- **TRIZ** (pronounced "treesz") is a Russian acronym for "Teoriya Resheniya Izobretatelskikh Zadatch," the Theory of Inventive Problem Solving, originated by Genrich Altshuller in 1946. It is a broad title representing methodologies, toolsets, knowledge bases, and model-based technologies for generating innovative ideas and solutions. It aims to create an algorithmic to the innovation of new systems and the refinement of existing systems and is based on the study of patents of technological evolution of systems, scientific theory, organizations, and work of arts.
- **Value Analysis**—The analysis of a system, process, or activity to determine which parts of it are classified as Real-Value Added (RVA), Business-Value Added (BVA), or No-Value Added (NVA).
- **Value Proposition**—A document that defines the benefits that will result from the implementation of a change or the use of an output as viewed by one or more of the organization's stakeholders. A value proposition can apply to an entire organization, parts thereof, or customers, or products, or services, or internal processes.
- **Vision**—A documented or mental description or picture of a desired future state of an organization, product, process, team, a key business driver, activity, or individual.
- **Vision Statements**—A group of words that paints a clear picture of the desired business environment at a specific time in the future. Short-term vision statements usually are between three and five years. Long-term vision statements usually are between ten and twenty-five years. A vision statement should not exceed four sentences.

Appendix B—Innovation Maturity Online Survey

INNOVATION MATURITY ANALYSIS FOR YOUR ORGANIZATION

We strongly believe that any new improvement initiative should not be started until there is a good understanding of the organization's strengths and weaknesses related to the type of improvement. Your impression of the organization's innovation performance is very important to you and your organization. As a result, we have developed a very short online survey that provides a snapshot view of how you believe the innovation activities within the organization are functioning. In addition, it will provide your impression of the strengths and weaknesses of the major innovation drivers within your organization.

Although your impression of the organization's ability to be innovative is very important and may or may not reflect the organization's actual performance, to have sufficient confidence in any survey, a much larger sample needs to be analyzed and has to be a homogeneous sample of the population being surveyed. As a result, we recommend that this analysis be used primarily as a weathervane to determine whether improving the innovative systems within the organization will result in a significant bottom-line improvement.

You can get to the survey using the following link.

www.hjharringtonassociates.com/

When you get to this web site, just click on breaking news. After you take the survey, the computer will analyze your inputs and provide a free customized report back to you within several minutes.

I hope you will find this report useful. Please let me know what you think of it.

H. James Harrington hjh@svinet.com

Appendix C – ISO 56002 International ISO Standard Summary

The following ISO 56002 International ISO Standard Synopsis was provided by Rick Fernandez Vice-Chair and Frank Voehl, US TAG Administrator for ISO TC 279 Innovation Management Standards

 COPYRIGHT PROTECTED DOCUMENT

EXECUTIVE SUMMARY

ISO 56002[1]

The 56002 International Standard Innovation Management—Innovation Management System—Guidance, consists of ten (10) sections with an introduction in the beginning. The introduction is summarized as follows: "An organization's ability to innovate is recognized as a key factor for sustained growth, economic viability, increased well-being, and the development of society. The innovation capabilities of an organization include the ability to understand and respond to changing conditions

---

[1] The International Association of Innovation Professionals (IAOIP) is the United States TAG for ISO 279/56000. This document is intended to be a summary report for the use of our members only. All copyrights that apply to the original ISO document shall remain in place. For the complete document, you will need to purchase a license from ANSI and or ISO.

of its context, to pursue new opportunities, and to leverage the knowledge and creativity of people within the organization, and in collaboration with external interested parties. An organization can innovate more effectively and efficiently, if all necessary activities and other interrelated or interacting elements are managed as a system.

An innovation management system guides the organization to determine its innovation vision, strategy, policy, and objectives, and to establish the support and processes needed to achieve the intended outcomes. This document provides guidance on why it is beneficial to implement an innovation assessment, what you can expect from a good one, how to carry it out, and act upon its results."—ISO Standards Doc Introduction

THE POTENTIAL BENEFITS OF IMPLEMENTING AN INNOVATION MANAGEMENT SYSTEM (IMS)

- increased ability to manage uncertainty;
- increased growth, revenues, profitability, and competitiveness;
- reduced costs and waste, and increased productivity and resource efficiency;
- improved sustainability and resilience;
- increased satisfaction of users, customers, citizens, and other interested parties;
- sustained renewal of the portfolio of offerings;
- engaged and empowered people in the organization;
- increased ability to attract partners, collaborators, and funding;
- enhanced reputation and valuation of the organization;
- facilitated compliance with regulations and other relevant requirements.

THE FOLLOWING PRINCIPLES ARE THE FOUNDATION OF THE IMS

- realization of value;
- future-focused leaders;

- strategic direction;
- culture;
- exploiting insights;
- managing uncertainty;
- adaptability;
- systems approach.

INNOVATION MANAGEMENT SYSTEM (IMS)

An innovation management system is a set of interrelated and interacting elements, aiming for the realization of value. It provides a common framework to develop and deploy innovation capabilities, evaluate performance, and achieve intended outcomes. Innovation isn't just having a few bright ideas. It's about creating value and helping organizations continuously adapt and evolve. ISO is developing a new series of International Standards on innovation management, the third of which has just been published. Innovation is an increasingly important contributor to the success of an organization, enhancing its ability to adapt in a changing world. Novel and innovative ideas give rise to better ways of working, as well as new solutions for generating revenue and improving sustainability. It is closely linked to the resilience of an organization, in that it helps them to understand and respond to challenging contexts, seize the opportunities that that might bring and leverage the creativity of both its own people and those it deals with.

PLAN–DO–CHECK–ACT CYCLE

The Plan–Do–Check–Act (PDCA) cycle was initially developed by Dr. Edwards Deming and can be applied to the innovation management system as a whole or its parts. Figure C.1 illustrates how clauses 4 to 10 can be grouped in relation to the PDCA cycle. This cycle is informed and directed by the scope and context of the organization (clause 4) and its leadership (clause 5).

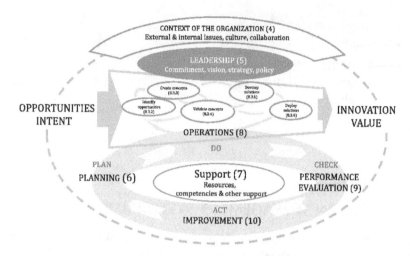

FIGURE C.1

Representation of the framework of the innovation management system with references to the clauses of this document. (This figure is from ISO 56002:2019(E) and is copyrighted by ISO.)

SECTION ONE: SCOPE

This document provides guidance for the establishment, implementation, maintenance, and continual improvement of an innovation management system for use in all established organizations. Many companies that want to become certified according to ISO 56000 have already gained their ISO 9001 certifications, or at least have plans to implement ISO 9001:2015. This is usually because it is the most general Quality Management System standard, and it is demanded by many customers in various industries, including the medical device sector. This means that an integrated management system encompassing the requirements of both standards will require the determination of the context of the organization, as well as the identification of any necessary actions to be taken.

SECTION TWO: NORMATIVE REFERENCES

The following documents are referred in this standard:

ISO 56000, Innovation Management—Fundamentals and Vocabulary; the PDCA Cycle.

SECTION THREE: TERMS AND DEFINITIONS

For the purposes of this document, the terms, and definitions that are given in ISO 56000 apply.

Note that ISO and IEC maintain terminological databases for use in standardization at the following addresses:

- ISO Online browsing platform is available at: www.iso.org/obp.
- IEC Electropedia is available at: www.electropedia.org/.

SECTION FOUR: CONTEXT OF THE ORGANIZATION

The organization should regularly determine:

- external and internal issues that are relevant to its purpose and that affect its ability to achieve the intended outcomes of its innovation management system;
- areas of opportunity for potential value realization.

SECTION FIVE: LEADERSHIP

This is an extensive section, and it is recommended that you acquire the complete document from ANSI/ISO to obtain a clear understanding. Leadership is probably the one key element that must be present in order to implement a successful IMS. Top management should demonstrate leadership and commitment with respect to the innovation management system by:

- being accountable;
- ensuring that the IMS vision, strategy, policy, and objectives be defined in line with those of the organization;
- fostering a culture that supports innovation activities;
- ensuring adoption and integration of the IMS;
- supporting leaders at all levels in the implementation;
- ensuring organizational structures support innovation;

- creating awareness and communicating the importance;
- ensuring the IMS achieves its goals.

SECTION SIX: PLANNING

Planning for the implementation of an IMS must include adequate planning that considers not only the opportunities but also the risks involved. In addition, innovation objectives should be developed along with supporting plans to achieve those objectives. These plans need to be:

- in alignment with the strategy of the organization;
- defined with specific deliverables and expected results;
- properly resourced;
- adequately monitored and adjusted over time to assure completion;
- fit within either existing supportive organizational structures or within new structures that are specifically designated for the purpose of supporting the IMS.

Another concept that is critical to the success of an IMS is the creation and management of innovation portfolios. Similar to the planning these need to be:

- in alignment with and contributing to the innovation strategy;
- be consistent between individual initiatives within the overall portfolio;
- synergistic using existing structures and efforts and supporting those;
- balanced between risks and returns;
- communicated;
- lastly improved as time goes on.

SECTION SEVEN: SUPPORT

The organization should determine and provide in a timely manner the resources needed for the establishment, implementation, maintenance, and continual improvement of the innovation management system. The organization should consider as follows:

- a proactive, transparent, flexible, and adaptable approach for providing resources;
- the capabilities of, and limitations on, existing internal support;
- what needs to be obtained from external providers, e.g. by outsourcing or partnering;
- internal and external collaboration, e.g. sharing or re-use, to optimize the use of resources;
- securing resources for innovation activities separated from other activities;
- the long-term build-up of capabilities for innovation activities.

One of the most important aspects of an Innovation Management System is the development or acquisition of new Intellectual Property, its protection, and its management. The organization should establish an approach for the management of intellectual property aligned with, and supporting, the innovation strategy. This section of the standard has an in-depth description of the considerations that the organization should take while considering intellectual property. A separate standard is being developed to further define this very important part of an IMS.

SECTION EIGHT: OPERATION

8.1 Operational Planning and Control

The organization should plan, implement, and control innovation initiatives, processes, structures, and support needed to address innovation opportunities, meet requirements, and to implement the actions determined in Section 6.2, by:

- establishing criteria for innovation initiatives and processes;
- implementing control of the innovation initiatives and processes in accordance with the criteria;
- keeping documented information to the extent necessary to have confidence that the innovation initiatives and processes have been carried out as planned.

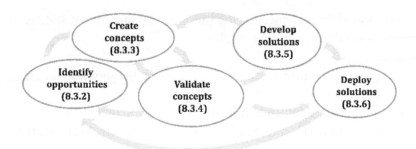

FIGURE C.2

8.2 Innovation Initiatives

The organization should manage each innovation initiative, as part of the innovation portfolio explained earlier. This section of the standard delves into the suggested considerations for the successful management of those initiatives including reviewing the scope and objectives, determining indicators of success, establishing management decision-making criteria, providing leadership support, and among others listed in this section.

8.3 Innovation Processes

"The organization should configure innovation processes to suit the innovation initiative.

The innovation processes can be flexible and adaptable, and form different configurations, depending on, e.g. the types of innovations and the circumstances of the organization."—ISO Standards Doc page 18.[2] Figure C.2 below from the standard shows the interrelationship between the different innovation processes and how the different sections of the standard where they are explained.

The standard explains each of the innovation processes and their interaction.

SECTION 9: PERFORMANCE EVALUATION

9.1 Monitoring, Measurement, Analysis, and Evaluation

"The organization should determine:

---

[2] This figure is from ISO 56002:2019(E) and is copyrighted by ISO.

- what needs to be monitored and measured;
- the tools and methods for monitoring, measurement, analysis, and evaluation needed to ensure valid results;
- when the monitoring and measuring should be performed;
- when the results from monitoring and measurement should be analyzed and evaluated;
- who will be responsible."[3] ISO Standards Doc page 15.

9.2 Internal Audit

The organization should conduct internal audits at planned intervals to provide information on whether the IMS conforms to its own requirements for its IMS and is effectively implemented and maintained.

9.3 Management Review

Top management should review the organization's innovation management system, at planned intervals, to ensure its continuing suitability, adequacy, effectiveness, and efficiency.

SECTION 10: IMPROVEMENT

"The organization should determine and select opportunities for improvement and implement any necessary actions and changes to the innovation management system, considering performance evaluation results."[4]—ISO Standards Doc page 24.

BIBLIOGRAPHY

This section contains the 22 related series of ISO Standards that are currently available for publication, or will soon be available by 2020.

1. BS 7000-1:2008, (Great Britain) Design management systems — Part 1: Guide to managing innovation.
2. CEN/TS 16555 (all parts), Innovation Management System.

[3] This quote is from ISO 56002:2019(E) and is copyrighted by ISO.
[4] This quote is from ISO 56002:2019(E) and is copyrighted by ISO.

3. EN 1325:2014, Value Management — Vocabulary — Terms and definitions.
4. FD X50 -271: 2013, (France) Management of innovation — Guidelines for implementing an innovation management approach.
5. ISO 704:2009, Terminology work — Principles and methods.
6. ISO 9000:2015, Quality management systems — Fundamentals and vocabulary.
7. ISO 9001:2015, Quality management systems — Requirements.
8. ISO 9004:2018, Quality management — Quality of an organization — Guidance to achieve sustained success.
9. ISO 14001:2015, Environmental management systems — Requirements with guidance for use.
10. ISO 18091:2014, Quality management systems — Guidelines for the application of ISO 9001:2008 in local government.
11. ISO 19600:2014, Compliance management systems — Guidelines.
12. ISO 21500, Guidance on project management.
13. ISO 22301:2012, Societal security — Business continuity management systems — Requirements.
14. ISO 26000:2010, Guidance on social responsibility.
15. ISO/IEC 27001:2013, Information technology — Security techniques — Information security management systems — Requirements.
16. ISO 31000:2018, Risk management — Guidelines.
17. ISO 37500:2014, Guidance on outsourcing.
18. ISO 50001:2018, Energy management systems — Requirements with guidance for use.
19. ISO 55001:2014, Asset management — Management systems — Requirements.
20. ISO/IEC Directives Part 1, Consolidated ISO Supplement, Annex SL.
21. NP 4456: 2007, (Portugal) Management of research, development, and innovation (RDI) — Terminology and definitions of RDI activities.
22. MANUAL Oslo 2018, Guidelines for collecting, reporting and using data on innovation. OECD, Fourth Edition.
23. SWiFT 1:2009, (Ireland) Guidance to good practice in innovation and product development processes.
24. UNE 166000:2014, (Spain) R&D&i management — Terminology and definitions of R&D&i activities.
25. https://committee.iso.org/home/tc176sc2 — Guidance on ISO 9001 and Resources/ Auditing Practices Group.
26. ISO 19011:2018, Guidelines for auditing management systems.
27. CEN/TS 16555-7, Innovation management assessment.

Note: The International Association of Innovation Professionals (IAOIP) is the United States TAG for ISO TC 279/56002. This document is intended to be a summary report for the use of our members only. All copyrights that apply to the original ISO document shall remain in place. For the complete document, you will need to purchase a license from ANSI and or ISO, which IAOIP will be happy to facilitate for its members at no charge.

Index